Live The Risk

Escape your excuses and enjoy life!

Joel S. Levinson

Jeffrey A. Steele

ISBN-10: 0991184106

ISBN-13: 978-0-9911841-0-1

Cover Design: Jack Solomon
Editor: Kari MaKenna
Interior Graphics: Saul Rand Productions/Hana Ruzsa
Cover Photos: Shutterstock/Olga Danylenko, Siraphat, and Sergey Nivens

Live The Risk is about living life the way you always wanted, but never had the courage to pursue.

It's not about taking risks for the sake of saying you live on the edge. It's about taking risks to break away from your comfort zone and get to the place you want to be in your life.

To Jackie, Jaime, and Sarah,
you are what makes my world revolve.
I love you all.
~ Joel

To Trina, Jordin, and Tiphany,
every good thing in my life
is because of you three.
~ Jeff

THANKS

Nothing is ever written without help, advice, and truths from other people, and this book is no exception. We wanted to take a moment and give thanks to the folks who have provided the encouragement to grow, to take a chance and write what we were thinking. It is always dangerous to attempt to remember everyone that has helped, so please forgive us if we have unintentionally forgotten you:

Kari MaKenna, Brian Cocherl, Patrick Lewis, Chris Sparks, Mikki Gordon, Inez Tenzer, Rick Tilley, Sean McHenry, Peter Acosta, Jea & Lawrence Robinson, the Attitude First family, Debi & Kirk O'Malley, Hellen Davis, Lauren Rees, Will & Tammy Rees, Scott Dessenberger, Tim VanDeGrift, Rick Miller & Kids At Hope, Mike Datema, Caroline Wood, Monte Montemayor, Casey Clark, Byran Zarnett, Eli Lopez, Skip Hancock & the Path to Excellence, Irene Clegg, Steve Smith, Cody Lambson, Brian Oakley, Corvin Walker, David Mohler, Chris Collins, Emil Cicogna, Barbara Bond, Brynn & Bill Kenyon, Shane Kenyon, Britnee Ruscitti, Matt Rohrs, Todd Schwartz, the amazing students and staff at Barry Goldwater High School, Carolyn Andrews, Mark Lutes, Nick Gelormini, John & Laura Correia, Michelle Howard, Nicole Deshaw Ansley, Brealyn Nenes, Alma & Paul Shrigley, Joe & Faye Marek, Miranda Tinney, Ruth Brubaker Rimmer, Brian McCluskey, Marcine Coburn, Taylor McCormick, Joel & Amy Carbajal, the EDS family, The Wentzel Family, Jodie Marek, Jodi & Mark Hardiek, Barbara & Lou Gennarelli, Steve Kytola, Kim Bissell, Raffi Simonian, Matt Crego, Eric Pohl, Shannon Oughton, Teresa Leighty, Robyn Interpreter, Robyn Kreitl, Joe Stempniewski, Kory Jensen, Fiona & John Rivard, Karen Marshall Akins, Darius Venclauskas, Peter & Grace Zadrozny, Omar Marhaba, James Chance, the HighJump team, Rylan Springfield, Vince Ely, Paul Simms, Ron Benigo, Jim Pitrowski, Brad Vergin, Charlene Jensen, Patrick McHale, Brenda Johnson, Mike Wallesen, Susan Johnson, Keith Yellin, Kirk Anderson, Mark Aument, Joe Blauert, Stan Chew, Mike Harris, John McCain, Tim Morton, Pat Sculley, Neil Jarvis, Lemuel Amen, and Pete Jacobs.

We thank you all for being a part of this adventure!

Contents

Journal Entries

Preface

Before we begin, we should say a little about ourselves. First and foremost, we are both blessed with very understanding wives and children! Jeff is married with two teenage children and Joel is married with two grown daughters. Collectively, they have listened to us moan, complain, dream, and take educated (and some not-so-educated) chances. They have propped us up when everything seemed to be going to heck-in-a-handbasket, and helped keep us grounded when things were going far too well.

That is why we dedicate this book to them.

But who are we, really? Okay, we'll give you a few personal details. We are both devilishly handsome, virile young men (wink, wink). Jeff (age 45) is 6'2" (in boots) and Joel (50) is 5'9" (in sneakers). We both still have our hair (kind of), but Joel's is turning grey as fast as Jeff is losing his. We are both martial artists. Well, one has a black belt and the other looks good in black. We are both runners and hikers at different levels of mileage. Neither of us comes from wealthy families – we both claim working poor as our upbringing.

As for our career paths, we each come from different ends of the employment spectrum – one from the public sector of education (Jeff) and the other from the private sector of large corporations (Joel). We do, however, share the want and desire to be *very* successful in life and to have the financial freedom, flexibility of time, and ability to provide for our families. Ultimately, our definition of "very successful" is *having the freedom to do what's important to us.* Making it happen was a matter of choice, and once we figured it out, the path opened before us, and life has never been better. We want you to have that freedom, too.

Introduction

You really can't *Live The Risk* without taking the first step towards your new future. So let's just get started. Yes, *now*! As you read the next two stories, highlight or underline items that you're currently experiencing in your life. Be honest.

Ready, set, go!

Story #1

The alarm goes off and you slap the snooze button because you didn't sleep well and the thought of the day ahead is too much to bear. Finally, without leaving enough time to get up and get ready, you crawl out of bed. The whole family is dragging, and as usual no one is excited about the day except the dog that gets fed in the morning. You eat a fat-filled pastry and chug an energy drink (coffee takes too long to make and there isn't enough time for the drive-thru) while shouting at the kids, "Get up! Do you have your homework? What's taking you so long? Why aren't you up?" You aren't surprised when they yell, "Oh no, I forgot!" and "I didn't sleep very well!" It's too late now. Everyone rushes out the door to face the long day.

On the road to work, your temper starts to flare. The stupid and selfish drivers who share the road seem to be doing everything they can to slow you down and make you late. "If these idiots weren't on the roads I'd be able to get to work on time," you grunt under your breath, along with, "Why are they so slow...no turn signals... cell phones up to their ears...they're all so &%!* rude!" Then you notice an accident up ahead and can't help but think, "These people are going to cause me to be late again!" You speed up to get in front of one of the slower vehicles, swerve your black SUV into their lane, and hit the brakes a millisecond before striking the car in front of you. "Whew, that was close!" you say exhaling in relief. "This city has the worst drivers!"

Introduction

After dropping the kids off at school, you arrive at work late. "Just great! But it's not my fault!" you think as you begin another inner tirade against all of the problems you're experiencing this morning. Forced to park in the farthest spot from the building you start the long walk in. All the while, a pain is developing in your gut – and it's not from the crappy breakfast that you had, but rather the feeling of despair you get when doing something you feel forced to do. You think of all of the useless activities you will complete today because, after all, that's life, and the bills aren't going to pay themselves.

The day drags along as you sit at your desk attempting the same repetitive activities you do every day. You can't help yourself; you keep watching the clock hoping it will move faster.

Somehow you made it. Lunchtime.

You and your coworkers crowd into the drab cafeteria, and while eating their tasteless meals everyone takes turns complaining about his or her life. Time is up...Whew! That was a refreshing and rejuvenating lunch – not! Back to work you go. Back to the grind that threatens to suffocate you. Back to watching the clock. Back to wasting your life. Back to the misery. Sigh!

As the boring day continues, you attempt to find escape from the tedium through social media. You can't believe how your friends spend their time, money, and energy. You find it deplorable how they are wasting their lives. You're not surprised.

The day crawls along until it's time to go home. As you follow the exit signs to your escape, your boss catches you and asks if you have a minute in the morning to talk. "Yeah, sure," you say, forcing a smile. Once your boss is out of sight, you grumble, "I'm probably getting fired!" Finally, the doors to freedom are within your reach and you race for the parking lot. Too bad you had to park so far away.

And to think, it's only Monday.

You and the spouse decide that the day was so tough that it would be easier if you picked up some food from a drive-thru – again.

While speeding home, you know that there isn't enough time to get everything done that you need to do, not when you are once again subjected to those who are plotting against you. As you finally walk into your sanctuary, you're ready to relax. In one fluid motion, you plop your rear end on the sofa while picking up the remote. The rest of the family arrives at home over the course of the next few hours, and everyone takes turns complaining about their day. Stupid people, hard teachers, too much homework, why can't we have a chef, I'm sick of fast food, when are we getting a maid, it's not my fault, and the list goes on and on. Somehow, through your exhaustion you help the kids get on task. "No, you're not allowed to go to your friends on a school night!" "You'll be grounded for life if you don't bring up those grades!" "Will you do your chores sometime this week?"

"Ugh!" you exclaim into the dark hallways of your home as the kids escape to their rooms to play video games. It's just in time too; you're too tired to fight anymore. Why do they love those games? Nothing seems to relax them as much as killing everything that moves, in an alternate world, of course. Maybe it's therapeutic.

After attempting to relax in front of the TV while taking out the day's frustrations on the food wrappers, you loosen your belt to allow the greasy food to pass, and begin to agonize over what the boss will say tomorrow and what excuses you will use this time. You can't lose your job now, not when the kids need braces. As weariness takes over you slip into your bed and exhale deeply. You are almost scared of the images that your mind will release, and spend the night twisting and turning in an attempt to find a comfortable position.

The last thought of the day as you pull the covers over your head: "Only four more days before the weekend, if I'm still employed."

Story #2

You wake up early totally refreshed and feeling quite a sense of satisfaction knowing you beat the alarm clock's shrill buzzing. Nothing like being reenergized after a great night's sleep. You're anxious to get the day started – but not in a hurry. You have arranged your life to include time for your personal space and health. You slip on your running gear and get out of the house in time to see the sunrise. As you stretch, you have a heightened level of awareness of life going on around you, the neighborhood cat watching from the top of the wall, the bunny in the front yard, the fellow runners making their way from down the street. You wave as they pass. You notice the tree that is getting ready to bloom (you love the way it looks in the spring). You set your GPS watch to track today's exercise, and off you go.

Back from your run, showered and dressed, you sit down with the family for a healthy breakfast. As you eat, everyone talks about the day and what each will be doing. Someone makes a joke and the entire family enjoys a good laugh. There's energy in the air that makes you feel like you're living the best life possible.

You and the kids hop into the car, and you look forward to visiting with them on the way to dropping them at school. Once there, you watch them walk away and know they will be doing their best. At times such as this, you can't believe how fortunate you are to have such an amazing family.

On your way to work there's the regular traffic and angry drivers. You decide to remain calm and centered, and you allow those who are *late for their accidents* to cut in front of you, especially one black SUV. He seems to be mad at the world! He keeps speeding up to the car in front of him and then slamming on the brakes. You know you can't control his actions, only yours. You've already made the decision to get to work safely rather than attempt to compete for the front spot in the morning's freeway race.

When you arrive at work, you discover that you have to park in the last spot in the second parking lot. Not a problem! You use this opportunity to plan your workday. It could turn out to be one of the hardest days this month, but it's the challenges that keep work interesting and satisfying. You always put in the effort to accomplish what is needed. You enjoy what you do so much that you have figured out how to always have a good attitude no matter the task.

After a productive morning, lunch seems to come quickly. You join your fellow workers for a meal. Nobody complains. You share your morning goals and accomplishments with your peers, as they do with you. You gain more energy and insight on how to do an even better job. You have some great friends in this place; their passion fuels your own. Time well spent.

Back to work and the day continues to fly by. In fact, you're surprised when it's time to go home. You feel great. You send a text to your spouse confirming that you will be home in time for dinner. After packing up your work, you make your way out of the building. Passing your boss's office, he calls out to you before you can say goodnight and asks if you have a minute in the morning to talk. "Absolutely, looking forward it!" you answer, with a friendly wave.

You're out the door to your car. Sure, traffic crawls along, but what else do you expect? You use the time productively – say, to practice with a foreign language MP3 or listen to an audio book of a recent best seller.

You're home before you know it. You even have a chance to bring in your neighbor's garbage cans from the street. Once inside you start dinner, get both kids' gear ready – one has volleyball practice and the other has a basketball game. Your spouse arrives with the kids. Everyone washes up and sits down to dinner as a family, sharing their stories of the day.

After dinner the kids do their chores, and you and your spouse clean the kitchen. It's agreed that you will drop your daughter off at volleyball practice, while your spouse takes your son to his basketball game. As soon as practice is over, everyone will meet up and watch the second half of the basketball game. Nothing like cheering as a family! You don't even know what shows are on TV that night because you're too busy living your lives and aren't concerned about the latest dysfunctional reality TV family and what trouble they're up to this week.

Once home, everyone talks about the effort that they put into their day, the actions that they took, and the results that they got. Then while the kids do their homework, you and your spouse put on your favorite music and get things ready for tomorrow. Your mind wanders as you think about the meeting with your boss in the morning. Does he want you to head the new account, or maybe take over as the department manager? Wouldn't that be great. You'd probably get a raise and the extra money sure would come in handy now that the kids need braces. It doesn't matter because whatever it is, you'll be ready to give one hundred percent, as always.

The last thought of the day as you pull the covers up: Tomorrow is going to be a great day.

Yes, both stories are extreme. Most of us have days that are somewhere in the middle. We could have written Story #3, #4, #5, … #20 to represent all the possibilities in between, but we're confident that you can get over not having a perfect match. Plus, we all know where this is going. If we could choose to have an extreme day, wouldn't we choose to have the great extreme day over the mundane crappy day? Wouldn't we all like to be able to approach life with the attitude that every day is a gift and to appreciate every moment on this space rock rotating around that ball of fire in the sky? Perhaps we should just strive to enjoy each and every day.

Did You Relate?

Did you relate to either of the stories? Count the number of times you underlined words or sentences in Story #1 and then do the same with Story #2. Before you wonder if there is a right or wrong, there isn't, so count and place your numbers in the following boxes.

Story #1 ▢   Story #2 ▢

Before we go any further, which number is higher, the number on the left or right? Is your life one where everything that surrounds you seems to be going wrong? Is the world against you and nothing ever seems to go right? Or is it an "everything keeps coming up roses" kind of life, where life is being pointed in the right direction – even the bad moments? We both hope that you had a higher total in #2. The reality is that story #1 plays out more often on a day-to-day basis than most people like to admit. In fact, we've had more than our share of #1 days, so many that we got to the point where we had to make changes.

Here comes the pitch: If you're like us, you have gone to a bookstore, or online, to find the answers you seek in order to improve your life. You're hoping to find something, anything, to help you on your journey out of story #1 and into story #2. You're not looking for a bunch of fluff, pomp or circumstance. You don't care if the newest TV doctor writes it; you want something that can help on your journey.

We believe what is presented in these pages will help you accomplish your goals, achieve your dreams, and allow you to live the life you desire. We want to help you be the man or woman in Story #2! (Heck, if you followed through with putting the numbers in the box, you can handle what's in this book!)

Part I: It's All About You!

I Want to Grow!

You may be wondering how two guys from significantly different backgrounds came together to write a new method for living a fuller, richer life. A book that can help you grow from Story #1, what we call "Dying on the Vine," to Story #2, "Living Your Life to Its Fullest."

It all started on a hike with a simple conversation between friends attempting to answer the age-old question: What's the secret to life? The subject being discussed was how can you get what you want when your current circumstances seem to be putting up roadblocks.

Over the past three years we have been walking, hiking, running, exercising, and having breakfast conversations about how to be successful in business, in life, with family, and at play. These questions led us to converse on the why and how to handle the ups and downs of money, which then allowed us to commiserate on what worked and what didn't. What surprised us most was at the end of these conversations came an epiphany on how to help us achieve our goals.

We both know what you are thinking: "Wow, they did it, so can I!" Or maybe, "Really? Is this just more stuff that doesn't work?" If you are part of the first group...thanks, we needed that ego boost! If you are in the majority with the second group, we appreciate your healthy skepticism and ask you to keep reading.

In an attempt to figure out our own lives, we made a list of the reasons we needed to improve. We found ourselves categorizing our lives by the following descriptive sets. Do they represent you too?

The abandonment of me

- ❑ Life seems to get in the way of my future.
- ❑ I view my life as wasting away (time flies and little to nothing changes).
- ❑ I talk about what I want, but never accomplish it.
- ❑ Rely upon luck as the answer to achieving goals.
- ❑ I'm doing something other than what I want to do (feeling trapped).

Life gets in the way of a perfectly good time

- ❑ Responsibilities continue to pile up (seem to be never-ending).
- ❑ Reality never seems to be what I hoped it would be.
- ❑ I work to pay the bills (the bills never end).
- ❑ Not (never) enough hours in the day.
- ❑ All work and no play, no time for hobbies, or "me" time.
- ❑ Less time, sleep, sanity, or money keeps me from doing.
- ❑ Usually feel two steps behind.
- ❑ Bound by society's expectations of me (feeling trapped . . . again).

Never juggle running chainsaws in the dark

- ❑ Unable to recharge (no matter how much vacation).
- ❑ The daily grind is not rewarding (not looking forward to more of the same).
- ❑ Too stressed out to make a change.
- ❑ Successes seem few, far between, or not at all.
- ❑ Always adding to the list, but never taking anything off (priorities, commitments, expectations, etc.)

The haunting of past decisions

- ❏ Took the wrong fork in the road.
- ❏ I'm following the crowd and taking their path - letting someone else make my decisions.
- ❏ Not choosing any path, making no decision.

Any one of these topics could be hard, but to have them all happening to you at once could be a real challenge. The lessons learned from all that talking between huffing and puffing on the mountain... okay, it was really a hill...is what we are sharing with you.

What Do We Want to Do?

As we have found during our personal transformations, change didn't come knocking at our door. In both cases we had to go find the changes we wanted and kick those doors in. We both decided that we could not stay put; the status quo was no longer an option.

Jeff felt stifled by the teaching profession. While it was a noble career and had brought him satisfaction (many students and parents had thanked him for his dedication), what he really wanted was to be responsible for his own future; to provide for his family while forging his own path. He wanted to have the freedom to work toward his goals on his terms, which is where the self-employment angle came into play.

After many years as a business consultant for corporate America, Joel believed that if he remained in that sector others would eventually step over his corpse to get to the next level of management. Still, he continued to succeed in helping companies achieve their goals. He continued to receive high marks for leadership and strategic abilities, but inside a part of him began to die. Joel's dream was to write and mentor others in achieving their own goals.

Both of us understand that our initial paths were good ones, and we are grateful for the successes we have achieved and the people that we met. It has been those successes that have placed us on top of our games and onto this path. But we were both unsatisfied with accepting that this was the best it was going to get. We both kept coming back to that question: What do we want to be when we grow up? Why would two middle-aged guys be asking that question? Why can't the status quo be enough? Why can't what we had yesterday be okay for tomorrow? Why would anyone want to change what already works? Why ask why? For us the answer was: *We didn't want to let others choose what path we took or stayed on for the rest of our lives. We wanted the freedom to choose.* We owed it to ourselves to live our lives. It's that simple.

The truth is, life never stops changing. The world of forever jobs, retiring with pensions, and housing prices that keep appreciating are gone forever, or at least evolving. Every day that we awaken is an opportunity to take a look at the changes we desire before the world changes it for us. This is not a doomsday prophecy; it's reality. It's not meant to be negative; it's meant for us to take control of our lives. It's a chance to plan what we want and figure out a way to achieve it. It's to have the freedom to make our own future. We have found that it takes as much energy to choose for yourself as it does to follow what others would have you do.

At any age we all need to keep asking: *What do we want to do when we grow up?*[1]

Personally, it hit us both square in the face that at the moment we became complacent, expecting everything to stay the same, we stopped growing.

This pretty much sums up our philosophy (so you might want to highlight it because we'll refer to it again and again): ***If you're not living, you're dying***. . .and dying isn't much fun. When all of our energy goes into maintaining what we have, we're not thinking

---

1 As kids we used to be asked, "What do you want to be?" which we have found is nothing more than a point-in-time destination. We have altered the statement to "What do I want to do?" to give it more of a journey and continued learning experience.

about change, but about survival. It forces us to the bottom of Maslow's hierarchy of needs[2].

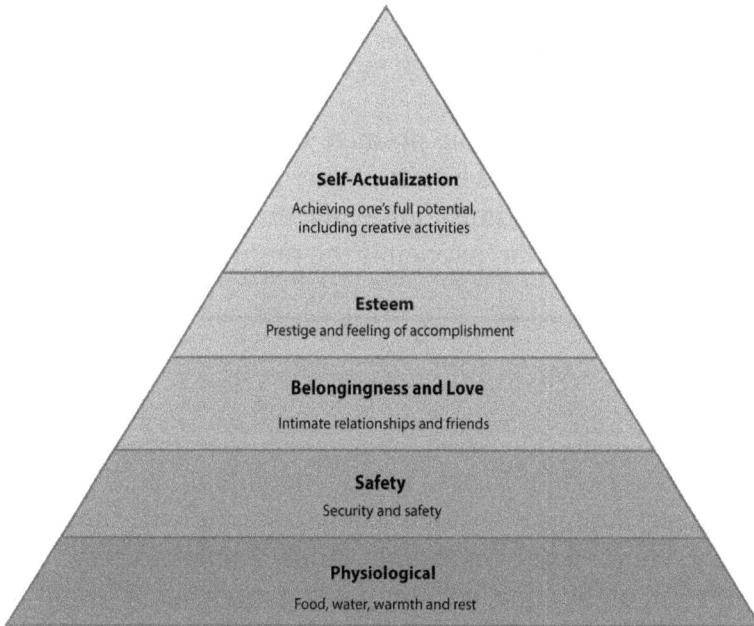

Let's be honest: This idea wasn't a lightning strike from the heavens. Rather, it was analyzing where we were today and where we wanted to be tomorrow. Our goal was not about coasting to the end of our days, which starts the process of dying until we end; *it was about living until the end of our days.*

> It really was that simple. It was all about *living versus dying.* We chose living and so should you. Rumor has it that too many people are dying with regrets.
> Don't let it happen to you.

When attempting to dive deep into how to really live life to its fullest, we needed to prove to ourselves (and hopefully to you) that we as human beings are meant to live. That doesn't mean looking at a pretty picture of what we wanted. We wanted to prove that it was our destiny (a great word, huh?) to take this path.

---

2 Maslow, A (1954). Motivation and personality. ISBN 0-06-041-987-3

I Want to Grow!

Our hypothesis is that we are meant as people to do more than survive; we are meant to learn and grow. We have an inherent need in our biological makeup to expand our horizons.

Can we prove it?

Well, we began with a simple premise that all of us start the same way: we are born[3]. And, we all have the same guaranteed ending: death. There's a lot of time (hopefully) to fill between those two milestones, and what can happen is the premise of this book.

●————————————————————————————————●
Birth   Death

We think it's important to note that as individuals, we don't want to be remembered for how we died. Those last moments should not be important. We want our wives, kids, family, friends, and strangers to remember all of the times *before* that last moment. We want to live our lives so fully that when the final moment comes (no matter how it comes), we are not wondering if we did everything we wanted to and were supposed to do – because we have! No regrets! We actually cringe (yes, we really do make that scrunched-up face look) when we see a marker on the side of the road only reminding people of where somebody died. What about where and how they lived? That is something we could celebrate instead of mourn.

We begin our quest by looking at the perfection of babies. They have it made, don't they? They cry, and we as parents get up and solve their problems. They experience without the worry of remorse or mistake. They don't hate or have prejudices. They learn about everything in front of them and they absorb it all. They even discover on their own most of the laws of physics such as gravity and how to at least prevent it from standing in their way (pun intended). Actually, they start using these lessons to achieve some movement and then a lot of movement (we call it a fast waddle). As they grow, they begin to

---

3 We will leave out the details prior to birth and say we had some help. We promise we were born. Ok, have a good

laugh at our expense, but it's not true that we were hatched, discovered, or from some other kind of experiment.

mirror their environments, which is sometimes sad because this is when they pick up their likes, dislikes, hates, prejudices, and habits without realizing it.

One of the greatest advantages a child has over an adult is that they can envision their future without boundaries, responsibilities, expectations, or guilt. They can become anything they want to be because they haven't yet learned that it could be impossible or at the least, unreasonable. They have the freedom to be anything they want to be and can do anything the want to do (as long as mom says it is okay). They can tilt their lifeline to the clouds.

Do you remember the answers that you gave when your parents, aunts, uncles, or grandparents asked you what you wanted to do when you grew up?

When we started asking the question of our friends and family, we had visions of that Monster.com commercial from a few years ago where kids replied with facetious statements like wanting to be in middle management, achieve low expectations, and push paper around (it still makes us laugh). We added a couple of our own: using the restroom on a bell schedule, wanting to be told how to think, needing to be taught how to be a number instead of a name, and how to be a follower.

The truth is that all kids have a future, even if they don't know how to achieve it yet! A child is not thinking about his or her demise when answering the simple question. None of the kids we asked gave a single thought about what they *couldn't* do, because everything was possible.

Dancer

RACE CAR DRIVER VET POLICEMAN

Writer

ARTIST SPORTS PLAYER

NINJA CURE CANCER Magician

Doctor SKATEBOARDER

SUPER HERO Journalist

Fireman MUSICIAN CHEF Comedian

Preacher Nurse Astronaut Teacher

MERMAID

World Traveler

Every time our parents and their parents used supportive statements such as, "You can be anything you want to be if you set your mind to it," and "You can do it if you put in the effort," they put us in a growth mindset.[4] Every time they supported us in our activities and encouraged us, they helped solidify our future efforts. They were even helping by sharing their own dreams with us. Of course, as parents questioned our dreams (hoping to keep us safe) they also had the opportunity to limit our thinking about what we could, should, or would become or do. Think about it.

---

4 Mindset: The New Psychology of Success by Carol Dweck (Dec 26, 2007) ISBN: 978-0-345-47232-8

Don't get us wrong, parents know their role: to guide, mold, and teach their young apprentices and protect them from the harsh realities of life. Parents are doing what is best regardless of how it limits their young apprentices' minds. We beg you, don't close off your children's imagination.

We agree that at some point in time realism will creep into the psyche and start giving us limits as to what we can do or even want to do…so superheroes might be out. (Of course, Batman is a great martial artist with some really cool toys and unlimited wealth. It could happen.)

We're Wired to Get What We Want

We believe that the design of our minds supports the "we are wired to get what we want" concept. In our search for proof we stumbled upon the human brain, and yes, everyone has one – it's just that not everyone uses it. For those that don't know, it is made up of three distinct sections.[5] Here's what our research revealed:

❑ The *reptilian* brain controls the autonomous features of our body, the instinctual part of our DNA – breathing, digestion, heart rate, body temperature, and balance to name a few. It includes the brainstem (autonomous items) and the cerebellum (fine motor skills, balance, timing and muscle memory). This part of the brain is rigid and compulsive. In other words, it does what it does when it wants to do things. It is not asking for permission or requests. This part of the brain is very territorial. It represents about ten percent of the brain's weight and the cerebellum alone has more than 3.6 times the neurons that the neocortex has (that is the big

---

5 Neither one of us is a brain scientist and where we use flight as an example, we are not rocket scientists either. However, we do use the internet and research when we don't know something.

part of your brain, see below). In the end, we really need to work hard to make sure that we don't go on automatic.

❑ The *limbic* or *mammalian* brain controls behavioral memories from positive and negative experiences; emotion (obviously, the pleasure center – laughing: yay, pain: boo!); flight, fight, or freeze reflexes; and value judgments. There are three major areas of the limbic brain: the hippocampus, hypothalamus, and amygdala. These will all be talked about in Part II. For now, believe that this part of the brain is really, really important in how we deal with risk.

❑ Now for the big behemoth portion of the brain, the *neocortex*. It is approximately 76% of the weight of all three portions. It contains 100 billion cells each with up to 10,000 synapses, and about 62,000+ miles (100 million meters) of wiring. It's responsible for language, abstract thought, reasoning, imagination, and consciousness. This is why as kids we can be anything we want to be; the majority of the brain lets us imagine it! The neocortex is very flexible and is considered to have infinite learning abilities. Meaning, we can learn anything and, in turn, grow! Think about it: we as a species have been given the majority portions of our thinking ability to learn about new things and grow because of them. Wow! We can, if we want, apply it to anything we want. That's powerful!

Here is where the rubber meets the road or the brain matter meets our control. If we have the capability and the capacity to *think* of anything, then in turn we have the capability and capacity to *do* anything. Simple, huh? The good news is that we are programmed to learn, grow, and expand our horizons. If we want (told ya we could prove it) we can have the upward trajectory to any future we desire. We can, if we so choose, manifest any desire upon which we take action. We have to figure out ways to *Live The Risk* and *REACH*[6] for what we want.

---

6 Shameless plug for what we ended up calling the five major supporting parts of our book.

Over-the-Hill Versus Up-the-Hill

The next question we faced was: do we continue learning, growing, and expanding over a lifetime, or is there a limit? We first focused our research on ourselves. When we asked ourselves this question we wandered into several mind-altering[7] answers. We both acknowledged that, like most people, we assumed we'd have the same type of life that our parents and grandparents had (or would have). When we looked at the generations of those in the family who made it to retirement, it appears they learned what they needed, they grew to a certain level, and then they leveled off. They didn't really expand their minds with anything new; they seemed happy enough to "coast until retirement," where the expectation to learn ended. We both doubted that this was a conscious decision, but more like an expected cycle:

❑ From childhood "everything is possible"
❑ Settling of expectations
❑ Reap the fruits of their labor
❑ Time to rest the body
❑ Done learning
❑ "Over-the-hill" taken literally

Their lifeline goes from their uphill climb to this:

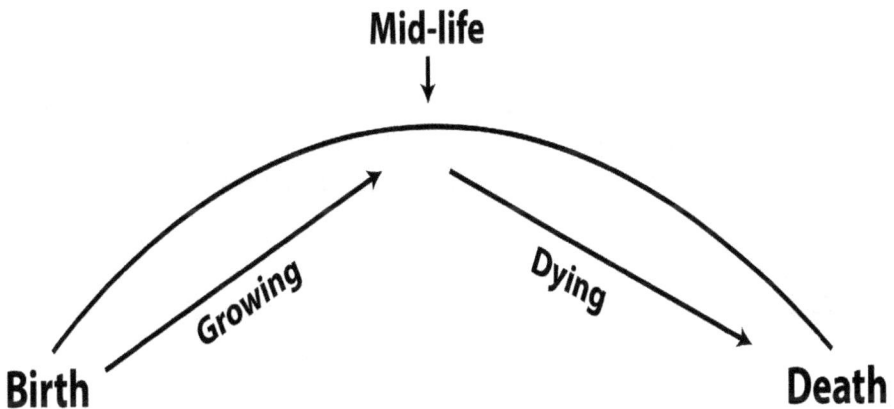

Mid-life

Birth   Growing   Dying   **Death**

---

7 Sounds like a drug reaction; it wasn't, we promise.

Of course, when we drew the model out on paper, it was obvious that if we're not growing, we're dying. Dying might not be in a physical final sense, but the process will start at the moment we stop learning. Quite frankly, we didn't like the answer we found. We saw that our folks and grandparents were living to work. Well, we were attempting to do the same exact thing. Ugh! After all, it's what we were taught.

We also figured out (this might frustrate some people) that there is no neutral on our lifeline road, just living or dying. There is no "middle." There is no "good enough." The top of the hill was the starting place to pick up speed for the end. We were both working to live, to pay the bills, to get to the grand old age of retirement, to relax, and then...well, you know...die.

We came to the amazing, profound, and honest opinion: This model sucks!

As we normally do, when we don't get an answer that we like, we look for a better one. We looked to see what others had said and then figured out what we should say. We came across some of the studies that bluntly told us if we don't *use* our minds, we *lose* our minds, so it pushed us to finding a different model. And a new model is what we discovered.

We chose to skip dying all together! Well, of course, that's not really possible, but what we mean is that we don't want to follow the path of growing, plateauing, and dying. We want to apply those neurons in the neocortex to help us live so that each and every move (or at least most of them) helps us maintain an active mind so we can keep applying it to new and different problems and situations.

OUR GOAL WAS TO SEE OUR TIME WELL SPENT IN AN ACTIVE FUTURE.

Quite frankly, we plan on taking the "living to work" motto of past generations and flipping it around to "working to live." At least it sounds better and looks better. In our own model, we altered the angle of the line, removed the hill, added a last moment, changed the assumption of entitlement, and fixed one word. The result is the "Living" model:

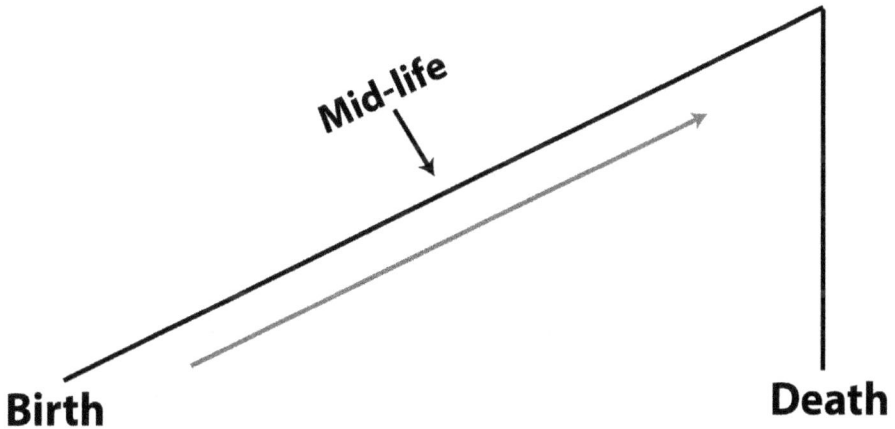

Mid-life

Birth

Death

Here's how it works. As we have already proven with the perfect baby story at the beginning of this chapter, we need to continually apply our inherent abilities to keep learning and growing. We can't think of mental limits as our stopping point. We also need to remove our defenses that nature developed for us, as well as the manufactured ones that will develop over time. We need to continually push ourselves toward a new goal by not looking at reaching one goal as finality, as much as the next goal being a new beginning.

We guess we can't even take credit for the Living model because every young generation that came before us was already using it. We are just extending it to the rest of our lives.

Honestly, we want our last words to be "Goodbye, I'm done," then shut our eyes with no regrets and no worries. Which means that *we will need to live in the now and also plan our future.*

Back to the Start

Do you know what you want to do when you grow up?

And now the more important question: *Do you have the fortitude to be willing to take action to leave the comfort of your current life to get what you want?*

Obviously for us it was a resounding "yes." It doesn't mean it wasn't scary, that we didn't question our abilities, or didn't worry about the outcome. It also didn't mean that we jumped without looking. It did mean that we went on a learning binge! We read everything we could get our hands on that might help guide us on our quest. We talked to our wives, kids, friends, mentors, and anyone else that would listen.

We learned: if you are not in control of yourself, making decisions for yourself, and living life to the fullest, you will not be able to say that you are *Living* your life. The path will be frustrating at times, but you will learn how to handle and welcome that frustration. We will help you to move outside your comfort zone, and in the end, grow from it!

To *Live The Risk* requires you to take positive action toward your vision of life. It's time to establish a goal, set forth a path, understand the topography, and put one foot in front of the other until you get there. And when you do achieve that goal, make another, then another, and then another! Doing so is called...**Living.**

If you are still fighting the urge to hold onto the exact life that you have, hoping and praying that nothing will change, or are putting your future on hold for a better time, then we have two questions:

IF NOT NOW, WHEN?
IF NOT YOU, WHO?

We have great faith in you and we know that you can do it. Of course, **you** need to know that you can do it. We suggest that you record what you are about to go through. Write your answers to our questions directly in this book. Record your thoughts and any epiphanies that might suddenly hit in its margins to track your journey. Keep good notes, write down your questions, and get some answers. This journey that you are on may be filled with obstacles that you have never faced before. Obstacles are often opportunities in disguise, and when you are making decisions for yourself, you'll be able to recognize them as such.

Of course, we are hoping and praying that in response you said, "Now" and "Me!" because there comes a time when, sooner rather than later, you need to decide that it's time to do something, anything! The time has come for you to make the ultimate commitment to yourself. You need to accomplish a project, activity, or task for yourself, not for fame or fortune, but because it's time you do so! Don't feel remorse for not starting any sooner. Don't make excuses to push it off until a little later. It's time to take control!

Remember, *if you are not Living, you are...Dying.*[8]

---

8 We sure hope that you want to follow the Living model; it does make the rest of the book a lot more fun.

To help make your choice a little smoother, here is a side-by-side comparison of the two models:

Living	Dying
No regrets	Unsatisfied, unfinished
Taking responsibility	Not feeling in control
Happy	Working toward others' goals
Healthy	Looking forward to the end, whatever/whenever it may be
Not worrying about what others think of you	Too busy to enjoy the moment
Goal-driven (having a plan)	Constant complaining. Not taking responsibility
Continually learning	Spending time making excuses so you can find someone else to blame
No excuses and owning your mistakes	Can't remember childhood dreams
Seeking opportunities to challenge yourself	Dreading each day
Making every day count	Not in control of your destiny
No such thing as retirement	"If only" and "I wish" instead of actions
Never trying, always doing	Too much energy spent talking about others
No one wants more for you than what you want for yourself	Remembering the past versus looking toward the future
Enjoying every new moment	The only exercise you get is jumping to conclusions
Never quitting	Never starting so you're never a quitter

The Top Reasons We Don't

We could snow you and say all you have to do is utter the magic question of "What do you want to do?" and all will come true, but we all know that isn't how it happens. Not only are there actions that need to be taken to get you to where you want to go, but there are barriers in the form of comments that are said and expectations from others that are laid in our psyche and are placed in our way.

Go back to your past; find a moment when you first blurted out to your mom or dad what you wanted to do. Now ask yourself, why didn't you become what you wanted? Here are the most popular word barriers and expectations that we found:

❑ That's just not realistic!

❑ You're not normal or our culture doesn't approve of that!

❑ Get a real job! That's just a hobby.

❑ Kryptonite (and any other excuse).

That's just not realistic!

❑ When Henry Ford told his mom that he wanted to build cars, do you think she said, "That's great, dear! Go forth and conquer the world! Don't forget to create the garage." It was probably more like, "That's nice, dear. Remember to wash your hands for dinner."

❑ "Maybe you should be the straight gal to my funny man," Desi Arnaz said to his redheaded wife, Lucille Ball.

❑ Can you imagine Isaac Newton's conversation with his dad? "Dad! Dad! This apple hit me on the head and I discovered something I'll call gravity!" Can you imagine his dad's reaction? "Son, what you discovered was the headache and a soon-to-be kick in the rear end if you don't get back to your chores!"

- ❑ How about Einstein? "Sis, I wonder what it would be like to ride a beam of light." "Oh, Albie, you're so stupid!"

- ❑ "Picasso, I don't know what you call that, but it sure isn't painting," said the neighbor kid to his friend upon seeing his "artwork."

- ❑ "I don't know what you think you're doing, but you need to be home cooking, cleaning, and learning to be a proper lady like your mommy," said the other little girls to their odd friend, Florence Nightingale.

What amazes us, for most folks, is that these situations[9] would have ended their future right then and there if they chose to believe what people said to them. Here you think you know what you want and you have the courage to say it out loud, but then you abandon what you want because you didn't get the response you expected or desired from friends and family. Really? Why give that much control to others? Your imagination could contain the next big thing, or not. But if you don't have the courage to make it a reality, who will?

Honestly, your future can't be foreseen. The unknown is just that... unknown. Realism has a mental limit, and its limit is the present moment. This means everything that comes after it can't be realistic; it can only be optimistic or pessimistic, and we don't know why anyone would be pessimistic when they are imagining what they can do. However, too often we allow others to dictate what direction our lives will take. We are, after all, social creatures and want to be accepted. Who would want to be on the outside looking in? Everyone we mentioned above: Henry Ford, Lucille Ball, Sir Isaac Newton, Albert Einstein, Pablo Picasso, and Florence Nightingale had to be on the outside for a little while before they defined the new "in."

> There isn't another animal on earth that thinks about the future the way we do.

---

9 We don't know what conversations really took place, but you get the point. Not to mention it was fun to make it up!

You're not normal
or our culture doesn't approve of that!
(Or social expectations say you should or shouldn't)

To start, here are some questions to answer:

- ❑ Which culture fits being an accountant or CPA?
- ❑ Which culture should trade in diamonds?
- ❑ Which culture has really good dancers?
- ❑ Which culture produces good doctors?
- ❑ Which culture fits being convenience store owners?
- ❑ Which culture makes good laborers?
- ❑ Which culture has strong and great lifters?
- ❑ Which culture is known for great basketball players?
- ❑ Which culture has bad teeth?
- ❑ Which culture makes great bartenders?

Now let's fill in the blanks:

- ❑ Blondes are _____.
- ❑ Models are all _____.
- ❑ Politicians are all _____.
- ❑ Girls are ____ and boys are _____.
- ❑ Dads are good at ____ and moms are good at _____.

We suspect that some of our readers gave really specific answers; they knew exactly the type, group, culture or gender that would provide the answers to the questions. Good news is that they are probably wrong. We expect that most of our insightful readers are all worldly individuals and that everyone answered the culture questions with: "Who cares as long as they are good at what they do," and filled in the blanks with: "smart," "representative of the real people," "tall," "awesome," "icky," "cooking," and "fixing things." Now, if your answers don't match ours – it's okay, not everyone can be everything (especially tall). It doesn't matter, because it has nothing to do with culture or stereotypes.

We know that many people don't want to hear it, but in our recent past, men and women had specific roles in the working world. Men became doctors and women became nurses; never did the two switch roles. And then they did. Someone of either sex had the idea that maybe they fit better in the other "normal" role. Well, good for them! They didn't let stereotypes and out-of-date ideas stand in the way of getting what they wanted. In case you wondered, the first woman to graduate from a U.S. medical school was Elizabeth Blackwell, MD, in 1849. Until 1930, men were excluded from the American Nurses Association. It took until 1993 to have the first U.S. woman fighter pilot, USAF Col. Jeannie Leavitt. In the progressive industry of the movies, it wasn't until 2010 that a woman won the Best Director award from the Academy of Motion Picture Arts and Sciences. It goes to show you that "normal" means nothing, and that amazing things can be accomplished when you choose not to allow others to place restrictions on your future.

We have all seen or have experienced stereotypes from our culture, history, gender, religion, clothes, etc. And just so you know where we stand: We think it is wrong. No one gets to say we are this or that because one is Jewish, Christian, was in the army or not, has the ability to grow hair or doesn't. (Jeff is still upset at that last one.) No one gets to pigeonhole us because of what they think our DNA is or isn't. No one! If we don't make this clear we are doing a terrible disservice to ourselves; if we don't help dispel the rumors, we are encouraging them. We need to treat everyone – and we mean everyone – as the human beings that they are; each with an optimistic and unlimited future regardless of any categorization method (gender, sex, race, creed, color, religion, etc.) that might exist.

Get a real job. That's just a hobby.

It's one of the most frustrating things to hear – but in honesty hearing "real job" and "hobby" are only in comparison to what the speaker knows. It has nothing to do with the listener (you). At the end, it doesn't matter what the other person says. The question becomes, what are you going to do about it? Are you willing to not ask anything from anybody while you travel your path? Have no bills? Take the bus? Take jobs that provide the capital so you can get the things you need? Will you take on the struggles of being on the outside of your family and friends' expectations of you? Can you handle the criticisms and shrugs?

We are really serious. If you want that answer to, "What do you want to do?" then you need to be willing to work for it.

> If you haven't figured it out, we are not about sugar-coating anything for anybody. We want everyone to go in to his or her future with his or her eyes wide open in order to see the obstacles and avoid or at least not be surprised by them.

Kryptonite (and other excuses)

This subject is *huge!* We give you our personal guarantee that we will devote an entire chapter to this subject later on. But just to whet your appetite here is our thought: **excuses do nothing**. Sure they fill time and space, and take energy to create, but they give you nothing in return. They don't make you any more successful in whatever you do. Actually, they prevent you from attempting new things and doing your best. They stand in the way of your taking responsibility for your own actions because they give you an escape route. Under no circumstances do they help you answer your question: *What do I want to do when I grow up?*

You know that Superman had the best excuse in the world (actually multiple worlds). He would become powerless when he came into contact with Kryptonite. Now, if it had been a real excuse, every time he was with Lois Lane instead of answering his call, he could have excused his behavior by saying, "Can't help, Lois. There will probably be Kryptonite there. I would be powerless! Let's just go to the movies." Of course, he never said it. He didn't shy away from a fight or saving someone, and as far as we know, he never made an excuse – except for when he had to change into his blue tights and red underwear. Rumor has it that he was once heard to say, "Does this outfit make me look fat?"

Living - It's Good!

Too often we forget this one simple fact:

IN REGARD TO LIVING,
THE CHOICE HAS ALWAYS BEEN YOURS.

Keep in mind that if you are not living then you are surely dying, and dying sucks. It means that you won't get the chance to have the life you really want, game over! We believe that we have shown beyond a shadow of a doubt[10] that living and growing is what your DNA expects. You have been encoded to succeed. You can achieve *anything* to which you put your mind.

> We know that it seems we are taking significant liberties with the "living" and "dying" words (and we probably are). Each time we use this model with folks they tend to get a wake up call in their own lives because they realize that they have been conditioned to accept (yep, *accept*) the Dying model. We are not about accepting the norm. In fact, that we can choose between the two is what we accept. So should you.

We are going to put some misbeliefs of the Living model to rest right now.

First, you can still grow in retirement and rest!

Second, growing doesn't mean work – it means positive challenges within your mindset!

Third, you don't have to be physically strong, just mentally strong.

Fourth, there are plateaus within the Living model and no massive downhill descents. You get to stop and smell the roses.

---

10 Or at least a shadow under a moonless sky.

Fifth, who wants to be dying?

Sixth, the choice is yours, always has been and always will be.

Seventh, living is all about action, so what are you going to do about it today?

Most people we know actually are more worried about the process of dying (the time, the pain, the problems) than death itself. In truth, what we learned while researching this section was that *thanatophobia*[11] is the abnormal fear of death and dying, and there are six major fear issues associated to it:

❑ Unknown - not knowing what happens next.

❑ Non-existence - being nothing after it is all over.

❑ Loss of control - not in control of your life.

❑ Pain and suffering - will death be slow and miserable.

❑ What will become of loved ones - the future of those that you leave behind.

❑ Punishment - will I be judged for the things only I know I did wrong.

Here is the interesting part (yes, we do find everything interesting): We found that the above list is exactly the same reasons why people want to live. These are the same reasons that people want to make changes in their lives. The only difference in the Living model is that they are not in fear of it; they embrace it. They expect it. They want answers to the six questions above, not because they will die from it, but because they know that they will grow from it.

Take a moment and let's reframe and represent these six items so they can co-exist in the Living model. Examine the six items; determine for yourself how you can represent them in your life so

---

11 Thanatophobia is a big word - hard to spell, harder to pronounce.

they are not fears, but powerful goals.[12] Here is our example:

- ❑ What item that is **unknown** to me can I learn about today?

- ❑ What can I do today that will reinforce my **existence** in this world?

- ❑ What actions can I take that will allow me to take **control** mentally, physically, emotionally, spiritually, and perceptually of myself today?

- ❑ What should I do/not do to remove, avoid, or eliminate any **pain and suffering** today and in the future?

- ❑ What plans can I put in place today that will make sure my **loved ones** are taken care of when my time is up?

- ❑ What will I start or stop doing today so that I am not in fear of **punishment**?

You don't have to accept what we wrote (actually, you probably shouldn't). You can rewrite any of these questions in any fashion that you want; just make each question a stepping stone to help you live and to get to where you want to be! When you think about it, how you present something to yourself becomes the divide that separates the two models.

Can You Answer the Question?

We are going to help you exercise what you have learned. This will require you to get into your time travel machine and go back to your past. Attempt to remember your first real serious image of your future; something that you knew, if given the chance, you would do for at least a few years. Go back to that moment. For some it was being an actor, being in a band, maybe a doctor, anything will do. What's important is that it is in *your* past.

---

12 Remember, we are not religious scholars - so think about it on an earthly level. If you can apply the same

process in a heavenly sense - go for it!

Take a moment and attempt Journal Entry (JE) number one:

Journal Entry #1: Your Youthful Future.

What did you want to do?

What did you do after you imagined your future?

What energy did it give you?

What personal expectations did you set?

Results: a) Did you succeed? b) Did you fail? c) Did you give up altogether?

Did you ask and answer the questions? If yes, please skip to the next paragraph. If not, we love when people skip over the exercises in the book. Why waste your time thinking about what occurred in your past and why it occurred? You're a different person, doing different things. You are no longer calculating the time mom and dad will be home so you can figure out when to party at the house. You don't have to worry about hiding your grades from your parents, forging a signature to take sex education in school, or wanting a better reason to wake up early on Sunday than "you have church." You are your own person (really); you can look at your own grades (and be as embarrassed as your parents were), you can sign your own permission slips, and if you don't want to go anywhere you don't have to (sounds faintly like story #1). Even the world has figured out (including some notably smart people like Jorge Agustín Nicolás

Ruiz de Santayana y Borrás[13]) that those who are not students of history are doomed to repeat it. We get it – you are different. But even so, would you look at the questions and answer them anyway? It's part of the Living model.

Let's look at your answers and add a few more questions.

1. <u>What did you want to do?</u> Was it far-reaching? Did it stretch you as an individual? Was it clear and concise? Would it have changed your world? Would it have lasted only a little while? Did you only want it because someone else also wanted it? Did someone else want it for you and you went along for the ride?

2. <u>What did you do after you imagined your future?</u> Here is where you find out if you have traction or not. How much time did you commit to your future, each and every day? What actions did you take? How much progress did you make toward your future?

3. <u>What energy did it give you?</u> When you chased (ran, walked, or crawled) to your future, did it give you the energy to keep working on it? When you were at your lowest moments did your dream provide you with that added boost just by thinking about it? When thinking about your future, did you feel a sense of freedom, that this would be the beginning of something wonderful?

4. <u>What personal expectations did you set?</u> What bars did you raise to achieve your future? What did you learn about yourself? What risks did you take? What challenges did you overcome?

5. Results: <u>Did you succeed?</u> Are you doing it today? Has it evolved? Are you still energized when pursuing your future? <u>Did you fail?</u> If so, why? Did you really want to achieve your future? Was it a future filled with passion or a passing fancy? Was it truly your future?

---

13 Spanish-American novelist, philosopher, poet and essayist, (Dec. 16, 1863 – Sept. 26, 1952). Santayana is known for famous sayings, such as, "Those who cannot remember the past are condemned to repeat it."

For some you may find it difficult to look at the one thing that you really wanted and see why you did or did not take action to make it a reality. Sad to say that for most it was a cool thing to achieve and then your mind shifted to the next shiny item...and you moved on. Your imagined future was a minor moment that you wanted to have. Be honest: What really held you back? Did reality trap you? Did the normal life keep you from achieving? Was the imagined future what you really wanted? Was it worth your time? Was it something that was a hobby versus an oh-my-gosh-I-have-to-have-it future?

For the minority who do go after their futures – congrats! We are hoping that you are wildly successful and are still doing it today. We hope you have continued to morph your original dream into the next big thing that your universe needs and wants.

I Believe, I Can, I Am, I Will

The process that you are about to embark on is one where you get to reimagine what your future will be like. You are going to take the simple question of "What do I want to do when I grow up?" and make sure that you are aligned to achieve it. This alignment will include your dream, which will lead you to your passions, purpose, and finally to your immediate vision of your life. Together they give you a solid foundation to stand on. We have written this section in the order that seemed to make the most sense to us:

Dream	Dreams are the mental and/or emotional representation of what I want, need or desire
Passion	Passion is the internal drive (energy) to continuously pursue my endeavors
Purpose	Purpose is the continuous self-discovery of why I exist
Vision	Vision is the compelling long-term view of my desired results

Of course, if you have decided that the order will be different, fine by us. If you want to accomplish passion first, so be it. If you understand why you exist, start with purpose. If you can see your long-term future, by all means start with vision. Package them differently and use what you will (we are glad that you are using it). Just make sure that all four are a united front all pointing in the same direction when you are done with this section. *They are your compasses for obtaining your future.*

Still don't believe us? We pulled out from the babbling brook of amazing knowledge (better known as the internet) some amazing examples across all age groups. History doesn't break down where they started for us, just that they had a direction, lived through their risks and challenges, and obtained something great:

- ❑ Ludwig van Beethoven. His teachers thought that he was hopeless and that he would never succeed as a composer or at the violin. But Beethoven kept up with his passion. He eventually composed some of the best-loved symphonies of all time. Five of these were composed when he was completely deaf.

- ❑ Eleanor Roosevelt. Did you know that she was one of the first women elected to the Senate in 1911? After her husband's death in 1945, she was able to continue her work when she was named a delegate to the newly founded United Nations the following year. In 1947, she became the first chairman of the Commission on Human Rights, during which time she helped draft the Universal Declaration of Human Rights. By the time of her death in 1962, she had also authored four books.[1]

- ❑ Lieutenant Colonel Tracy Onufer, Commander, 16th Special Operations Squad. Only the second woman operational commander in the ultra-selective Air Force Special Ops, Onufer supports global undercover missions with a staff of 165 — most of them men. Over nine deployments, as of this writing, she's won seventeen medals and a Distinguished Flying Cross, the military's highest aviation honor, for protecting her aircraft on a 2003 mission in Iraq.[2]

---

1 http://www.toptenz.net/top-10-most-famous-women-in-history.php

2 http://www.marieclaire.com/career-money/jobs/women-on-top-tracy-onufer

❏ Elvis Presley may be known as the King of Rock and Roll, but back when he was still unknown, he got fired after one performance. His then-manager, Jimmy Denny, told him, "You ain't goin' nowhere, son. You ought to go back to drivin' a truck." Millions of fans were sure glad he didn't listen and pursued his dream.[3]

❏ Harrison Ford. You have seen him in many movie blockbuster hits such as *Star Wars* and *Indiana Jones*. There is no doubt that he can act convincingly. In 2003, he received a star on the Hollywood Walk of Fame. However, in his first film, Ford was told by movie execs that he did not have what it would take to be a star. As a struggling artist, he did carpentry work. Helping George Lucas in his house landed him his first starring film role as Han Solo in *Star Wars*.[3]

❏ Madame Marie Curie. She was a largely penniless student who worked as a governess and tutor while pursuing her dream of becoming a physicist, an unheard-of occupation for a woman in the nineteenth century. Besides being the first woman to win a Nobel Prize in science, she became the first female head of the Laboratory at the Sorbonne University in Paris and went on to win a second Nobel Prize, this one in Chemistry, in 1911 (a feat not repeated until 1962).[4]

❏ Winston Churchill makes the perfect role model for the advice that you're never too old to get started. He was defeated in every election for public office until he finally became the prime minister at the age of sixty-two. He said, "I am an optimist. It does not seem too much use being anything else." We're willing to bet there are a lot of people who are glad that he didn't give up on his passion for public service.[4]

You've got to admit all of the stories are quite amazing. These average folks had a direction, cultivated it, and made it a reality. They didn't let realistic expectations, safe thinking, stereotypes, or excuses get in their way.

---

3 http://www.abundancetapestry.com/21-role-models-for-success

4 http://www.toptenz.net/top-10-most-famous-women-in-history.php

Let's answer the big question up front: Can this quad of items (dreams, passion, purpose, and vision, which are better known through the rest of this book as DPPV) change over time? As our Minnesota friends like to say, *youbetcha* (it means yes). Let's be perfectly clear. It does not change because the wind blows, the birds come back in spring, a new movie comes out, or because of what you had to eat last night. Change normally follows great introspection (think significant emotional events). We will share a secret (so say this to yourself quietly):

> ### *IF WALKING YOUR TALK ABOUT YOUR DPPV INTENSIFIES OVER TIME, THEN THIS PATH OF EXISTENCE IS VERY TRUE FOR YOU. IF IT FADES OUT IN A SHORT MATTER OF TIME, IT IS A FALSE PATH.*

And we have got to tell you, if you are walking your talk, you are unlocking the portion of the human spirit that most keep locked away. It is your personal path to your future.

Now it's your turn to determine your starting place. You need to think of the four items as a wheel of fortune, except there are no bankruptcies and you cannot lose. You can spin and no matter where it lands it will give you a prize, which is a starting place to find the others. No matter where you start, each question that you ask yourself will give you hints to your direction and future.

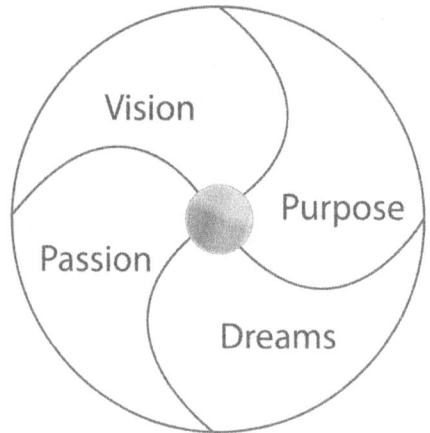

Time to spin the wheel.

Wheel Portion	Determination
Are you able to define "What you want to do," and are you still chasing it? What was it? Would you call it your dream?	As you will learn, Dreams are timeless and boundless. If yes, start with Dreams, Passion, Purpose, and Vision. Read and participate; it is going to be fairly easy for you to figure out the rest. Now don't be surprised if as you go through the other sections you find yourself needing to refine the dream.
You don't know what you want to do, but you do know what gives you energy and excitement in your life.	Now this is not something that you *think* gives you energy; this is something that *does* give you energy – something that you have actually done and can't wait to do again. If so, we recommend going to the Passion section first and see where the section takes you. There is a test of nine questions that might help you determine if your passion is really your passion. We suspect that you will go to either Dreams or Vision afterward.
Do you know why you currently exist in this world? (It can't be survival or a generic item – be specific.)	Most will claim only their current role like mom, dad, brother, sister, worker. Why you exist is much more. To a pastor it might be to bring the message of God to their flock "right now." To a martial arts teacher it is to teach children to protect themselves from bullies "right now." Folks who start with Purpose normally have the sense of what they need right now. It will be important to make sure that this purpose will also transcend into a future (i.e. vision or dream) and be backed up by passion.

Do you know what you want life to be in fifteen years?	If the others are tough to answer we suggest starting at Vision. The only caveat is that you have to have a view of your future results in two or more of four distinct areas: Home and Family, Education and Career, Community and Service, and Hobbies and Recreation. It is okay if you can't see fifteen years out. Keep reducing the timeframe until you can see your future (though please make it more than five years). After Vision, we recommend taking your direction into Passion, Dreams, and lastly, Purpose.

At the end, when the DPPV support each other (in whatever order you start), they propel you forward to begin your journey. If one is missing it will be painful and a waste (like jumping many stairs at once and missing the landing).

We request that after you find your starting point, come back around and review the other sections. Each one has been designed to help test your own resolve and commitment. No need to cheat yourself (remember, no one needs to know if you tell yourself the truth).

DREAMS: Setting My Direction

We need to make sure that we allow our minds to dream in order to grow, because dreaming really unlocks our opportunity to align who, what, why, and where we are going. First and foremost, dreams are the door to an amazing world that only you can see, which is why it can be anything that you want it to be. Your dreams are always about the future; they have no limits, boundaries, or worries.

We know, we know, that nagging thought of not having enough money, skills, or time will get in the way of your dreams. **Don't let it!** Remember, you could pick any dream,[5] and given access to the right resources you will achieve your dream. Money, skills, and time are nothing more than excuses (which we will talk about later). If you really want something, you will figure out a way to make it happen. You might not be able to do everything at once. You might have to invest in your own education and take night courses over years; you might have to save every penny and learn the process of fundraising to achieve what you want, but it is possible. Self-made millionaires, such as J. K. Rowling, Madonna, Bill Cosby, Ben Franklin, Andrew Mason, Ronald Reagan, and Catherine Cook started with nothing and made it big despite the odds. Good old Benjamin Franklin ran away as a teen and became America's first self-made millionaire. Even Superman himself, actor Christopher Reeve, after having a devastating and paralyzing accident, was able to contribute and raise funds, support, and awareness for paralysis victims. Here is a man that could not move anything below his neck and he fought his body for the right to move it again. It took years of painful exercises to help retrain the brain to accomplish what he did. Even though it was only small movements, it was what he had hoped for, movement. He didn't allow the accident to be an excuse to not live anymore. Yes, his dream changed after the accident, but his desire to achieve his dream did not[6].

You need to have the same drive if you are going to achieve your fullest potential, because if you don't, then you start coasting

---

5 Because who are we to say which dreams can or can't be realized.

6 http://www.christopherreeve.org/site/c.ddJFKRNoFiG/b.4431483/

downhill. No future means you have started your slide into "die" mode and we don't think you need to let it happen because you have a choice (personally, we didn't let it happen). Oh, and when you're coasting downhill you begin picking up speed to... a grave. Yuck! We also want to make it very clear that just dreaming the big dream and not taking all of the appropriate actions to get it makes no sense. This is when reality smacks you upside the head – you can't pay your bills as an actor if you aren't getting any acting jobs. So just dreaming is not good enough; you have to follow up and follow through to achieve what you want (but we will get to what you should be doing in later chapters).

> Dreams are personal in nature, so you shouldn't care what others think. It's more important that you care about what you think.

Now before everyone gets up in arms, let's put a positive spin on this. We want you to have an outrageously great dream to pull you forward through the current muck. We don't want you to give up on what matters most to you (and yes, the dream needs to be so powerful that it matters most, right after responsibility, family, and spiritual needs). On the flip side we also don't want you to allow life to get in the way of a perfectly good time. And dreams need to be good times. (Honestly, who is going to spend their life's work on having a bad time?) We need to start elevating our dreams to the future pedestal that they belong on and then moving toward them each and every day.

Beware: the biggest pitfall in life is waiting patiently on the sidelines and *settling.* Yep, we said it! Dreams dissipate when settling becomes your norm. Settling occurs when you lower your standards of yourself and you stop taking action to improve.

SETTLING = STOP TAKING ACTION + ACCEPT LESS

All of a sudden you wake up one day, and being average or even below average is okay. You no longer want to change and grow and you are okay with the status quo. And when you settle, it isn't like the world stops moving and everything stays the same. Nope, you start accepting less from your life, less from yourself. Less becomes the new normal. Then later you accept less than before and lower and lower you go . . . on the downward slide. Think of a toilet flush and the swirl that goes around and around and then down the drain. That's what it's like when you allow less to be your normal.

Those folks who are entering this process with us should not be thinking about average dreams. Your dreams need to be grand, great, and amazing! Let's define what dreams really are:

> # Dreams are the representation of what I want, need, or desire

Think of a dream as a special long flying dart that has the capacity to be thrown past the horizon. You pick its direction by the way you stand and hold the dart. You throw it. You are really not sure where it lands; it's too far away and is out of sight. You search it out by walking the path that the dart took. Each step brings you closer to the end objective of finding your dart. Some might never find it, others might get close, and some will retrieve it to one day throw again. The goal of your dream is to have a lofty, timeless, boundless objective in life. It doesn't have to be overly specific; to some it will not be realistic or believable. It doesn't matter because it isn't their dream, it's yours.

> **Journal Entry #2: Your Dream. Close your eyes and think about your dream. If you have more than one, pick the one that you are most passionate about, then open your eyes and write it down here:**

Ask yourself if your dream helps you develop tenacity. Does it provide you with the opportunity to focus on your future? Does your dream allow you to think big? Does it allow you to break the bounds of realistic, normal and stereotypical? Does it ignite your energy? Does your dream keep you moving forward?

> If you find that your current dream doesn't answer all of the questions, please keep refining (expanding, altering, changing) until it does. It's important that your dream fill your heart up, because if it doesn't, you'll never have the courage to overcome every obstacle that will inevitably get in your way of getting it.
> Dreams must be potent!!

For example: If you want to make movies then you better learn the trade. Paraphrased from *Reader's Digest*,[7] here is a story about a man named Steven Spielberg who followed his dreams:

> "He was no scholar and his classmates teased him. Rather than read, the kid really preferred running around with a 8 mm camera, shooting homemade movies of wrecks of his Lionel train set (which he showed to friends for a small fee). In his sophomore year of high school, he dropped out. But when his parents persuaded him to return, he was mistakenly placed in a learning-disabled class. He lasted one month. Only when the family moved to another town did he land in a more suitable high school, where he eventually graduated.
>
> After being denied entrance into a traditional filmmaking school, Steven Spielberg enrolled in English at California State College at Long Beach. Then in 1965, he recalls, in one of those serendipitous moments, his life took a complete turn. Visiting Universal Studios, he

---

7 http://www.rdasia.com/how-famous-people-achieved-their-dreams

met Chuck Silvers, an executive in the editorial department. Silvers liked the kid who made 8 mm films and invited him back sometime to visit.

He appeared the next day. Without a job or security clearance, Spielberg (dressed in a dark suit and tie, carrying his father's briefcase with nothing inside but "a sandwich and candy bars") strode confidently up to the guard at the gate of Universal and gave him a casual wave. The guard waved back. He was in.

"For the entire summer," Spielberg remembers, "I dressed in my suit and hung out with the directors and writers [including Silvers, who knew the kid wasn't a studio employee, but winked at the deception]. I even found an office that wasn't being used, and became a squatter. I bought some plastic tiles and put my name in the building directory: Steven Spielberg, Room 23C."

It paid off for everyone. Ten years later, the 28-year-old Spielberg directed *Jaws*, which took in $470 million, then the highest-grossing movie of all time. Dozens of films and awards have followed because Steven Spielberg knew what his teachers didn't — talent is in the eyes of the filmmaker."

His dreams, if compared to others, were probably bigger than he was (just like it should be in your case), but it didn't stop him and it shouldn't stop you. Sure, some might say it was luck, though we believe it was more than that, because Spielberg took action to achieve what he wanted to achieve. He threw his dart and then walked his path to the best of his abilities. He was able to do, improve, and achieve, over and over again until he got what he wanted. How do you think he would have answered the following questions:

- ❑ What do you want to do?
- ❑ What did you do after dreaming the big dream?
- ❑ What energy did you give it?
- ❑ What personal expectations did you set?

We can pretty much guarantee that based on his direction and the results he obtained, they were all very detailed and positive. Now, we all know that it probably wasn't easy; there were doubts and some big falls. Each time, he got back up until he achieved what he wanted! History says that his mind, body, and breath (spirit) were aligned with his direction.

> We don't care what any book (including this one) promises. Without choices, determination, and guts, you aren't going to get what you want. Period. If you want your dream, you have to start walking toward it! No one wants you to achieve your future more than you. It is, after all, yours.

PASSION: Have the Energy to Take the Next Step

To some, passion is an act,[8] while to others it's a clue from beyond. For us, it means "energy giver." Passion is the internal drive to continuously pursue your endeavors. It is our internal drive to succeed. Think of it as the power to take the next step.

> # Passion is the internal energy to continuously pursue my endeavors

Imagine what it would be like if your passion were disconnected from everything else: Your time and energy are spent in activity A when you really want to be doing activity B. You are wandering through lackluster events hoping and praying to find a way through your life. Who wants that? No one. But when passion is ignited and it is connected to your dreams, purpose, and vision – look out world, here you come! Passion also has the capability to help you test if your dream (vision, or goal for that matter) is right for you. As you have figured out, if a car doesn't have fuel, then the car is useless[9]. Passion can test if what you are doing in life is an energy giver, if it will help raise the bar for yourself, if it can help define who you are, and if it can most definitely navigate between successes and failures.

When you are passionate about what you do and where you are going, then you can accomplish anything. It doesn't mean there aren't timeframes, rules, and obstacles. It does mean you have the power to keep going until it is done. If you are one of the folks who started in a different place, then passion can also provide you with a clue as to what your life should be about. As Joel tells his daughters: Do what you love.

---

8 Now we can make some crude jokes and trust us, we wrote many.

9 In other words, passion gives you gas... to succeed.

It is also important to remember that passion is not an excuse. There are times when we are full of energy and the best thing we should and could do is to slow down and enjoy what is going on around us.

> There is no better way to figure out what you love than by looking at where you put your energy.

Though we wish there were a physical test to prove passion, it really comes down to how you respond when passion is turned on toward a particular subject – in this case, your dreams, purpose, or vision (wherever you happen to start). So think about your subject and answer the following questions (you will find more details about The Passion Questions[10] in Appendix A):

Journal Entry #3: The Passion Questions. Answer "yes" or "no" to all of the following questions:

1. Does my passion fill me with energy?

2. Am I a student of my passion?

3. Am I becoming an expert in my passion?

4. Does my passion force me to raise the bar on myself?

5. Are my 'values' and 'culture' in support of my passion?

6. Do my friends identify my passion in me and see the positive results that it brings?

7. Am I willing to fail at my passion and then keep on attempting?

8. Does my passion apply to both work and home life?

9. Am I willing to give up material things to obtain my passion?

10 The Passion Questions © 2005 – 2013 L.E. Robinson II & JS Levinson.

If you can answer "yes" to all, then congrats! You have passed one of the tests that have stumped most people. You can maintain control, keep moving forward, and handle the successes that you will have. You don't see failure, because problems are nothing more than annoying hurdles that need to be cleared. You can see and obtain your future by constantly making choices. Most importantly, you accept responsibility for what you want to be and where you are going. Congrats, you are able to take the next step along your journey.

If you can't answer "yes" to all of them (and we mean *all*), then we would tell you that your passion isn't going to support where you want to go. Sure, you will make some progress, but at some point in your future – the batteries will run low and you won't have the energy to keep moving forward. Go back and really think about your dream or vision, strengthen it, and make sure it's yours. If your starting place was passion, we suggest that you refine what you think until you can answer "yes" to all nine questions.

From Jeff:

I had always wanted to be an entrepreneur, but I was afraid to take a risk. I listened to others tell me what was best for me – that the safe path would guarantee my future, and of course, happiness. By taking the safe path I could provide for a family, have a home, and that ever-important pension. During my tenure as a teacher I found I really loved helping others find success. While on the path that others had directed me to take I was always looking at what success meant to me. When I answered honestly, I found that I wanted freedom and that I couldn't worry about what others thought. I had to live my life, as I wanted, in order to really live the life I desired.

PURPOSE: Keep Walking Strong

As you start on your journey you must have the courage to keep walking. Understanding the *whys* of your life can help magnify the courage required, especially if your current *why* is the impetus for helping you take the next step (and of course, all of the steps after that). The *why* we're going to discuss now is *purpose*. It is the linchpin to keeping your DPPV aligned. Purpose keeps giving you a reason to take the next step because it is directly related to your current life.

If your starting point is here, then by answering what the purpose of your life is right now will give you the hint of what your dreams, passion and vision are. In more esoteric words:

> # Purpose is the continuous self-discovery of *why* I exist

As we researched this topic we came to the conclusion that purpose allows you to keep making progress as you refine yourself. Purpose gives you the opportunity to keep asking *why,* to ensure that your direction continues to drive you toward what you believe you want from where you are today.

- ❏ *Why will what you do now help you?*
- ❏ *Why does it pull at you with such force?*
- ❏ *Why are you willing to work so hard to get it?*
- ❏ *Why are you in this world, doing these things?*

Purpose gives you immediate answers to these questions directly from your core (gut and heart) and points you in the right direction. It's a great tool to use when results aren't what you expected or you don't feel like you're making any progress at all, yet you know you're on track and just need more time. It's hard to keep going when you don't see immediate results. Purpose keeps you going.

Mother Teresa is a great example of someone who went through this entire process:[11]

❑ What did she want to be when she grew up? Her dream by the age of twelve was to become a missionary and commit herself to a religious life.

❑ Was she passionate about what she wanted to be? Oh, yes. She continued to learn, understand, and pray. By the age of eighteen, she made her final resolution while praying at the shrine of the Black Madonna of Letnice, Kosovo.

❑ Did she find the *why* and *how* to her existence? Several times. Her purpose kept evolving. At age eighteen, she joined the Sisters of Loreto as a missionary. At nineteen, she went to India to teach children. At twenty-seven, she devoted her life to the Catholic Church as a nun. And at thirty-six, she took up her calling to help the poor of Calcutta while living amongst them. Yet all steps supported the same two dreams: to serve God and help people.

❑ Until her death at eighty-seven, she lived her dream, fueled by her passion, and focused by her purpose. She had trials and tribulations, but she never abandoned her dreams. She left behind a legacy that included the establishment of 610 missions in 123 countries.

Now, here's the difficult aspect of purpose. When you strongly believe in what you are doing, you may start barreling down paths and become myopic[12] in method and thought. You start bypassing what could be very important steps that could help you in the game for the long term. Your awareness can drop. When you get tunnel vision, you do the next easy thing, though it might not be the right thing. You're taking steps, but more automatically than by choice. Avoiding choices will make your dreams, passion, and vision stagnant...or worse, disappear. (It is right up there with dying.)

---

11 http://en.wikipedia.org/wiki/Mother_Teresa

12 You become near- or shortsighted, unmindful of future consequences.

As always, there's a way out of it. Make sure you constantly review your DPPV and ensure that your actions support it. Keep an eye on the final prize (that dream and vision) so you don't get distracted by shiny objects that pop into your line of vision now and then. Yes, you always have the power of choice, but allowing yourself to be distracted from the main goal lengthens the time for achieving it. At the same time, don't pass up an opportunity to stretch yourself if it supports the overall goal.

Keep recreating and refining this new you, so that it will support your future. Purpose helps keep your dreams and passion in motion in the now, and that's Living!

> If you want to be an artist and an opportunity presents itself to learn photography – which interests you – follow that up. Photography teaches you how to see things with a unique perspective, and that not only teaches you a new skill, but also supports your overall dream. As a result, your artwork could become even stronger. On the other hand, if an opportunity presents itself to learn how to make quick, low-calorie casseroles....well, not so much.

For a friend of ours, he so strongly believed in providing hope to children that he created an entire organization to help deliver his *why* across America. It's called Kids At Hope.[13] Another friend found his purpose in knowing Jesus Christ, to grow in Him, to serve Him, and to help others do the same. He found his *why* by joining a seminary. Now he lives his life accordingly and preaches the Gospel.

Joel's purpose is to be a catalyst in life and to help his family, friends, strangers, organizations, and businesses achieve their future. He wants to continue growing and learning so he may change his life to achieve financial freedom, flexibility of time, and an awe-inspiring life with his wife, family, and friends.

---

13 You are welcome to learn about Kids At Hope at kidsathope.org.

Journal Entry #4A: Defining Your Purpose - Describe yourself right now:

Who are you?

What are your likes, dislikes, hates, loves, prejudices?

What fears do you have?

What successes? What failures?

What makes you feel great about yourself?

If you had to describe yourself in eight seconds what words would you use? If you had to pick one word that describes you what would it be? ("Sexy" or "stud" is not exactly what you're looking for; dig a little deeper.)

What do you have to change in yourself to achieve the things you want to achieve?

Journal Entry #4B: Defining Your Purpose - Significant people, decisions, and events

What significant people, decisions, and events help or helped alter your life? Why?

a) For people: what did they say or do?

b) For decisions: what choices did you have and why did you pick one over the other?

c) For events: why do you remember this as a game changer?

Journal Entry #4C: Defining Your Purpose - Details of you, Part I

What or who inspires you? What qualities are you inspired by? (The more the merrier, and please don't limit this to the famous or infamous).

What actions make you lose track of time?

What are your favorite things to do? How much of your 168 hours in a given week do you spend on your favorite things? (Think carefully about this. You might get a rude awakening that what you spend your time on isn't a favorite or healthy thing to do.)

What are you naturally good at?

What would you regret not doing in your life?

Journal Entry #4D: Defining Your Purpose - Details of You, Part II

If you could solve any problem in the world (remember, dreams are limitless), what would it be?

What causes do you strongly believe and participate in (this is about the time you invest, not the money)?

If you could get a large group of people to do exactly what you say, what would you say to them? Why?

What makes you smile?

Look for the common themes that developed when you answered the questions in JE #4A-D and define your purpose in the following journal entry. It needs to be powerful, compact and very current:

Journal Entry #5: My Purpose

My purpose right now is to (fill in the blank):

_____.

Ask yourself these questions: Does my purpose help link what I am doing today to what I want to do in the future? Will my purpose help establish my legacy when I look forward twenty years from now? Does my purpose help pull me forward into my future?

If you answered "no," then please go back and refine what you wrote. We are hoping you answered 'yes' to all of them, because there is no doubt in our minds that if you have a strong purpose in life it will allow you to focus on what you want to accomplish!

As you review what you have written ask yourself this last question: *Have you started walking your true path to get to your future?* If yes, fantastic! Keep moving forward. If not, when are you going to start? If you are standing still and time is still moving, aren't you essentially falling behind?

VISION: Can You See the Path to Your Future?

Picture this:

> You have the courage and determination to find the door. You know that it says "MY FUTURE." You have the passion and energy to open that door and understand your purpose is to walk through. But as soon as you are through, the door shuts behind you with a loud slam! You jiggle the doorknob, but it's locked from the other side. You bang on the door, but no one hears you. You don't have a phone to call anyone in your past so there's no way to get a message out to your old world, and as you turn to look forward all you see is this white fog that has filled the room. Fear takes over.
>
> No, you haven't entered the Twilight Zone. Even if you can't see a way out, you instinctually know there is another side to every room. You can even imagine what that other side looks like. You take a step and start moving. You extend your hands out before you and gingerly step into the fog hoping you don't hit the wall. Curiously, as you step, the fog separates momentarily. It's not enough to show you the opposite side of the room, but it's enough to show a clear path for the next couple of steps. You take a tentative step forward and then find that by waving your arms in front of you, the fog dissipates just a bit to make another opening. You take another step.
>
> After a while of this, you come to a chair, a welcome respite. You sit for a while and look over your shoulder to reminisce about where you came from, but notice that the fog has swallowed up the path. You have no choice but to look forward to plan the next part of your journey to reach the other side. That picture of the unseen side of the room is clear in your mind. You get up again. For many moments you clear a path, move forward, find another chair, sit and look back, see nothing but memories of where you once stood, and look forward to plan the next step of your journey

again. Finally, you reach out, and this time your hand touches something solid. A door on the other side! With excitement you brush away the fog and see this new, different door, with a different lock, with another sign that says, "MY NEXT FUTURE." You know you will now need to have the courage and energy to turn the knob and walk over the threshold so you can continue on this journey.

This is exactly what we want your mind to be thinking: Enter the door of your future, keep your past in the past, and you find your way to the next door. The Living model is very specific in saying that growth is the only way to fend off the dying model; you must keep making progress. Now for some, even when they have their dream, passion, and purpose aligned to achieve what they want, it might be too big for them. As usual, we have chosen a word (with a definition) to help break up the journey. That chair in the story (no, the word isn't "chair") where you can sit down and not only reminisce about your past but also plan the next part of your future, is *vision.*

Vision, for us, means the compelling long-term view of our desired results. These are your intermediate steps within your larger dream. Vision can represent any (we repeat, *any*) number of years; we have found that it tends to fall into fifteen-year segments of a great dream. It might be shorter, especially when dreams are narrow, risk averse, or the age of the individual is older. For others, it might be longer because of gaps between where the person is and where they want to be.

> # Vision is the compelling long-term view of my desired results

Here is what is cool about vision...it's mental time travel.[14] When we were first described this method by Rick Miller[15] it was for helping children (of all ages) understand that *hopefulness* is defined as going to their future, seeing their life in four distinct destinations, returning to the present, and planning their journey to obtain it. He also imparted on us that hopelessness (the opposite of hope) is when we have terminal thinking – when we can't get past today in our thinking.

Time travel – it's good to live

We have shamelessly adapted (with permission) this awesome process for adults. Your vision (if you chose to accept it) is the next big step in your dream acquisition process. You need to go to your future (at some time that you set – the longer the better – let's say fifteen years), and look at your future with the same *no boundary* and *no excuse* method as you dream, and then return to the present so you can plan this journey. When you go into the future you need to see your life in four distinct destinations: Home and Family, Education and Career, Community and Service, and Hobbies and Recreation.

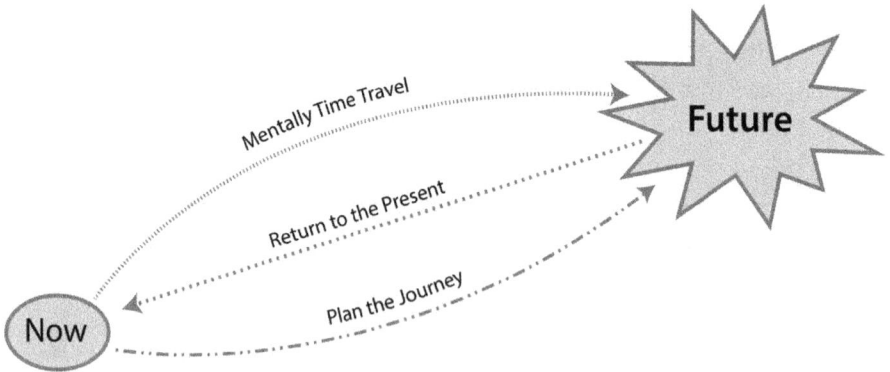

---

14 Mental time travel™ Kids At Hope, LLC.

15 President and Chief Treasure Hunter of Kids At Hope.

Destination	Definition
Home and Family	The area of my life that contains house, location, and close relationships (this includes family and friends).
Education and Career	The area of my life that creates, uses, and/or provides skill and professional knowledge for the purpose of employment and income.
Community and Service	The area of my life that uses time, skill and labor to improve others or other things.
Hobbies and Recreation	The area of my life that provides an outlet to play and enjoy, to learn and exercise skills for the mind, body, and/or spirit not directly connected to work or income.

We have to learn to time travel to our future if we are ever going to make it happen. We have to be able to break down our dreams into portions that are powerful, but obtainable. We need to know that it is okay to break the bounds of current circumstance and past memories to go after something even if it will stretch us, as long as it is on track with our overall self. It's really important that you create your next rest stop in a destination that will thrill you. A destination that will stretch your imagination of what you can achieve and remove the boundaries that so often get in your way. It must give you permission to see yourself in a different and more positive place! It needs to provide you with the room to move around and help avoid any type of tunnel vision that might occur. Most importantly, Mr. Miller is right: When you see your future, you can have hope in your future today.

Journal Entry #6A: Time Travel to My Future - Go back through the JE #2, 3, and 5 and reread your dream, your passion, and your purpose answers. Now close your eyes and time travel to your <u>future</u> some fifteen years (let's see if you can do it) from now.

Where has your dream taken you? What have you gotten done? How do you feel? How has it affected your life?

What is your home and family life like?

What happened in your education and career because of this journey?

What have you accomplished in the community?

Did it change your hobbies?

Here's the biggest question: Does this vision align with your dreams?

There is one small twist. While you're in your future, you need to determine how much of your dream you have accomplished (don't forget this part – it is very important!!) Because when you return to the present and plan for your journey (which happens to occur in the rest of this book), you will need to make sure that what you desire in the four destinations of your future matches your dreams, passion, and purpose. Yep, you in the back row with your hand up, we know the question: What happens if it doesn't align? Well, we think by now you have the answer: If your vision of your future life doesn't align with your dreams, passion, and purpose, then either the future you envisioned needs to be tweaked (or could be wrong) or your dreams, passion, and purpose are not really aligned with what you want your long-term vision of life to be.

Journal Entry #6B: Scoring Your Future Vision

Let's use an arbitrary scoring method for our little trip: Was your trip to your future poor, okay, good, or great? Please score each destination from 0 through 10.

0 – my future me is *not aligned* at all to what I want as my life's plan; 10 – my future me is an *exact match* to my life's plan:

- ❑ I can see my dream supported in my home and family vision. _____

- ❑ I can see my dream supported in my education and career vision. _____

- ❑ I can see my dream supported in my community and service vision. _____

- ❑ I can see my dream supported in my hobbies and recreation vision. _____

Now add up your total score:

< 30   Your vision of your results doesn't seem to get you where you truly want to be. Go back, modify your DPPV, and revaluate your future destinations. Really examine why you could not see your future self on the path that you had chosen.

30 – 34   You need to give more time to your dream, passion, purpose, or vision. Not seeing your future self in one or more areas will cause you great concern as you move forward in your life. Fix something; make your future world better.

35 - 37   You will probably be able to see most of your future world very clearly. If you reduce the amount of time between now and your future, you will clear up any issues that are outstanding. We recommend producing a detailed plan to accompany your vision.

38 - 40   The results of your vision of life are in alignment. Now go out and execute your plan. Enjoy your future!

Review any single destination that scored 7 or less and please look at that area more closely. Ask yourself why isn't your future able to provide what you are looking for in your life. Reread, refine, and reframe your dream or vision. Keep in mind that seeing your life fifteen years out in some areas is not possible; so pull back the number of years to twelve, ten, or even five. Or maybe your dreams sound really good, but you have found your imagination limited as to what it means to you. This is not really a problem. Most adults have spent a lifetime capping their imagination with that dream-killing "realistic barrier." So shorten the vision. Remember, when you reach this vision you get to make a new one. We really recommend that before you move on you are clear on *who* you want to be, *where* you are going, *why* you want to go there, and *what* you want to do.

Before we go any further, the number one question that we received from all that have taken this personal test is: *Does my life have to be all tens?* If you are talking about your current life, the answer is "no." If you're talking about your future life, we did put significant thought into this answer: "Absolutely yes!" Why would you *not* want a future life to be all tens? (The key word is "want.") We should always want our lives to be tens. When you compare your plan to where your future is going to be, we hope you can say that you are planning your life to be a ten. We hope that you see that the actions you are taking will get you a life of tens on our scale. Now we will grant you that there are some moments in life that are bad moments, but like all moments, bad ones don't last forever. It is also true that one area in life might dip down because of some of the choices you need to make. Remember that when you mentally time travel to your future you should see what you want – a life of tens! **Anything less should not be acceptable**.

Plan B: What Is This Good For?

We are going to have to make an assumption that you have done each of the other sections of the DPPV. You have answered all of the questions, dug deep into your soul, and have come out the other side. If not, *stop right here*. Don't continue, because it's just going to anger you. Non-alignment, lack of imagination, and not following through will show you that you are not living your Plan A. Don't be embarrassed; many of us have fallen for *surviving* life but not *living* it. Plan A and your definition of personal success are tied up in the DPPV! Any other direction or plan is...Plan B, C, D, E... Z; it's just not your Plan A. And Plan A is what will make you the happiest. Nothing less should do.

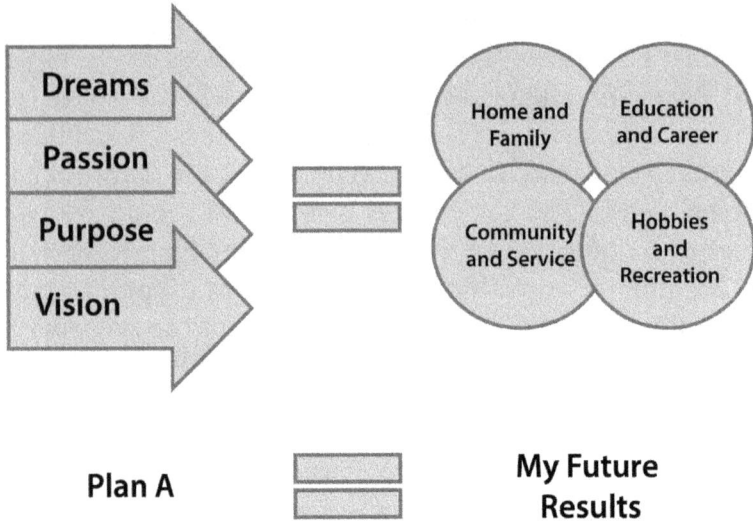

Dreams
Passion
Purpose
Vision

=

Home and Family | Education and Career | Community and Service | Hobbies and Recreation

Plan A = My Future Results

Sounds kind of restrictive. Well, it is! Really, we meant it that way. We had the same problem as most of you. We talked a good game and could tell anyone who would listen that everything in our life was aligned. Sometimes we fooled ourselves that we were heading in the right direction, but in reality our world often looked like this:

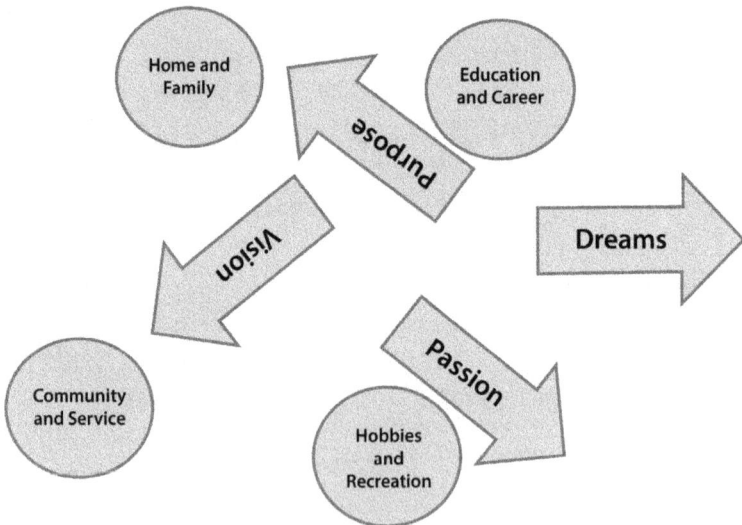

Nothing was aligned at all! Everything was there, just not working in harmony. Yes, we were executing Plan B (or whatever letter we happened to be on). We were not even sure that we could say we

were hoping for the best. It was like we were hoping to survive another day. Perhaps, one might say, we were coasting...and you know where that leads.

How did we escape our conundrum? First, we discovered that when we mapped out our *current life* (the one we are living right now) against the four destinations, what we found gave us a wake up call.

This was the hard part – we had to be really honest for this to work. We took where we were *currently* in our four destinations – Home and Family, Education and Career, Community and Service, Hobbies and Recreation – and measured them against our *future* dreams, passion, purpose, and vision, and found out something very surprising: we had each lied to ourselves!

> We are going to give you some heart-to-heart advice: Don't lie to yourself! Don't start letting your ego get in the way of a perfectly good time. There is no doubting that this process is going to make you think about where you are going, where you are now, and how you got here. It might be a little sad and depressing, but it will definitely be an eye-opener. And you can only fix it by facing it.

Jeff's example:

I was raised to believe that a person found a job or career that they could do until retirement. During that time, they would raise a family, buy a home and be happy. By the time a person was ready for retirement, their home would be paid for, the kids would be out raising their families, and all would be wonderful. I did my best to follow the examples set by my grandparents and parents. Every time I found myself questioning this approach I'd fall back on the idea that it was a problem I had to deal with and overcome because it obviously has worked for others and so it should work for me. I was afraid to go against everything I'd been taught. I was afraid to take a chance and follow my dreams. When I finally acknowledged to myself that I didn't want to follow the path that my family before me had taken, I was able to break free from the cycle and find my own path to success. That path was being an entrepreneur. Now I no longer worry about my future because it's within my control. Looking back I often ask myself, "What was I afraid of?" and the answer is always the same. I was afraid of going against what I was taught.

Journal Entry #7A: Mapping Your Current Life

Time to score your *current* position in each of the four destinations: Home and Family, Education and Career, Community and Service, Hobbies and Recreation.

Measure the four destinations against what you are doing now as it relates to what you want your vision of your life to be. The scale is:

- ❑ 0 – currently not aligned at all to what I want as my life's plan; have not achieved anything.
- ❑ 10 – currently a perfect match to my life's plan. I continue to be amazed by what I have, can and will achieve.
- ❑ You can define any score in the middle, excluding a score of 5… It doesn't exist. It's too easy to say, "I'm in the middle of the road." It's too easy for people who don't want to make changes. People who have a score of 5 are probably *not* happy. They may not think of themselves as unhappy either, but if you are at a 5, we strongly suggest you dig a little deeper into your world and really examine who you are and where you are going. Remember, we want you to live your life at a ten! You deserve it!

Home and Family score: _____

Education and Career score: _____

Community and Service score: _____

Hobbies and Recreation score: _____

Journal Entry #7B: Put the four *current* **destinations in order based on your score (from highest to lowest).**

1st Highest Destination: _____ Score: _____

2nd Highest Destination: _____ Score: _____

3rd Highest Destination: _____ Score: _____

4th Highest Destination: _____ Score: _____

First, place the name of the highest destination from JE #7B on the corresponding horizontal line along the top of the PIT graph on the next page (JE #7C) and do the same with each corresponding destination title, 2nd through 4th. Then, plot the results (your score for each one) by placing a dot that represents that score on the dark vertical line beneath each destination. Now, connect the dots by drawing a line between them. (It will probably be a little curved.)

Next, go back to JE #6B (your vision of your future) and transfer those scores onto your PIT graph (JE #7C) using a different colored pen or pencil. Remember to align the destinations appropriately. For example, if your highest destination in #7B is Education & Career, then you would use Education & Career's score from #6B in the first position. You have just completed your PIT graph.

There is a completed example on the following pages.

Journal Entry #7C: Make your Point In Time (PIT) Graph

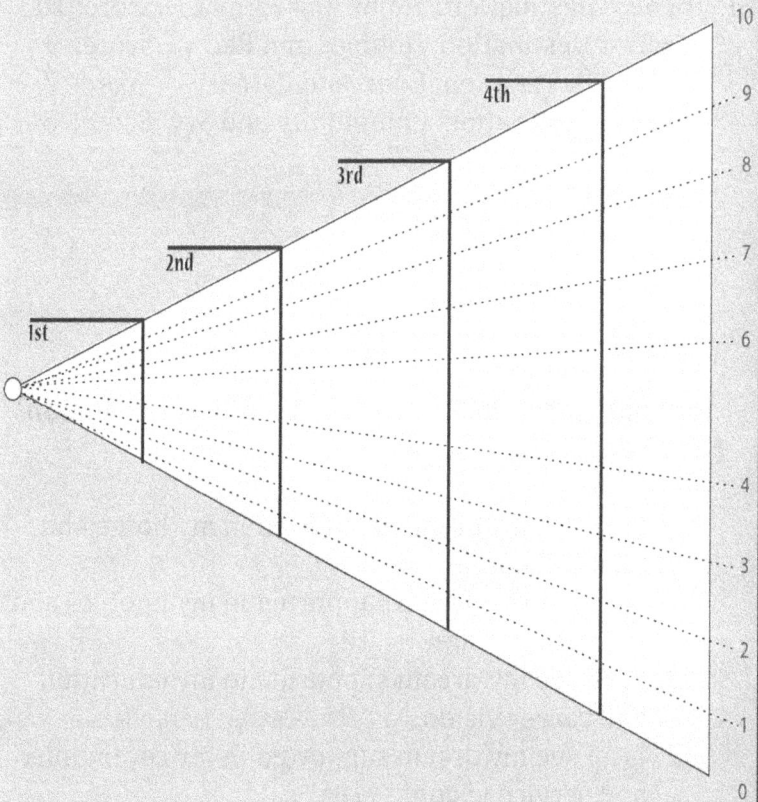

As an example, we decided to create a composite of several models and present the results for a person we will call "Mr. I. M. Complacent." Here are his results:

Journal Entry #7B: Put the four *current* **destinations in order based on your score (from highest to lowest) (EXAMPLE)**

1st Highest Destination: Home and Family   Score: 10
2nd Highest Destination: Hobbies and Rec   Score: 9
3rd Highest Destination: Educ. and Career   Score: 7
4th Highest Destination: Community and Srv. Score: 6

Journal Entry #6B: Scoring Your Future Vision (EXAMPLE)

❏ I can see my dream supported in my home and family vision.   10
❏ I can see my dream supported in my hobbies and recreation vision.   10
❏ I can see my dream supported in my education and career vision.   9   (won't have his Ph.D. in time)
❏ I can see my dream supported in my community and service vision.   10

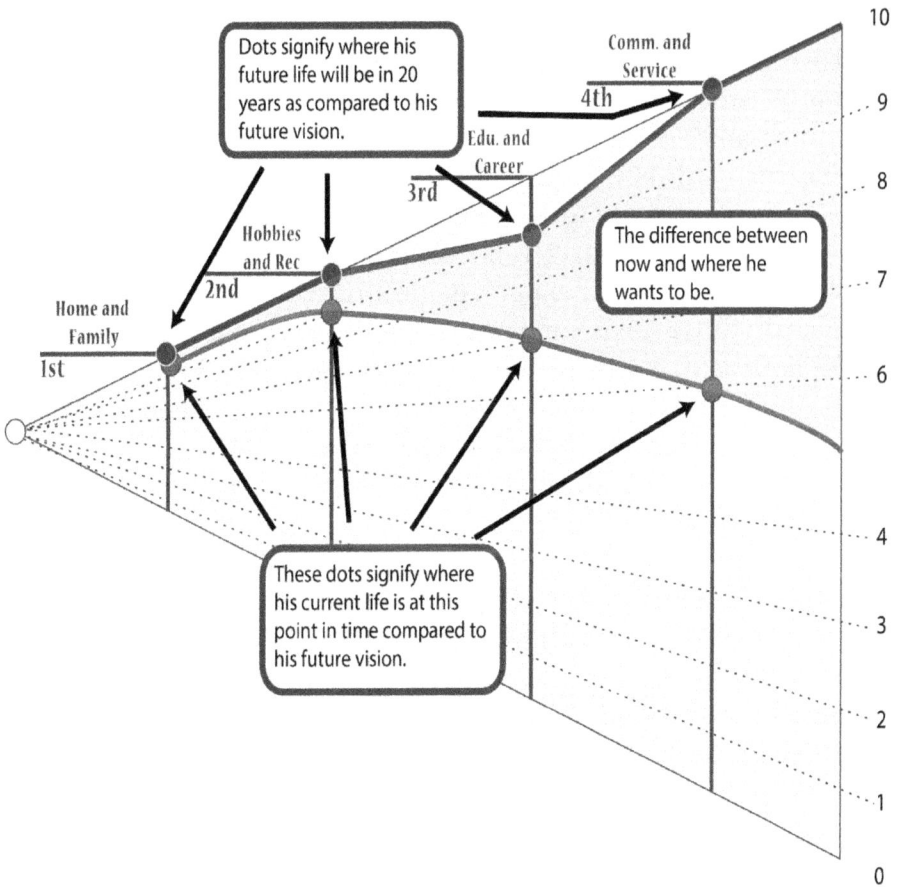

Mr. Complacent had an epiphany when he saw his current PIT curve. It was very reminiscent of the dying model and it upset him. (Recognize that curved line?)

Actually, everyone who used the graph had that same reaction: mad that they knew the life they wanted could exist, but that they haven't been able to capture it yet. Each had thought that they were living Plan A, only to find out that they were actually in Plan B because they had let go of their alignment and their desired future. When this happens, it means that a refinement to their actions is in order, nothing more. Obviously, the clue is in the areas that are seven and below on the PIT graph. Take a look at them and make the necessary corrections to your Plan A. (Become who you want to become!)

Back to Mr. Complacent: He had done the right thing by comparing his current life to his future dreams, and 10 being a perfect match means he has some work to do to become aligned to what he wants. His Home and Family is exactly what he wants it to be now and in the future. His Hobbies and Recreation are right now pretty close to what he wants his life to be like. Though for Education and Career and Community and Service, his current actions are trailing behind what his vision of his life expects in the future. Which means he needs to work on those areas – if he wasn't taking action to improve those areas, he was living Plan B. The good news is that he can see that his future life matches perfectly to what he wants to do (knowing that his Ph.D. goes to 10 when it is completed). He sees that his gap between his current world and future world is where he will spend most of his time.

To those who took the time to plot their current and future worlds, take a moment to write up what you believe the PIT graph tells you. Determine if you have a plan to get you where you want to go. Also, remember it is your plan, dream, and actions. If you never plan to do anything in the community or if what you are doing today is all you desire then your life is a 10 in that category (now and in the future). No guilt involved, no preconceived expectations.

If it helps any, only three percent of the people we interviewed are living their Plan A in all four of their destinations! They had the plans and took the actions to keep achieving the life they wanted. They recognized that their DPPV is their Plan A and the results from their actions are the proof.

Seven percent of our informal test group are achieving their Plan A in some of their destinations. When they have to detour off their Plan A it doesn't last, but they tend to find their way back.

Thirty percent of them had a Plan A, at one time. Their detours are more prevalent; their Plan B is what life is now about. They have settled (there is that nasty word again: settle) for a different life than the one they had dreamed about. They tell themselves they are happy and fulfilled, but aren't. They are starting to believe this is the way life is supposed to be.

A whopping fifty percent of our interviewees have had more detours with their Plan B. They are spiritually, emotionally, mentally, and physically out of balance. Life for them is not about living; it is about surviving (both of us were here once!). The feeling of having no control is almost overwhelming. The days drag into weeks, months, and years of no action. Nothing is defining their lives.

The final ten percent have no plan, no dreams, and no hope. They can't see beyond a day or two. Life has no meaning or direction.

Now take a moment, shut your eyes, and think about what stands in your way. What feelings creep up into your mind or body as you think about why? Do you feel guilt? Shame? Nothing? **Are you okay with those feelings?**

Hopefully, your eyes are now wide open (figuratively and literally). We found that detours from Plan A to Plan B are normally minor moments that turn into big hairy deals. They start harmlessly and end as potential life changers. There is a quick list that we compiled on the following page. Let's see if your *why* is on it.

Let's get real; some detours are very valid. A newlywed couple may find themselves pregnant three months into the marriage when they thought they were going to wait five years. Did they have the control to avoid it? Yep. Did they take a chance? Yep. Did it alter their plan? *Youbetcha* (yes). Did they regret it? Never. Will they return to their Plan A? Eventually, and they did (true story).

Of course, the same circumstances could be devastating. A couple chooses to have sex in their first year of college and she becomes pregnant. (Awkward if they'd both become pregnant; there'd be some 'splaining to do.) Both have to quit school, one to raise the child (can't seem to balance kid, classes, and homework) and the other quits to work full time to provide diapers, food, formula, and shelter. Did it alter their plan? Yep. Do you think they will return to school? Don't know. We do know that their Plan A probably changed – not because of the child, but because of the missing education, which may have been in the area of their passion (also a true story).

The Why List			
Too much partying	Health	Culture	No one else does it that way
Unplanned pregnancy	Time availability	Skills	Believing others
Distracted from school or work	No help, support	Smarts (brain trust)	They couldn't, you can't
Video games	Age: too young or old	Didn't believe	Keeping up with the Joneses
Debt/bills	Trans-portation needs	Didn't trust	Caught up in "reality"
No money	Fears: yours and others'	Didn't really care	Beyond your control
Family respons-ibilities	Perceptions of ourselves	Not realistic	Doesn't pay the bills
Job(s)	Expectations from others	Guilt	Entertain-ment more important
School	Morals	Guts	My time is more important
Routine	Values	Afraid of change	Need to relax

To end this little foray into Plan B, we shall return to the beginning. What is it good for? The answer as some of you have guessed is: absolutely nothing! Plan B is our best excuse to not feel guilty for not achieving our real path in life.

Everyone who finds themselves in Plan B does so not because of a lack of intelligence, education, morals, or ethics. These folks (and remember we were some of them) are good people. Most don't rob banks, cheat on their spouses, or use drugs and alcohol as if they were Tic Tacs. They just don't have the tools, processes, and experiences to get what they want. They should recommit to their DPPV because it is showing them a future that they absolutely want! (And if it isn't what they want, then they need to redo their DPPV.) In most cases, Plan B'ers are being held back by a lack of action and commitment to themselves.

> If you are a plan B'er and have already made a list of why you can't possibly get to your Plan A, then hold on to your hats, because what is coming up in *Live The Risk* was made for you.

Plan A: Returning and Staying There

Remember, Plan A is obtainable right now because it only sets direction and a path. Plan A is about not wandering through all of the detours aimlessly. It requires you to make sure that your life is pointed and executed in the direction that you have set.

We have some questions for you (and none of them are trick questions). There are only two answers available for each question: Yes and No. We want you to answer from top to bottom and stop at the first "No" answer:

Journal Entry #8: Are You a Plan A'er or a Plan B'er?

1. Are you refusing to give up?

2. Are you willing to take the next steps to get what you want for a complete life?

3. Are you willing to create a plan and excited to learn?

4. Can you see what path you need to get to your first vision?

5. Do you feel strongly that your Plan A will take you where you want to grow (go)?

6. Are you prepared for the opportunity to keep growing until your last breath?

7. If you were to re-ask the passion questions, could you still answer 'yes' to all of them?

8. Does your PIT graph for your future accomplish your current Plan A and get you to where you need to be?

9. Are you willing to learn?

10. Are you prepared to take responsibility for your actions?

11. Are you prepared for the benefits and rewards of executing your Plan A?

12. Are you prepared to keep updating your DPPV (especially your vision)?

13. Will you be smiling when you accomplish Plan A?

So let's see where you ended up. Give yourself one point for each "yes," and remember you must stop answering after the first "no."

0-1 -   Please go back to the beginning of the book, reread it, and determine which model you want to follow. Because right now you are on the wrong path!

2-4 -   You are hanging on by the skin of your teeth. Survival is fine in the really short term, but it is not possible to stay here and still get the life you desire. Please, please, take some time and plan well. Then start executing what you plan; we don't want you to fall or fail!

5-7 -   You have a chance to make the best decision of all time. You can decide to open the door to your future or keep it shut. We are rooting for you to open the door and keep moving forward. You can't stay here too long, because as we said, staying still means you are really falling behind. Time keeps moving.

8-11 - Wow, you are almost there. You know what to do, but probably get a little sidetracked by some detours. You know perfectly well how to avoid them. Keep planning your life and keep walking in the direction of your choosing. You can make the commitment if you choose.

12-13 - This is too exciting! You can do it! If you are at a score of 12 you are probably attempting to tune and refine so you are all smiles at the end. If you have a score of 13, congrats – you have figured it out! We are darn proud of you!

To close, regardless of where you started and how you ended we congratulate you on getting your dreams, passion, purpose, and vision (DPPV) aligned to support where you want to be. There is no better proof of why so many people shy, hide, crawl, or run away from their own dreams – it's hard! We know that you are different. We know that you now have the capability to keep yourself on track because you believe in yourself, you have the energy to accomplish it, and you are clear about the results you will achieve because of it.

Repeat after us:

> I have dreams, therefore I believe.
> I have passion, therefore I can.
> I have purpose, therefore I am.
> I have vision, therefore I will.

See you in the next chapter!

Part II: The REACH Philosophy

At the risk of sounding like a broken record,[1] this simple soul-searching method of aligning your dreams, passion, purpose, and vision gives you the opportunity to make sure you're starting to create and focus on your future. To begin living life!

With the big stuff out of the way, it's time to focus on the nitty-gritty. We will be providing you with the tools, processes, and knowledge for your journey. And it will be up to you to bring your dreams and aspirations. Together, we'll be concentrating on your goals, actions, and results that allow your DPPV to equal your wanna-be future results.

It works on any dream or vision. It doesn't matter if it's at work, home, or play. It's not prejudiced against money, fun, or family. There are no limits to what it can help you achieve. Really, the philosophy isn't choosy. It allows you to be successful, period. It doesn't require:

- ❏ Specific education
- ❏ Community stature
- ❏ Being in good shape
- ❏ A particular cultural background
- ❏ Being able to bake a ten-minute brownie in two minutes
- ❏ Money in the bank
- ❏ Good spelling and grammar
- ❏ Ability to drive a car

Part II of this book is all about how goals, actions, and results stay interconnected with your dreams, passion, purpose, and vision. Our mission is for *you to keep improving you.*

> A word of caution: If you have made your bed we expect you to sleep in it. Don't use "following your dreams" as an excuse for not keeping up your end of the bargain to your family, friends, and bill collectors. Don't use yourself, your behaviors, or habits as an excuse to not finish what you've started.

---

1 For the streaming generation that is a really big vinyl disc that doesn't use an advanced form of technology, not even the internet, to get the information off of it.

Let's continue our pledge:

I have dreams, therefore I believe.
I have passion, therefore I can.
I have purpose, therefore I am.
I have vision, therefore I will.

I have goals, therefore I see.
I have actions, therefore I do.
I have results, therefore I live.

We are going to simplify our language a bit. We are going to combine Goals, Actions, and Results into one word: Mission.

The Mission

A mission lets you break down that long-term vision into more manageable portions. There will probably be many missions required to accomplish your next vision, just as there are probably multiple visions to accomplish your dream. Each mission will be three to eighteen months long and each is a step along your path. Every mission will have multiple goals and accomplishments. We are also going to add contingencies to our definition. This will allow you to plan for any and all barriers.

None of the barriers are impossible to overcome. In Shane J. Lopez's book, *Making Hope Happen,*[2] he hits the nail on the head when he writes that "high-hope people *have* the ability to plan for ifs, the ability to anticipate obstacles, and create multiple pathways *[contingencies]* to each and every goal." In other words, being realistic about what might stand in your way will actually help you succeed. If you put all of your eggs in one basket, assuming everything you

---

2 Making Hope Happen, Shane J. Lopez, Ph.D., ISBN:978-1-4516-6622-9, pg. 160. Italics were added for readability.

do will work the first time and to your standard, then you are in for a rude awakening.

Don't take missions lightly; they need to paint a picture of what direction you are headed and of the attitude, altitude, attention, and intention that you are planning on applying to get you there. If it's something that you want, maybe you need to invoke the patience, focus, control and discipline to wait for it. You need to have the courage and fortitude to stick with it because it was important enough to be included in the first place. Don't abandon what you need to do because you are not getting the response you want at the present moment.

> A mission is my personal collection of interrelated goals that provide significant steps toward my vision of life

Our current mission happens so fast that it's important that it can be achieved by what we now know. (This is better known as being realistic.) Sure, future missions can stretch our senses and comfort zone, but current ones need to be possible and you should be confident in your ability to complete them.

It really has been amazing to learn that if a person doesn't have alignment of DPPV, then the missions that they are on are scattered, non-directed, and somewhat wild. Their own results will be nothing more than a mishmash of attempted journeys. Some folks will literally say they are doing a lot of things as a part of a plan, but when they look back, they are not sure what they accomplished and those "things" were nothing more than a waste of time.

Look into your past and ask yourself this: Did you accomplish what you thought you should have? Yes or no? Hopefully the question is an eye opener for some. It is really easy to keep busy and not to see any real results. It is easy to excuse your behaviors, making up reasons why you didn't do what you promised. Though if you want to *Live The Risk,* now is the time to take immediate action to bring that vision and dream to life.

So let's start with an exercise to review your dreams and vision from the previous section:

Journal Entry #9A: Remembering.

My dream (JE #2): _____
_____.

To obtain my dream , my future life needs to be well on its way in (JE #6a):

Home and Family: _____
_____.

Education and Career: _____
_____.

Community and Service: _____
_____.

Hobbies and Recreation: _____
_____.

Take a moment and think about the big steps that need to be taken to achieve your vision of life in all four destinations for the next three to eighteen months. For example: You want to finish school in eighteen months, which will help meet your education and career destination. And you also want to buy a condo, which will help you on your way to establishing your home and family destination. So that would be your first mission.

If you can't put your hands around what is first, start backwards at Mission #10, which should represent you obtaining your vision. So if you know you want kids in college in twenty years and don't want them to have to work to pay for it, you should probably start thinking about finding a spouse, having kids, or at the least start a college fund. Regardless, if you use a forward (1 to 10) or backward (10 to 1) approach, you need to do your best to break down your entire vision.

Journal Entry #9B: Your Missions. If I want my future, I know I will need to achieve these big missions:

1. _____ by: __/__/__
2. _____ by: __/__/__
3. _____ by: __/__/__
4. _____ by: __/__/__
5. _____ by: __/__/__
6. _____ by: __/__/__
7. _____ by: __/__/__
8. _____ by: __/__/__
9. _____ by: __/__/__
10. _____ by: __/__/__

On a separate piece of paper break down each mission from JE #9B into its unique combination of goals, actions and results (i.e. going to class, buying the first suit for interviews, saving for a down payment, making the call). Don't feel bad if there is a lot of detail in Mission #1, and then in the future missions, which get further and further out, things get a little blurry. That's okay... you'll get better at it (we did). The goal of mission planning is to give you a rough outline so you can see the steps you need to take to make significant progress to your future. From here on out the book is only going to concentrate on that first mission. (If you are an overachiever you will be able to apply each and every topic to all of your future missions.)

Let's test our resolve. Answer yes or no:

1. Do I have the attitude, confidence, and strength to achieve my first mission?
2. Do I have the will to succeed?
3. Do I have the skill to succeed?
4. Can I keep myself focused?
5. Is my mission between three and eighteen months?
6. Does my mission have my absolute attention?
7. Does my mission paint a detailed picture of my next logical step to my vision?
8. Does my mission stretch my comfort zone, but not trigger my excuses?

Scoring: All should be "yes." For any "no" answer, ask these questions:

- ❑ Why?
- ❑ What do you need to know (or do) to change it to a "yes"?
- ❑ What is standing in your way?

New Year's resolutions are made at an alarming rate every December 31st and abandoned before the end of the next month. There is an unsubstantiated figure on the internet (and everything on the internet is almost true) that 80% of all New Year's resolutions are abandoned by January 20th. Now, even if this figure is wrong by five, six, or even seven months, that they are abandoned at all is a travesty. In a study from the University of Scranton[1], it was discovered that about 45% of Americans actually make resolutions. Personally, we don't know why most people pick New Year's as a starting point. (We suspect that it's right after the party and gift giving seasons, so weight loss and saving money seem to be on top of most people's minds by the new year.) We actually recommend that once you have determined it's the right thing to do, whether it's February 9th, April 21st, July 18th, November 3rd or December 24th, start doing it! The top 10 resolutions are as follows:

1. Lose weight
2. Learn something exciting
3. Get organized
4. Quit smoking
5. Spend less, save more
6. Help others with their dreams
7. Enjoy life to the fullest
8. Fall in love
9. Stay (or get) fit and healthy
10. Spend more time with family

Self-improvement or education-related resolutions represented 47% of the resolutions made; weight loss, 38%; money related, 34%; and relationships, 31%. So here is a bunch of people that wanted to change something in their lives. The bad news was that only 8% actually achieve their resolution. Eight percent - Wow! Another

---

1 Journal of Clinical Psychology (accessed on 12/13/2012).

73% have infrequent or no success in achieving what they want. (That is sad.)

Now, what about age groups? 39% of those folks in their twenties will achieve their resolutions (given that they make them). And those over fifty? The percentage comes way down, literally: 14% of the people over fifty that make resolutions achieve them.

Neither Jeff nor Joel make New Year's resolutions. We never have and never will. We're part of the 38% of Americans who don't. It was kind of interesting when we started talking about this section of the book and found out that both of us create "themes" versus resolutions for the year. For Joel, 2011's theme was: "Be uncomfortable – to find the excitement, energy and challenge of the moment." 2012's theme was: "Find a new level of fear and remove it from existence!" 2013's theme is: "Living the risk."

Jeff's themes: In 2011, "No risk, no reward." In 2012 it was: "The year of opportunity," and in 2013 it is: "Growth."

What is your theme?

What is REACH?

REACH stands for **R**adical Persistence, **E**xcuses Removed, **A**ccurate Missions, **C**hip Away, and **H**abit Forming. It's a process/philosophy/ acronym that helps you structure your relationship with your vision of life so you can accomplish your missions. It supports you as you make the necessary steps toward your future, and helps to identify the barriers (both physical and manufactured) that stand in your way. *REACH* is designed so that you are ensuring that your mind, body, and breath (spirit) are in tune with what you want. *REACH* is based on building good habits so that taking small, logical, interconnected steps become your new normal. The best part is that you can inject any aligned dream, vision, or mission into the model. Thus, given the time, commitment, and energy you can accomplish what you want.

As usual (or maybe it is with us), you can start at any spot in this model. We suggest that you start on the R in *REACH*. Of course, since we like being flexible you could start with E, A, C, or H. It doesn't matter as long as you get through all of the sections.

Imagine, as we did, that your DPPV is liquid gold that gets dropped into the center of the model (represented by the center dot) and a small ripple begins to move and reverberate to the outside edge (which is your vision of your future life). This analogy represents how the model works:

❑ Each distance that the wave moves from the center to the edge is representative of the progress you are going to make (or the progress you are making) as you achieve your missions.

❑ Like the wave touching all areas of its circle, the individual parts of the *REACH* process should never be considered separate and distinct parts, each doing their own thing, in their own way with no contact with or connection to the other parts. Life doesn't work that way, so why would the model?

❏ The wave keeps moving forward. We have yet to find a way that we can make any dream come true without movement. The *REACH* model works the same; you have a responsibility to yourself to keep moving through your missions.

❏ The wave keeps getting bigger as it gets closer to the outer edge (small movements combined equal big distances). This is the same for you. As you continue to make progress, you should be able to look back and see the big changes that have occurred.

Are you ready to make some waves? Let's start with the five equally important sections of the *REACH* model:

	Section	Chapter
R	Radical Persistence	No one wants this more than me!
E	Excuses Removed	I will eliminate all obstacles
A	Accurate Missions	It is all about the choices I make
C	Chip Away	Small stones build big pyramids
H	Habit Forming	Continually *REACH* in order to live!

A quick summary:

Radical Persistence contains the personal tools that you will need to complete your mission. This includes anchors and sails (hey, we like boats). Think of anchors as the things that hold you in place and sails as the things that propel you forward. A boat needs both, but too much of any one thing and the boat either won't move or will sail out of control. Anchors are the absolutes, fears, perceptions, and expectations that we hold near and dear to our hearts and which keep us safe. Sails are the tools you need to keep moving in a direction of your choosing.

We will be spending time in making sure that you are spiritually, emotionally, mentally, physically, and perceptually aware of what is going on. Now we are not assuming that everyone has to be a Zen master. We don't expect anyone to have a clear handle on this part of his or her life. We know from our own personal experience that without balance of our inner self, our outer self doesn't handle anything well. We're not talking about some mumbo jumbo poufy thing or a new exercise program. We're talking about the simple fact that we, as human beings, spend a significant amount of time out of balance. Our bodies, minds, and spirits are often in no condition to help us achieve our current mission, let alone our future vision. That must change.

Excuses Removed is all about those pesky little defenses that stand in your way. This section includes the basic natural barriers that our bodies impose on us (i.e. that gut feeling, that nagging issue, or headache from overthinking). Most of the areas are actually healthy for you – they keep you out of big trouble, if you listen – while some, such as the limbic region of the brain, which controls fight, flight or freeze, sometimes get in the way of a perfectly good time. The limbic region actually becomes invoked without you even thinking about what it's stopping; it's designed that way.

The other area includes the manufactured defenses that you create all by yourself (yes, you!). We don't know why anybody would be scared of a drop of liquid gold in a bucket. It's a drop. But for some it's a tsunami – a giant-sized tidal wave that is going to wash out their existence. We want to hit this area head on. We want any problem to be removed before it hampers what you want. From personal experience this was the biggest area of growth for both authors, the reason being that it's easy to hide when you give yourself the opportunity. If what you want is strong enough, then you need not let anything get in your way. We will expand our conversation on the natural defenses that our bodies create (i.e. the limbic system) and make sure that you are aware of the manufactured defenses so you'll know how to deal with them. The expectation is that nothing you can control will interfere with your mission to obtain your dreams.

Accurate Missions is having a clear and concise view of how your choices connect to your past and future steps. It's to create your immediate plan to give you direction on how you are going to get where you want to go. Plans can't be cursory; they must be specific, detailed, timely, measurable, and attainable. They need to show the interconnection between the past, present, and future activities, and they need to describe the results that you want and how they will impact your future. This is a major area that most conversations gloss over. What are the expected results that you want and demand of yourself?

The steps that you take are not expected to be a "write it once and never look at it again" moment. Each of the processes that we will show you will be ones that you will hopefully want to update on a day-in, day-out basis. Remember, it takes a significant amount of energy to make positive change. It's going to take a lot to channel the exothermic reaction to power you while you're attempting to plan, execute, and obtain your results.

Chip Away is actually the first piece of the model that we created. This section was the catalyst for everything else we wrote in this book. It was the answer to not only what we have dealt with personally, but also our solution to halt the limbic region of our brain from taking over the rest of our mental capacity and preventing us from doing what we needed to do. Every part of our progress has been attributed to understanding that thinking is useless if not followed by actions. Put up or shut up! How simple, and yet so difficult.

Even if you abandon everything else we have and will discuss, having a clear understanding of this section alone will give you the ability to follow through and make some progress. This portion of the model contains the actions to deliver your mission. Remember, if you are not living you are dying, and the only way to live is to grow. These actions, regardless of success or failure, are very critical to your growth; they are the building blocks to construct that stairway to your dreams. Our expectation is that you won't see the actions that you are required to take as big. They should be nothing more than many small steps. Each action should build on the previous one.

Habit Forming is last, but not least. Simply put: to grow and improve means your actions compound like interest at the bank, but with a much better percentage rate. The goal is to determine what is worth doing permanently (yes, as in forever!). Trust us, we're talking from experience; we had to learn to make new and different habits our permanent choices in how we were going to live our lives. We had to rebuild our habits in exercise, money, business, and play. We know, it sounds kind of basic to say, "eliminate what hasn't worked and repeat what has been found to be successful," but it's true.

No One Wants This More Than Me!

Radical Persistence

Leo Tolstoy said, "Everyone thinks of changing the world, but no one thinks of changing himself." Simple, profound, and absolutely right. If we're going to change the world, then we need to change ourselves first.

Let's start this off right. Read the following and ask yourself if this is true:

I CAN ATTEST THAT NO ONE WANTS THIS MORE THAN ME AND I AM RESPONSIBLE FOR MYSELF!

It's really all about you! It's all about what you bring, hold, keep, shed, and need to have the life you desire. You have already proven that you can follow through; all of the journal entries that you made are proof. You know you can make choices that will solidify the foundation of your new life. Your DPPV is proof. All that you have already experienced will go into your You Toolbox.[1] Now here is the big difference between this toolbox and every other one you own:

---

1 Which is different than the YouTube box, where many people go to spend time instead of working on themselves.

Every tool – we repeat, *every tool* – that you are going to add to the You Toolbox requires your belief that it will work, and you have to use them. In other words, you need to both *believe* and *practice* what you say.

The next thing in your You Toolbox is the clear understanding that there is no one else but you to do the work. (You can almost hear it clank against the rest of the other tools.) Yes, you may have emotional support or some kind of cheering section, but it's all up to you. You are really the only major actor in your story; everyone else has a bit part.[2] You must take on the responsibility to make sure you are prepared to enter the world of your mission. You must have the conviction to stay until it's completed.

Actually, in thinking about it, who would start something and then not finish it? Too many people, that's who! Sometimes it's easy to forget what we promise to do, especially for ourselves. Come on, admit it, haven't you promised yourself something, and then for some reason as the days and months passed you suddenly looked up and said, "Oh yeah, whatever happened to that goal?" Oh, we know life gets in the way of a perfectly good time and causes us to change direction. We can't let it, if it's what we truly want. We can't let things go by the wayside; we have to have the guts to continue. It's your life and only you can live it.

We can't let things pass because they have fallen off the radar. We need, for the sake of our own DPPV, to complete what we have started. True, it's easier to ride the couch than it is to hike the mountain. Always has been, always will be.

> Obviously, one of the easiest ways to do all the things you have promised is *not* to take on more than you can handle. Remember, this model is very interconnected. Can't wait, can you? Don't flip ahead; there's still some great stuff in this chapter to be learned.

---

2 Of course, they are the only major player in their own story.

Piers Steel, Ph.D.[3] (no relation to Jeff) completed a five-year study and determined that 26% of Americans in 2007 considered themselves chronic procrastinators. About 54% of the procrastinators are men, but ladies, you're not off the hook; you represent the other forty-six percent. Dr. Steel says that the causes of procrastination combine temptation, sense of immediacy, the value of doing the job, and whether you believe you can get the work done. He also believes (and we agree) that technology (especially in 2013) diverts a person's attention (wait, someone just posted a funny picture of a cat playing the piano on Facebook) so easily that we never get back to doing what we are supposed to do.

RESULTS WILL BE THE PROOF OF YOUR EFFORTS.

Our way to avoid this problem is to take our antidote to procrastination, which is... drum roll, please... *persistence.* One of the dictionary definitions is: *(n) Continued effort or existence.* Now this might solve part of the procrastination problem: if I continue to "do" then I have a good chance of making progress. Our definition takes it to a whole new level. For the *Live The Risk* community, our version of persistence is the Radical version:

> Radical Persistence is the ability to have the willpower to stay focused on my mission, to be self-correcting in my behaviors, and balanced in my approach

Radical Persistence is not about "doing" in this world; it's about making sure you're doing what needs to be done. Let's set the record straight: we are not talking about taking advantage of others, hurting them on your way up the corporate ladder, or destroying your competitors. There is karma in this world and if you treat

3 http://usatoday30.usatoday.com/tech/science/2007-01-12-procrastination-study_x.htm

others like that, sooner or later they will do the same to you. We do believe that you need to treat others with great honesty and respect, and yes, still get what you want.

There are three significant areas that make up this section:

1. The Big Granite Block
2. The seven steps to your RADICAL self
3. The balance to achieve

The Big Granite Block

X-rays and CAT scans can't detect this part of you, though you know it's there. This piece of you is hard stone-like dense matter. See, this part of you is a big granite block (BGB) and was designed to house you…not like a sarcophagus after you're gone, but to house you while you are alive. This, our friends, is where we store every filter we have learned and collected to keep us safe from the world. *It's our comfort zone!* Of course it didn't start out that way. This comfort zone didn't exist at all when we were born. There was nothing when we started in this world and nothing is a lot easier to move around than a BGB.

We need to give thanks to our parents; they gave us enough rules to help grow this aura of protection around us (think of it as the outer crust). Mom told you that a behavior was risky, dad didn't like a type of food, and chances are you think the same way now. Don't get us wrong; most parents are doing exactly what all parents do (and we did the same), attempting to keep their children safe and helping them grow up into productive human beings. They take this perfect baby and mold them into…the perfect version of who they want their child to be.[4] They share their beliefs, likes, and dislikes; and some, if not all, become inherently the child's.

Now for the bad part: You continue to add to that outer crust and grow that BGB into something bigger and heavier. You add to your

---

4 We can hear you laughing and thinking, "Oh my gosh, I have become my parents!"

BGB by using that inquisitive mind of yours. You will add filters to keep you out of trouble. Everything you determine that is important to you (be it through action, guilt, success, or failure) gets added to the BGB either by taking up room on the inside and/or adding another layer on the outside.

We have found that four major areas (we call filters) make up the BGB:

1. Absolutes
2. Fears
3. Perceptions
4. Expectations

Over time, as we continue to learn about life, the walls of the BGB get thicker with experience, all in the name of keeping us safe and sound. We can only play within the walls of the BGB, and that is the problem. The thicker the walls, the less room we have to maneuver. The fewer options that we seem to have, then the less trouble we seek (a good thing) and the fewer calculated risks (a bad thing) we take. There are definitely more restrictions that we place upon ourselves. The BGB houses all of the methods, processes, rules, and regulations that are either self-imposed or imposed on you by work, home, business, or play. Its primary goal is to keep you protected from real or imagined danger.

Of course, *what keeps us safe also keeps us contained.* All of the filters (absolutes, fears, perceptions, and expectations) that we hold near and dear to our hearts, and control by our minds, need to be validated to make sure that they are the right ones for us.

Imagine that whenever you make a decision it only occurs within the center of your BGB: the smaller the area available, the less room for taking risk and obtaining mobility. Why? Because of the definition of the BGB. If you were to choose something outside of your comfort zone (filters) it would require more risk to be taken on. Of course, if you allow yourself to take on more risk, then you're at war with yourself. However, this is one war you must win!

There are some people who don't seem to have any problem in altering themselves; they seem to be able to turn off all of the body's safety switches and go for it. Professor David Zald has determined that risk takers get an unusually big hit of dopamine each time they have a novel experience, all because their brains are not able to inhibit the neuro-transmitter adequately.[5] We hate to burst anyone's bubble, but those people make up about two percent of the crowd; we are the remaining ninety-eight percent. We have every intention, come heck or high water, to survive to old age, and we definitely want to keep the risk out![6]

---

5 http://www.time.com/time/health/article/0,8599,1869106,00.html#ixzz2IH6rEJQY

6 Risk does not only mean life threatening; sometimes it means different/change.

If we did the DPPV correctly, it automatically sits outside of the BGB because it's supposed to stretch us to our new and lofty vision of ourselves. Which means we better figure out a way to deal with our BGB so that it doesn't stand in our way. By breaking through that BGB wall, you step outside the box and see the world for the first time in all its colors and possibilities.

Absolutes

Honestly, this is what makes you, you. Absolute filters are the items that we have collected over time that *will never change*. They're permanent residents of our comfort zone. For most, they will include irreversible medical conditions, unconditional faith, ingrained value/culture systems, and cemented beliefs. These items are *not* up for negotiation; they will not be changed based upon mood or whims. It's possible that after great soul searching or significant emotional anguish that you can decide to remove or change one, but it's not easy, and shouldn't be. This is important because everything we do and everything that is said to us goes through this filter. If it doesn't pass this checkpoint, then the chances of you accomplishing it are nil. Whatever is an absolute, must remain . . . absolute.

Some people may lump more items as an absolute that really aren't. They will place goals, objectives, and guilt-ridden behaviors within this filter knowing that they aren't planning to carry through with them. They might place beliefs within this filter that are never practiced. The question to ask yourself is: "When the going gets tough, will I follow through on *all* of my absolutes?"

If wanting a new sports car is so important that all of the things you say, hear, and do need to be bumped up against it to see if you will do it, then leave it as an absolute... if not, then take it out of this category. You must be honest with yourself.

What are the absolutes in your life against which you judge everything?

For example:

#	Absolute	Why is it an absolute?	Do you use this absolute in <u>every</u> decision you make?	When do you not use this filter?
1	I support my country's products	Because I live here I feel it's important to be patriotic.	Not really.	I do purchase products made in other countries because their prices are cheaper.
2	I will not kill Bambi	I think it's wrong to hunt Bambi (I am still upset from the movie that I was forced to watch as a kid!).	Kind of...well, actually no. Because I do like venison.	When someone makes me venison stew or jerky (one of my favorites).
3	My religious beliefs	I was raised with them and believe they will get me into heaven.	Yes.	When they stand in my way of having fun. Then I ask for forgiveness.

Please don't overreact – these are in jest. They are to make you think. We do find it interesting how easy one can shut off their absolutes when they are in the way of what one wants or likes. This is why this exercise is important to do honestly.

Take the time and determine what your absolutes are. Why is each one an absolute? Do you use this absolute in every decision that you make? And when do you not use this absolute?

Were you surprised by any of your answers? We suspect that you have figured out that if you are claiming absolutes in life, then the third question, "Do you use this absolute in every decision you make?" is always "yes." Nothing else matters; you are dedicated to your cause. You have no reason why you wouldn't use it. If it isn't "yes," then spend some time on why you think it is an absolute. There's no point in crowding your list or comfort zone with something that you already know is negotiable.

Fears

As many people before us have said, F-E-A-R is False Evidence Appearing Real. It can be a warning signal about what is going on around you (which we will talk about in Self-Awareness), or to say it as nicely as we can: it can be issues that your mind, body, and spirit have conjured up that are *not* based on experience, but on your mental prediction of what *might* happen. It was based on some internal notion that someone or something in your life *might* do this to you....*Even if there is no factual basis to back it up.*

The way we are using fear in this section is that there is no first-person factual basis. In other words, it didn't happen to you. It's just a thought that manifested itself into something so real that you filter what you say, listen, and do through it. (Yep, there they are again, those darn filters.) Now neither of us is going to provide advice for getting rid of your fears. We *are* going to ask you to make sure that they aren't holding you back.

If there are things in your life that hold you back, take a good look and make sure that they are real. Figure out ways to reduce them or remove them from your filtering process. It's going to take some time, effort, and guts, but if you start now it might one day be gone or at least minimized to the point that it doesn't hold you back from accomplishing your goals and dreams.

Joel's story: From the ages of ten to seventeen, I flew in airplanes often. At the age of seventeen I lost my father, stepmother, and two stepbrothers in a plane accident. From that day forward I had the fear that the same thing would happen to me. As an adult, I slowly worked through the crushing physical pain that I would feel when I was on a big jet by taking a flight on a small plane. Next, I worked through the angst and worry of the small plane by getting on an even smaller plane. Lastly, a friend of mine who is an instructional pilot took me up in a four-seat Cessna and had me fly over Dallas. (Really? Give the guy who is scared to death the controls to a plane?) It turned out to be probably one of the coolest things I have done. I am no longer worried about flying.

Your turn: Take a moment and look at those fears that play havoc in your life. You are probably going to have to go deep and be really, really honest. (Remember, no one else is reading this besides you.) Has it actually ever come true for you? What can you do to reduce or remove this fear? What would you accomplish if you didn't have this fear?

Take a look at your answer to, "Has it actually ever come true for you?" If you said "no," but you are still worried about it, then it really is a fear. If you said "yes," then it's a fact, not a fear. You have real life experience about the possibility that this action is going to happen again. The best thing to do is to make sure that you have learned from what occurred in the past, find the truthful lessons and apply them to your future. If you are feeling overwhelmed by your fears, look at the answer to, "What can you do to reduce or remove this fear?" and take the time to think about this. Read about your particular subject and determine steps you can take to reduce or remove your fear. There is a good shot that you are not alone in your fears. Someone in your life or in some book has had your issue before.

Take to heart the words of an unknown poet who said, "Replace fear of the unknown with curiosity."

Perceptions

Simply put, this category contains your internal representations of loves, likes, dislikes, hates, prejudices, and certainties. Perceptions are both good and bad. In most cases they are influenced by those around you (i.e. parents, siblings, friends, enemies, teachers, leaders), and you have accepted them as your own. In some cases, your perceptions are molded into final form by activities that are going on around you. They are seeded by what you have seen and heard.

For example, a father who doesn't like veggies has a child that doesn't like veggies. Do you believe that the child has developed this perception of veggies by himself or herself? Are we born with these perceptions, or are they learned? We can see it now, the "anti-veggie" gene has been discovered along with the "it's not my fault" gene. Whew, now the world makes sense.

The good news is that individuals control their perceptions. They can add, alter, or remove any of them at will. If you hate a certain veggie (i.e., Brussels sprouts), can you one day find a way to like them?[7] How about if you have a good friend and then find out that they are of another faith – one that you were raised to dislike? You can alter your perception, remove it and enjoy the friendship, or leave it in place and no longer be friends. It's up to you.

A question that we often get is: Are positive perceptions better than negative perceptions? You probably won't like the answer.[8] The answer is: not really. There are some negative perceptions that are valid no matter how the individual alters them; there are some things that a person will not like. And, of course, having a negative perception of arsenic is a rational choice for self-preservation. This discussion is not about commonly accepted things in the world that can injure you. We're talking about things that other people may find acceptable, but you do not. Our recommendation is to keep testing your perceptions. A perception that is never really tested and is blindly accepted is not necessarily good.[9]

---

7 Try them baked with a little balsamic over the top – YUM!

8 That's actually pretty funny! THAT is a perception!

9 For example: a political party's dogma.

The most important thing about perceptions is that any and all items in this category should be tested for validity by keeping an open mind. When you verbalize that you do or do not like something, ask yourself if there is any reason that you might change your mind. Ask yourself if you have any current examples that would actually invalidate your own perception. Ask if there is any way that you haven't tried to accept the opposite.

> The authors' intent is not for you to start hating a lot of items that you once liked. It's to realize that we make a lot of decisions on the basis of what someone else has told us and that we need to start making sure that we are making the decision for ourselves (good or bad).

Journal Entry #10: Perception Point-of-View. Think about your loves, likes, dislikes, hates, prejudices, and certainties in the following categories:

Social (includes friends, school, work, etc.):

Political (Republican, Democrat, Green, Socialist, Communist, Independent, Libertarian):

Economic (poor, rich, middle class, capitalistic, materialistic):

Race (color of skin):

Nationality (as other nations see you and as you see other nations):

Family (includes family members, values, religious views):

Now ask yourself the following questions: What reasons might change your perceptions? Do you have current examples that would actually invalidate your own perceptions? Why haven't you tried to accept the opposite?

The list of perceptions (and we all have them) need to be checked against the ones you want on your boat sailing to your destination. You need to decide if the added weight is worth loading. Look at how you answer the questions: "Do you have current examples that would actually invalidate your own perceptions?" and "Why haven't you tried to accept the opposite?" Determine why you have limits to your perception. Ask yourself: "Why does this particular perception matter? Can I get rid of it? What if it weren't in my life?"

It's important to consider how each of the perceptions will relate to your wants and desires in your DPPV and mission. Determine which ones will sooner or later get in your way or are diametrically opposed to your future. It's better to know now and fix them while you still have the time vs. letting them fester and get in the way of your goals.

Can you imagine your hero inviting you over to dinner, and because you found out he is serving the one veggie that you hate on everything, you decline to meet with him? Really? Would you? Of course not! You would suck it up, enjoy every bite and ask for seconds. You would go from "I hate" and "I won't" to "I choose not to," and finally to "I choose to." So, if you can control your perceptions then why have them at all? Why pack something for this trip that you don't really need? It's only going to slow you down.

Expectations

Let's start with a question: Have you ever gotten mad at someone else for something you thought they should do, but didn't tell him or her that is what you wanted? We bet you have at least once, and if you're like most people it's happened more than once.

Family expectations: "Why doesn't he send me a card for my birthday?" This is an actual example from Joel that resulted in his mother not speaking to him for two weeks. It wasn't until he asked her why she was angry that he found out that receiving a store-bought birthday card was important to her.

Friend expectations: Your friend isn't feeling well, so you bring them some soup on your way home from work. Another friend is bummed because they didn't get the raise they were hoping for, so you take them out to lunch and let them vent. Then, one day, you are home sick with the flu and get a call from your boss that you didn't get the promotion you had earned. You call or message your friends, but no one comes over with soup or stops by to visit. As a result you're mad at them for weeks and avoid them.

Work expectations: What about the times when an employee is put in a position where they must make a decision without input from management, and later they find their boss either mad at them or treating them differently. The funny thing is that the employee is thinking the boss is angry because of the decision, only to find out weeks later that the decision was the correct one and the boss was actually mad that the employee didn't contact them for input. (It would be funnier if it weren't a true story.)

Expectations are your external wants, needs, and desires of others and/or other things. You project your wants, needs and desires onto others and then judge them by those items. The receiving party may or may not even know about your projections, but they get your wrath if they don't meet them. Now, some might argue that "they" (whomever "they" are) should know or "they" should be able to read your mind. Well, the only reason we could come up with for allowing an expectation to be projected is that you want to *test* the receiver. And if you get mad or happy and it changes your opinion of them, then it was a test. It tests their resolve, knowledge, integrity, or commitment. But does it test them fairly?

Don't get too up in arms (and please don't email us). There are times when it's absolutely the right idea to have expectations (for a class, a driver's license, etc.). And it's okay to test others – as long as they know about it. It's not okay to make them guess what you are going to test them about or to see if they are going to figure it out with limited or no information (i.e. a MacGyver great escape). That is where discord and discontent breeds.

Take a moment and think about the following categories and the expectations that have surprised you: Home (spouse, family, kids), relatives (parents, siblings, aunts/uncles, grandparents), work (coworkers, team members, leaders), play (friends, sports teams), school (classmates, teachers, curriculum).

Now ask yourself: How does this make you feel to have these expectations forced upon you? Probably not very good; it feels kind of restricting, and definitely places you on the hook.

Let's look at the expectations that you are carrying around about others. Let's turn the questions around and ask the questions about home, relatives, work, play and school – except that *you* are placing the expectations on *them*.

Think hard about what you expect others to do for you. They all add weight to your BGB; they filter the things you do and that are done for you. Do you need to carry around the burden of test giving and grade keeping? If not, then it isn't an expectation. Personally, expectations seems like a lot of energy expelled and a lot preparation for future disappointment.

Ask yourself what your expectations are and why? Have you told others what you expect? How does it make you feel when others don't do what you want? When do you not place expectations on others?

Find anything interesting? Are you carrying a lot of expectations around that you don't have to? If you know the reasons why you have each expectation (especially if you couldn't answer why in "what your expectations are and why?"). Have you found out that you might treat others differently based on some criteria ("when do you not place expectations on others")? Are you consistent in how you apply your own expectations?

Don't get us wrong; we are all for expectation setting, just not by osmosis. We don't spend a lot of time making rules that others need to follow without telling them. We don't hold the weight and burden of testing and grade keeping – it takes too much time. We don't need or want people wandering around the earth wondering what they should do for us. We tell them, because if we don't there is a good chance that it might not get done.

What should be in your BGB?

Our BGB is too confining, too limiting. Frankly, it's holding us back; it's a cage. We must stage a revolt and abolish the BGB or at least alter it. We need to change our BGB to give us room to grow! Because if we are not growing, we are not living, and if we are not living, we are _____! (Did you say "dying"? Good.)

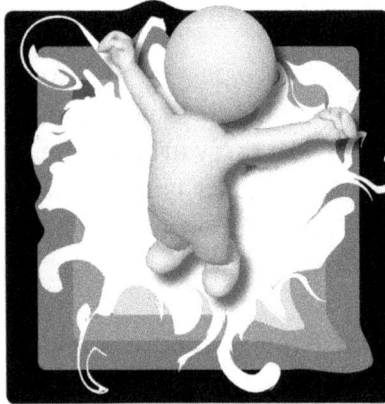

What if your BGB is not holding you back? What if the filters that you have placed in your You Toolbox are exactly what you need? (Not too many and not too few.) Our answer: Fantastic! You have probably already done the work that is required to give yourself the appropriate amount of maneuverability and flexibility that you require.

For most who need work on their BGB, we are not saying to throw everything to the wind, leave everything you know behind, and become a different person. We are asking that you need to make sure that you are holding onto the right filters. Even if you don't realize it, every action goes through each filter to make sure that you stay true to yourself and that you are staying within your comfort zone. Too many filters could equal a lot of wasted time, increased excuses, and missed opportunities.

Remember, everyone has a BGB and we all operate from within our own. Now is the time to compare yours to your DPPV and determine if it will support you. As we stated: If you have done your DPPV correctly, your dreams and vision actually sit outside your BGB. Stretch and stress should not occur inside the zone; they actually occur outside. This is a massively critical junction for most people, because it will be their first time to make sure that their comfort zone is flexible and pliable enough to grow, expand, and change. Think about it; if you have chosen a dream, vision, or mission that requires certain things of yourself that are contrary to your safe place, do you think you will change? Absolutely not. You will actually employ the opposite of what we will talk about in the E section of *REACH*; instead of removing excuses, you will use them to make yourself not feel guilty for not achieving what you want.

Use the personal inventory that you have collected in the previous questions for absolutes, fears, perceptions, and expectations and let's make sure that everything you keep inside of your You Toolbox is helping you.

Journal Entry #11: BGB Audit

Test your filters (absolutes, fears, perceptions, and expectations) with your friends (that you trust and listen to) and family to see if your BGB is correct. If not, why not? If yes, did you update your inventory? What were the top three changes?

What filters do you believe support your DPPV? Why?

What filters do you believe *do not* support your DPPV? Why?

What filters *do not* support your dreams and vision? Is it possible to change them? If yes, how and when? If no, do you need to change your DPPV so your comfort zone will support your direction?

Did you leave any filters out of your list because of embarrassment, annoyance, unwillingness to share, or too personal? Which ones are they?

The Seven Steps to Your RADICAL Self

We're about to share the seven steps of how to become a RADICAL Self. Each of these will be another tool in the You Toolbox. We suspect that you have already surmised that to live up to the new and improved you, to accomplish what you have set out to do, you're going to have to employ each of the seven items to achieve every future step that you take. Each of the areas helps energize you. Each one could be thought of as a spark plug in an engine. If you have none working you won't go anywhere; if you have one spark plug you will make very little progress; with two spark plugs even more progress, and so on, till you get all seven turned on and your dream car is speeding up the hill.[10] The components of the RADICAL Self are:

1. **Responsibility**
2. **Awareness**
3. **Determination**
4. **Image**
5. **Control**
6. **Affirmation**
7. **Listening**

We must tell you, RADICAL examples exist everywhere. Maybe you want to be a motivational speaker so you think you need a good body and great speaking voice. Look at a successful motivational speaker like Nick Vujicic. This is a man who has a great enduring story, but doesn't have a great body (really, go check him out on YouTube®).

Maybe the dream is to be a pro basketball player, but you need to be taller because the average height is 6'7" and being 5'10" just doesn't make it. Well, we have news for you: we found **ten** individuals who are 5'10" and even shorter[11]: Damon Stoudamire (5'10"), Avery Johnson (5'10"), Michael Adams (5'10"), Calvin Murphy (5'9"),

---

10 Yes, in our *Live The Risk* world, we drive a special seven-cylinder car.

11 http://www.toptenz.net/top-10-shortest-nba-players.php (accessed on January 21, 2013)

Nate Robinson (5'9"), and Wataru Misaka (5'7"), Anthony "Spud" Webb (5'7"), Earl Boykins (5'5"), and Tyrone Bogues (5'3"!). All of these guys had long NBA careers; they used their attributes not as excuses, but as a RADICAL way to get what they wanted.

What if the dream was to feed the poor, but you needed to be an adult to accomplish it? Guess what? Ten-year old Kadin Adam decided to make a difference in Portland, Oregon and fed peanut butter and jelly sandwiches to the city's homeless.[12] Well done, Kadin!

You see, it really doesn't matter how tall you are or how much you weigh. It doesn't matter how old or young you are or if you have money or not. The only requirement is to be RADICAL. Don't be held back by perceptions, images, or expectations (think back to the BGB filters) – because if you do they are nothing more than excuses (and that is the next big section). You really need to bring your RADICAL self to this endeavor!

> As usual, RADICAL is in no particular order, but it does spell out a great acronym.

Responsibility

The problem is no one can force you to be responsible. Sure, someone can ask you to be, but if you don't want to, it isn't going to happen. Self-responsibility doesn't require permission from anyone else, just you. You need to accept what you have to do (a job, a dream, chores, or a decision) as your own and do it to the best of your ability. You need to compare yourself to your expected result and at the same time ask for nothing from others.

---

12 http://www.examiner.com/article/portland-boy-staves-off-hunger-by-feeding-homeless-pb-js (accessed on January 17, 2013)

The rules of responsibility:

1. Set your expected result.
2. Determine how this expected result does not require you asking for things from others.
3. Balance the first and second rule so you can stay in control and lead yourself.
4. Don't complain about what you have decided to do. (It was your choice.)

For example: you want a 4.0 grade point average in graduate school, but also have to keep a full-time job to support yourself. If the 4.0 personal requirements cause you to need others to pay your bills so you can dedicate every hour to study, you are then violating the second and third rules of responsibility. Something has to give. Either you reduce your expenses or you reduce (or postpone) your expected outcome so you can support yourself. Perhaps you decide that graduate school isn't important enough to your future self or find some other solution.

Think of your friends, family, coworkers and acquaintances. Peer into their lives and see if they take full responsibility for themselves. See if they have followed all four rules. Easy to do when it's not you, huh? Now, let's look into *your* life.

We are sure you know this by now; it's up to you to put the details down. You can be superficial, dishonest, or bend the truth to the point where it's an out-and-out lie. You can pretend that your answer is, "I don't need anything from anybody!" But if you take one dime, require one favor, need one thing from someone else, then guess what? You need something from somebody.

What did you find? We suspect that there are some obvious responsibilities that require other people. The first one that comes to mind is raising your children (you need babysitters and teachers). Another might be making money (you need clients), and another is learning (buying/borrowing and reading this book). Did you find that responsibility is also about where you spend your time? Did you learn that some of your low priority items (things that don't directly impact your mission, but require a lot of help) are taking up too much time?

RADICAL responsibility doesn't have to be stressful and it's not meant to be difficult. **The secret is that you must own it.** If the list of responsibilities is too long, then shorten it (remember the moral, ethical, and legal compass that you should be using). If others need to help, make sure they know. Don't use guilt or knowledge by osmosis and assume they know. Tell them! (This is also taking responsibility for you.) At the end, to have Self-Responsibility you need to be accountable for what is within your own power, control or management.

Awareness

If you ask any police officer, martial artist, and army ranger what's one of the most important things in order for them to do their job well, they would tell you that awareness is high on their list, if not first. The need to be aware of what is going on around them can mean the difference between life and death. Their opportunities to avoid getting hurt are based on them seeing, hearing, or sensing what is going to happen around them and taking action prior to it ever occurring. The response could be anything from avoiding interaction to offensive or defensive engagement. The point is that they have listened to the information around them and made a choice. This particular section is not about that choice (that's determination), but about you being conscious and participatory.

Self-awareness is all about you being attuned to what is happening in your environment, which is defined by author and martial artist Skip Hancock as *what is going in you, on you, and around you.*

Let's give some examples. This was a true story for Joel that actually became debilitating. He got heartburn every night. He took one of those magic pills and the heartburn subsided. He was confident that it wasn't the spicy food he was eating or the extra thirty pounds that he had put on. That little pill made the symptoms go away, but not the underlying problem.

Another example: A gut pain actually made Jeff double over. Sometimes, it wasn't as extreme – just a constant nagging pain that never seemed to go away. It was there every day and every evening, interrupting his sleep and preventing him from accomplishing things he needed to get done during his day. He did the right things – he went to the doctor, he had a lot of tests, he tried some new drugs – but nothing worked and the pain didn't go away.

What did both of us good-looking and intelligent authors do? We listened closely to what was really going on. For us, it was the wake-up call to look past the masking of the symptoms, because it wasn't the heartburn and acid reflux that was the problem; it was being caused by our eating and exercise habits. We both discovered our real issue by doing the exact same thing: we became ultra-aware of what we were putting into our bodies by keeping track of what we ate and when the symptoms were worse. Of course, this led us both (on different occasions) to have a heightened sense of what was going in us, so we could determine what we needed to do to change to an outcome that was more desirable. For Joel, it was exercise and weight loss (thirty-two pounds to be exact). For Jeff, it was a diet change that required him to admit that certain foods didn't agree with his body.

When it comes to awareness, there is no better book than the *Gift of Fear* by Gavin de Becker.[13] In it the author talks at length about how awareness can help you avoid being a victim by keeping attuned to what is going on around you and listening to that little annoying voice in your gut telling you something is wrong or at least out of place.

---

13 Gift of Fear, Gavin de Becker © 1997; ISBN 978-0-440-50883-0

What we find very interesting is how this out-of-place information is actually delivered to our brains. The author calls them "Messengers of Intuition": nagging feelings, persistent thoughts, humor, wonder, anxiety, curiosity, hunches, gut feelings, doubt, hesitation, suspicion, apprehension, and fear (with fear being a good thing this time). We call them "awareness buoys" because when they start bobbing, then you should start planning.

Even though Gavin De Becker is using the information to keep you out of undesirable and violent circumstances, we are using the same material to help you see the world around you as clearly as possible. The buoys can be used for normal everyday activities in work or play. You can probably remember catching your kids in a lie by those buoys bobbing. Good things can happen too – some nice people met their spouses by being charming and offering a piece of gum at a bus stop.

Ask yourself the following questions: Have you ever seen the awareness buoys in practice (by you or by others)? What was the outcome? Did you know another individual's intent before they started talking? What do you think the other person thought about your intent? When the awareness buoys start bobbing, what do you do next? Are you aware of the weather before you go out? What about the temperature where you are going? Who is around you at the grocery store? What is under your car where it's parked? Do you pay attention to dark spots of oil in the driveway? Can you name all of your kids' friends? Do you have their phone numbers?

RADICAL Awareness is about being more knowledgeable, conscious, and cognizant of ourselves in our environment (in you, on you, and around you). It's about having a better opportunity to succeed at what life throws at you and the time to figure out what to do.

Determination

Choice, choice, choice, choice, and choice. You are going to make thousands if not millions of choices during the course of your lifetime. You are going to be pleased with some and annoyed with others. You will have the opportunity to reap the rewards, and on occasion (hopefully rarely) you will have to pay the price. Over time you will see some choices as fantastic, good, okay, and just plain bad. You will have moments in time where you have chosen not to make them, which will be fine. And there will be other times where you took too long to make them and missed the opportunity. There will be some that you will love and some that you will deeply regret. Such is the nature of things when given the beautiful gift we know as **freedom of choice**.

If you haven't figured it out, this section is about making sure that your choices are yours and they help you get where you want to go. Our goal and intent is making sure that *you* are making the choices that fit what *you* want.

> We are not so naive as to believe that you will only make good choices and decisions. (Not all of ours have been good either.) We only hope that what we are about to introduce will increase your odds of success.

There are a couple of issues when it comes to the topic of making choices. The first one is not to get fooled into thinking that anyone else can make decisions for you. You have the ultimate decision-making authority. You can say *yes* or *no*. People may not like hearing those answers. In fact, there could be some very serious consequences for not giving the answer other people expect. You cannot afford to let this scare you. The decisions you make need to work for you.

Secondly, when you don't make a choice and use this as a defense ("I didn't know what to do so it's not my fault!"), we say, "No choice is a choice." This will screw with some people's minds: *How is not making a choice a choice?* Think about it for a second. You choose to not make a choice. Obviously a choice needed to be made and you chose not to participate – thus it is a choice. The outcome normally means that you are probably going to get the results of someone else's choice. So rule #1 is (and it's actually the only rule for determination): *You make all your own choices.*

We discovered six items to help validate our determination to make the right choices:

Question	What is my objective with this decision?
Time	How long do I really have to make this decision?
Attitude	What is my frame of mind going into this decision?
Details	Is my data accurate and relevant?
Options	What are my options to accomplish what I want?
Choose	What is my best choice to help me accomplish my goal?

Question

"What is my objective with this decision?" is the #1 item on our list. The simpler the topic the easier it becomes to answer. Sometimes we forget the scope of what we need to determine; we start piling multiple requests together, attempting an all-for-one choice to be made. We can't tell you how dangerous this is. Remember, we are attempting to decide something that we consider critical to our well-being.

We need to bring to the forefront what we want to decide and why. Really, it doesn't get any more complicated than that. This single question will aim the bazillion neurons in your head toward a common purpose. It directs the brain to formulate an answer. It will keep firing answers until you accept one. Believe it or not, if *questions* make the brain come up with options, then *statements* have the opposite effect. They are treated as fact and the brain considers that there is no question to answer. We normally make statements when we have a preconceived choice in mind.

Such as: "This movie is going to suck because all chick flicks are dumb." Or, "I don't like anyone who supports a particular political candidate." Keep in mind that most decisions (thus the questions we want to ask) are really balancing out the risk with what you think the reward will be. For example:

Type	Verbiage	Result
Statement	I want a car.	Congratulations, you're buying a car! A choice has been made.
Good Question	Should I buy a new car?	The question isn't specific enough. Your brain will answer as it always does: with emotion, logic, and wants. Our guess is that you will waffle on the topic attempting to convince yourself to do what you want.
Great Question	Do I need a new car and the associated expenses at this time, or should I choose a good used car?	By separating out want from need (I want to eat a steak vs. I need to eat) you have cleared the way to process the risk and reward of a new car vs. its associated payments.

It's incredibly important to not regret the end decision, thus you need to make sure you are asking the right questions.

Time

How long do I really have to make this decision? How much time could folks save by asking, "Is this the *right* time?" Patience is key. There are three likely outcomes for using patience in this process:

- Don't take enough time and you might make the wrong decision,

- Take too much time and you might miss the opportunity, and

- Take the right amount of time and you develop the appropriate choices.

How do you know if it's the right time? Ask yourself: "Do I need to make this decision *now*?"

We'll admit that "patience" is an overused word in business and at home. Most of the time it's used as an excuse by others for not providing an answer to a question we have: "Have patience. It's in the works." In reality the word "patience" should never be told to you by others. The problem with hearing "have patience" as an answer when you have asked the question is that it provides no facts or assumptions by which to make a better choice (hopefully the reason for asking the question). If you were to tell yourself to have patience and wait for a better answer, *you have decided to wait for the details that will allow you to better answer your question!*

Ask yourself: Do I need to make this decision now? If not, how long do I have till I have to make it?

Attitude

Attitude is a very valuable, intangible, inner working that some call confidence, chutzpah, or guts. Webster's Dictionary defines it as: *"A mental position with regard to a fact or state.[14]"*

Your attitude can be positive or negative. A good attitude is the key to a successful life and a bad attitude prevents it. To us, attitude is the

---

14 http://www.merriam-webster.com/dictionary/attitude (accessed on May 4, 2013)

basic confidence that ensures success and it's the first thing brought to the fight called life. It's also the starting point to understand, "What is my frame of mind going into this decision? Is it positive, negative or someplace in-between?" Attitudes can be statements like, "I have the right to protect myself" or "This is going to be good!" Attitude gives you direction and permission to determine what choices you will make. It's a constant reminder that you can accomplish what you set out to do. Keep in mind it's much more than the way you think; it's in the way you walk, speak, and act. Attitude can be seen from a mile away.

Whether your attitude is good or bad is up to you. The first priority of attitude is to bring you up to a level that will allow you to solve the problem. There is no doubt that by understanding your current attitude, it will provide you an inside view to the choices with which you're going to have to live. Here are some questions to ask in order to determine yours:

❑ When I wake up in the morning, do I jump out of bed? Go back to sleep? Or lie there and think about things?
❑ How am I carrying my body (posture) while thinking about it?
❑ What is my mood – happy, sad, content, or tired?
❑ What is the last thing that I think about before I go to bed?

Details

There is an old saying that states, "garbage in, garbage out." In other words, the data that you put into your decision-making process makes or breaks your choices. The better the data, the better the decision. We see folks blindly following what everyone else has done and never asking, "Is my data accurate and relevant?" The best example that we have is the collection of sound bites, misinformation, and part-truths of political ads attempting to get us to make a choice with what could be considered garbage information. This is what we don't want to happen to you. We want you to have a clear line of sight to where your data came from. Let's say you're buying a car, and you wanted to figure the appropriate payment. You didn't use the right interest rate and your calculations gave you the wrong payment. With all other items being equal, this one piece of data could get you to make the wrong financial choice.

> We are not suggesting that all data can be known before any choice can be made. Search out and verify the data that you need for the decision.

What to do? Well, we can't define all of the appropriate places to get the most accurate information. However, we can give you some pointers on what to do when you get the information:

❑ Find an independent source for your information. Beware of bias.

❑ Maintain a healthy skepticism in what you hear and learn. Be cautious.

❑ Think about the other side of the coin (and there is always another side).

❑ Make sure you listen before you determine if it's garbage or not.

<u>Options</u>

Each of the other four portions of self-determination serves these functions: to arm you with the right question; to remove questions that aren't worth asking (yet); to make sure that you understand that your frame of mind influences you (by the way, bad mood or attitude probably means bad choices); and to make sure that the information that you are using to create your options is valid and balanced.

Given that you collected the right information and you jumped the hurdles, it's time to ask the question: "What are my options for this choice?" Now, this is the moment where your DPPV and current mission come back into play. Why would you make options or choices that violate what you want your dreams, vision, or mission to be? You wouldn't. We suggest you follow the very B.E.S.T. process that we could find to shift through your options:

- ❑ **B**rainstorm - Write down all possible options that come to mind. Don't apply rules; at this stage there are no bad ideas. Keep writing. Remember, if you find yourself saying "too risky" or "not what they expect," then go back to the BGB and Living models, because something hasn't been resolved.

- ❑ **E**liminate - Remove all of the ideas that violate your mission or DPPV, or go against any of the other RADICAL items (yes, you might need to read ahead so you know them all).

- ❑ **S**elect - Determine your top three choices and produce a pro/con list for each. Now, keep in mind that if you are attempting to make the data lean a particular way, you already have your answer!

- ❑ **T**rack - Go back through each of the other segments (Question, Time, Attitude, and Details) to make sure that what you have as possible answers to your question are valid.

Choose

You have done your homework. It may have taken you moments or days, but you have done everything you were supposed to and it's now time to decide what your choice is going to be. There really are only a few rules by which to abide:

1. Be sure to make a choice.
2. Be sure that you *own* the choice you have made.
3. Be sure not to regret the choice you made.

That's it! Self-Determination is the act of coming to a trustworthy decision after observation and investigation. It's a decision that you can live with, and one that doesn't violate your ethical, moral, and logical standards. It's one that allows you to take risks, moves you on your way through your mission, and gets you to your dreams.

> We will spend a lot more time on the subject of setting goals and enacting your choices in the "A" and "C" sections ahead. Get ready.

Image

There is a great picture of a kitten looking in the mirror and seeing the reflection of a full-grown lion. The caption says, "What matters most is how you see yourself." We couldn't say it any better. You cannot leave it up to anybody else to tell you what image of yourself to have. Their opinion really doesn't count, nor do their list of qualities or their desires for you. The only thing that matters is what you think about yourself.

According to psychologist Carl Rogers,[15] this sensitive area consists of what we think of ourselves (self-worth) and how we see ourselves (body image, personality, and our personal perceptions). Now, here's the hard part to hear. We have been conditioned to develop our image based on the wants and needs of others or someone else's expectations, and that is a mistake. Modern advertising plays on this misconception and capitalizes on this misguided need to be like others. The need to change your inside or outside image to be something other than you is a problem. To become someone else instead of you is plain crazy. You'll never find happiness or achieve your dreams if you are not true to who you need or want to be. There's no doubt you are probably okay at being someone else, but we'll bet you are perfect at being you. Look at those who've accomplished the impossible and who've made their dreams come true, and we know that you'll see people who are true to themselves.

---

15 http://www.simplypsychology.org/carl-rogers.html (accessed on February 2, 2013)

You can tell yourself that your dream, vision, or mission requires something to be changed on you or in you, and we suspect that with a quick Google search you will come up with at least one example where the opposite was true for someone else.

If you want to do it for yourself because you want it, then so be it; you'll get no argument from us, but don't use the image as defined by someone else as an excuse. If you are doing it so others will see a different you, we would really caution you to ask yourself if it's worth the expense, time, energy and pain. Ask yourself whether changing your outside (shape, size, looks) or inside (ethics, morals, logic) will *guarantee* your goal. For example: "When I lose weight I will get a better selection of dates."

Take a moment to think about your self-image. Don't be shy and don't hold back.

Is your self-image positive or negative? A poor self-image will prevent you from obtaining your goal because you don't feel worthy. A strong self-image will support your goal. You have the right to be as positive and powerful as you want. At the end, you need to decide for yourself what your self-image is. You need to be in control of your mental, emotional, and physical image: *Who, what and why you are you*. Here is a non-scientific quiz. By going through the process you will see items that you might need to work on:

Journal Entry #12: How's Your Self-Image?

Question	A	B
When you first see yourself in a mirror in the morning, are your thoughts good or bad? (Other good questions to ask: What do you think about yourself? Do you like or dislike yourself?)	Good	Bad
How do you compare yourself to others? 10 - Exceeds / 6 - Above Average / 4 - Below Average / 0 - You suck. (Sorry, there is no 5.)	6 - 10	0 - 4
Do you deserve to be happy?	Yes	No
Are you happy?	Yes	No
Do you have mostly good moments or bad moments?	Good	Bad
Do you think others like you when they first meet you?	Yes	No
Would people think poorly of you if you made a mistake?	No	Yes
Does your opinion matter to others?	Yes	No
If you do well at something, do you tend to put it down to luck rather than skill?	Skill	Luck
Would you prevent yourself from seeking a job or promotion based on how you feel about yourself?	No	Yes
Do you feel you are a leader or a follower?	Leader	Follower
Do you find it hard to take criticism?	No	Yes

Give yourself one point for each answer in Column A. Use the following chart to assess your score.

Score	Self-Image	Description
10 >	Excellent	Keep moving forward; keep believing in yourself.
7 - 9	Good	There is always room for improvement and you know where you need help.
5 - 6	Borderline	It might be worthwhile to dive deeper into how to improve a specific area (we always suggest getting professional assistance).
< 4	Not good	We suggest that you consult a professional; there are self-image issues that need to be worked on (and they are probably not skin deep).

Control

Think back to when you were a kid and you heard the word "control." For us, it was mostly from a teacher, parent, or sitter telling us to stop doing something we weren't suppose to be doing at that moment. They would yell to us to, "Control yourself!" It seemed to imply that we should have known better.[16] The word "control" to them was defined as:[17]

❏ Exercising authoritative or dominating influence over (i.e. ourselves).

❏ Adjusting a requirement (i.e. change what we thought we were going to do).

❏ Holding in restraint; check (i.e. put our hands in our pockets, or take our hands out of pockets).

❏ Reducing or preventing the spread of (i.e. the damage they could foresee).

---

16 It also usually included our full name, which from experience is never a good thing.

17 http://www.thefreedictionary.com/control (accessed on 1/21/2013)

Of course, as we got older and perhaps had a spouse, boss, or bartender utter the word *control*, it also meant the same thing, but the punitive damages were much greater than a smack on the hand or being grounded. Not having control over ourselves as adults means that we could end up divorced,[18] losing a job, or getting kicked out of a favorite bar.

Another form of *control* is when you are delivering (i.e. a task at work or play) what someone else wants, but you haven't accepted it as your own. Don't shrug this off too quickly because we all know we have done it. Our question is why? Why fall into this hornet's nest of ridicule, nonsense, and disappointment? If you don't care about the topic, reason or action, then our suggestion is: Respectfully tell them you're not doing it. Remember, if you take any action toward accomplishing someone else's goal (which hopefully is incorporated in your mission) you have created the contract with yourself to do your best (correctly, timely, and to their expectations) and you have assumed the responsibility to control yourself so you can deliver as promised. You have invoked all of the RADICAL selves to make sure you achieve your mission, which now includes their stuff. Again, it's your choice.

We don't care if it's their mission or yours; control is a very critical item. Control means that we maintain a dominating influence over ourselves. We take and keep control of our actions (whatever they may be) in order to have the focus to deliver.

Stop blaming yourself or others and start taking control of your life. It's quite a powerful feeling to know that you control you! Don't dwell on past mistakes, blame yourself, or regret your decisions – let it go! From this moment forward, *you are in control of your life!*

We trust that you won't lie to yourself, right? If so, when you do something that's wrong (or not so right), you will take the blame (what a novel concept, perhaps all governments should do it), learn from your mistake, set the mistake right, and then move on. But it starts with controlling the ability to make your own decisions (even

---

18 In which case she gets your 50% and her 50%.

if they're wrong). Now the question becomes, how do you maintain control of yourself? We have scoured our notes and narrowed it down to seven really important items:

1	Understand the intention	We know that you have control over your BGB - Absolutes (including moral, ethical, logical), Fears, Perceptions, and Expectations. As you start accomplishing your own dreams, you need to make sure that you have a clear intention of what you are signing up to do. You need to be concise and accurate so your mind and body know that there are no self-built obstacles in getting it done. This could be as easy as saying "I want/need a new job by January 2014."
2	Keep focused	Don't lose sight of the goal. Focus needs to be laser-like and on-target.
3	Give enough time	We know the realities of accomplishing what is on your list. It is important to note that you shouldn't stack and hope to accomplish everything within the same timeframe/deadline. It's an *excuse* waiting to happen.
4	Eliminate temptations	When you're focused on getting something done it's important to remove the things that steal your time and energy, especially if they provide no value to your overall mission. We are not saying that you eliminate everything else in your life; we are saying that to stay in control you must remove the temptations that take you away from what you need to do (i.e. social media has given us all an escape that seems to get in our way on a regular basis).
5	Keep some distractions	If you do #1 through #4, you are welcome to some distractions, especially if they help relax and rejuvenate your mind or body. If you are not doing the others well, then guess what this is? Nothing more than a temptation.

6	Take care	There is only one you. If by staying in control you are hurting yourself, then we suggest that you really look at what you are doing and why. Taking care of you should be rewarding in and of itself. Any of the *addictions* (i.e. alcoholic, chocoholic, druggie) seem to take this category and throw it out the control window.
7	Practice	We cannot tell you how important this is. To have self-control is to exercise restraint, direction, and command over yourself. To accomplish this on a regular basis means you need to practice it daily. Don't use it only when someone is looking or you're being judged. Use it all of the time. Exert self-control when you eat, sleep, work, and play.

Affirmation

For much of society, there seems to be a significant need for others to tell us how good we are, that we did the right thing, and that we put in the effort. Some people need to hear others say, "You do good work," "Your skills are great," and "You do that better than someone else." Some need the positive affirmations that friends, acquaintances, and strangers provide to keep going. The general compliments, the encouragement, and the flattery tend to fuel their engine to keep on moving, at least for the short time. Let's get real. It feels good when others compliment us and we are not going to ask them to stop. It's nice being noticed for having done the right thing, the right way, at the right time.

We are talking about the *need* to be recognized from an outside source to validate your existence on this planet. If they don't recognize you, your self-worth and self-image diminishes based on their lack of validation. Not good. You actually lose steam when others don't see you in a positive light. Or worse, when they say negative things it actually stops you from going after your dreams. The sad part is that we humans often face, on a regular basis, the need to have a form of validation from others – normally people that we trust, respect, admire, or with whom we are in competition.

We would like to help you break this need (or at least diminish it). You really can't afford to put that type of power into another's hands. We want you to learn to provide yourself with positive affirmations that give you the same endorphin rush as getting the statement from another. We want you to develop or improve on your self-talk, or as our great friend and mentor, Hellen Davis, President of Indaba, Inc. says, "To develop a strong sense of targeted and active motivation based on your intentions." Self-talk can be a powerful mechanism, given that you get control over it. Hellen writes:

> "Negative self-talk can actually inhibit your effectiveness and your ability to achieve your goals... It's no secret that we become what we most believe about ourselves. If we believe ourselves to be individuals capable of success, then it's much more likely that we'll actually go on to achieve that success. If we believe ourselves to be incompetent failures, however, then it stands to reason that we'll eventually become such...[With positive self-talk] we have more confidence in ourselves and more freely express and pursue our ambitions. Likewise, we tend to have confidence that these ambitions are worthwhile in the first place."[19]

Wow! What a powerful statement and thought. There are times when you have to go out into the world and achieve regardless of what others say (good or bad). You have the opportunity to change your outcome by making sure that you listen and change what you tell yourself.

---

19 Hellen D. Davis, Indaba, Inc. © 2008. Life Coaching / Self Talk.

Journal Entry #13: My Affirmations.

1. What positive statements do you make about yourself?

2. What negative statements do you make about yourself?

3. What positive things do you need said to you on a daily or weekly basis to feel good about yourself? (Be honest.)

4. What negative things, if said, make you feel bad about yourself and make you want to stop and change directions?

5. How can you reframe or reword them, so both the positive and negative items become agents of change?

6. What are the most powerful positive messages that you can tell yourself? Here are some helpful starting words: I acknowledge, I am, I allow, I am willing, I realize, I enjoy; and our personal favorites: I fully accept, I know without a doubt, and I take action.

7. Can you change any of the words to be more powerful? (Think about positive and negative adjectives.)

8. Pick the top three and go to a mirror and say them out loud. How did they make you feel?

Listening

More and more people surround us in our everyday lives and fewer of them are truly listening to what we have to say. Let us set the stage with two examples:

Example 1: After Joel's mom died in 2002, he would tell his story to anyone who would listen, attempting to get it out of his head. On occasion, he would hear the dreaded, "I understand…" He knew people attempted to commiserate with him, but felt that if someone hadn't been in his exact shoes, did they really understand? He was finding his angst, anger, and sorrow was being cheapened by others not letting his story stay his story.

Example 2: Years ago, we overheard a very excited teen tell his parent that he was finally able to break a board in his martial arts class. It's an exciting moment when it actually happens (in case you have never broken a board). The parent jumped in and described his experience when he broke not one, but *two* boards. We sat in wonderment that this kid's exciting news was now only a footnote. In one moment, the student's story was downgraded (i.e. not as good as dad's).

Each of these examples made us wonder about why we have this need to hijack another's story, whether good or bad. Why not let them finish and then pass the proverbial talking stick to the next person? Why are we compelled to explode on the scene with our own experiences? Why can't we listen?

We know it's good to share. It's nice to know that we have something in common. There is nothing wrong with sympathy. We are helping them to know they are not alone. Really? Do we interrupt what they are saying so we can help or to hijack? Maybe it is innocent: "I understand," or "The same thing happened to me." Maybe it's one-upmanship: "I've got you beat," or "You've got me beat." Each can be seen as helpful, and each is also designed to take the conversational off-ramp, so we can redirect their story into ours. In our personal experience, it's unintentional (as we believe it is eighty percent of the time). When we've done it, it wasn't because we meant to. It was only that the words started coming out of our mouths before we could take control of what we were saying, and that's not a good thing.

Sociologist Charles Derber says that redirection is a sign of "conversational narcissist" behavior. He writes, "People often enter into conversations seeking to receive attention rather than to give it. This norm is unlikely ever to change in a society that is increasingly impersonal and atomistic, and conditioned to award attention to those with status rather to those who might actually have something interesting to say."[20]

Personally, what we think it means is that real listening is a lost art! We have grown accustomed to looking for the opportunity to change who has the attention and/or focus. Our problem (and yes, we have this terrible habit) is that if we look for the moment in time to take the off-ramp from our friend's path, we have stopped listening to what they are attempting to tell us and definitely to what is going on around us. If it's a bad moment, we can only pretend to commiserate. If it's a good moment, we can only pretend to be excited for them...because you guessed it...we are not giving them our one hundred percent undivided attention to their story; we are not really listening.

External listening is one thing that we hope you will correct, but there is also another type of listening – internal. This is where listening to what your mind, body and spirit are saying to you. To continue running when your legs are past hurting is not listening to yourself (also see *Awareness)*. The good news is that there is a way out of this bad behavior, and the same methods work for everyone.

20 http://www.philosophicalsociety.com/Archives/Conversational%20Narcissism.htm

Here are some things you can do to be a better listener, both externally and internally:

❑ Ask the speaker if he/she wants you to just listen (be a sounding board) or provide help or offer an opinion. Respect that choice! Then, sit down, shut up, and concentrate on what they (mind, body, spirit, or others) are saying. Just listen; keep the speaker front and center.

❑ Let them know that you are listening and absorbing what they are saying by providing them with non-distracted feedback (i.e. active listening skills). Asking questions is a good way to stay focused on what is being said. You can also paraphase back to them what they have said to you.

❑ Don't look for common stories; be appreciative that they are sharing with you.

❑ Don't say, "I understand" (or any other phrase that is a comparison) because you are not them nor have you gone through what they are *exactly* going through. "I can appreciate what you are going through," is a valid response.

❑ Don't be compelled to "one-up" their story. Be in awe of what they have accomplished and not what you have accomplished. After all, you'll expect the same from others when you tell them about how you accomplished your goals and dreams.

❑ Check your ego at the door. Really, it's not all about you. (Unless you're listening to yourself; then it is *all* about you.)

We challenge you to listen to their story and to listen to your own stories. Give you/them your attention. Stay away from taking control. Keep reminding yourself that they are sharing for a reason. If they want your opinion, they will ask for it. Most importantly, listen; really listen.

The Balance To Achieve

This is the final section that makes up RADICAL persistence. Our version of balance is achieved by the interaction of five distinct areas, called fitnesses. In his book, *Kenpo: The Path of Excellence,*[21] author Skip Hancock describes these five fitnesses as:

Spiritual The proper use of *knowledge* in one's daily life and on the street. The courage to act according to standards of right and wrong, or life and death that one establishes for him/herself. (This is not the same thing as religion; it could be considered a superset or subset.)

Perceptual The quality of one's senses (seeing, hearing, feeling, smelling, and tasting) that determines the limits of one's ability to defend oneself or to take action.

Emotional The ability to internally represent experiences in such a way as to make oneself powerful and capable of taking decisive and effective actions.

Mental The ability to correctly interpret events and to focus one's attention at will, being aware of all relevant information, but oblivious to distractions, and to concentrate as long as necessary to achieve one's goal.

Physical The health and condition of one's body. When properly prepared and maintained, physical fitness will be a deciding factor in one's ability to benefit from each opportunity that comes in life.

It would be easy to see each section being separate and distinct, but they are not. They are all interconnected and part of the same structure. They work together and they are pulling for you to achieve

---

21 Skip Hancock © 1994 ASIN: B0006F5US6 (used with permission). We have added additional italicized words to the definitions to make each of them applicable to our daily lives.

what you want. For example, to think that "physical" only refers to your muscles but not to your mental or spiritual functions is wrong (ask any body builder what they rely on most). The five fitnesses need to work together to keep us going for the long haul.

> # Balance is when spiritual, perceptual, emotional, mental, and physical fitnesses are 100% in support of my life

Of course, you might be one of the readers who will replay their youth. Nothing was a problem, anything bad could be handled, and you didn't care if you had to stay up late, not eat, not work out, and drink like a fish to get whatever job you wanted done, done. We were the same (maybe without the drinking part). With age,[22] new thought processes crept into our psyche, leaving us with the question: Should we take care of our body, mind, and breath separately?

Trust us (actually trust yourself); each of the fitnesses – Spiritual, Perceptual, Emotional, Mental, and Physical – play a role in keeping you sane and upright. Can you imagine the toll it takes keeping a thousand plates spinning at the same time? It isn't any fun.

Out of balance

When all five fitnesses are in balance, they work in harmony, each doing their part of the job, none having to overwork to compensate for another. All of them support you while you move through life. But when one of the fitnesses is out of balance, each of the other fitnesses tries their best to fill the gap created. Some will stay in place

---

22 Which for us contained some important knowledge and wisdom.

and expand, and some will move with the out-of-balance fitness. But sooner or later, the other fitnesses also become fatigued and out of balance, unable to support and cover for the others, and that is when true body distress occurs, making any kind of movement or progress very difficult if not impossible.

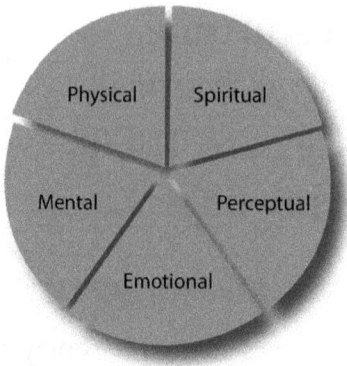

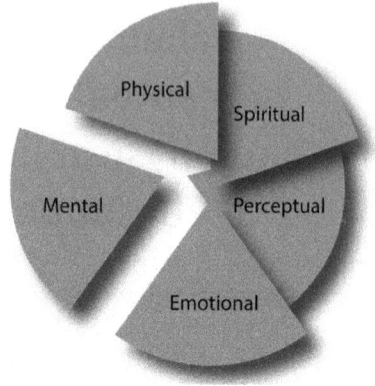

Balance   Out of Balance

Imbalances occur at work: long hours, low wages, unforgiving managers, and costly mistakes. At play: too much focus on training, not enough rest, no healing time. Each of these triggers will cause you stress and will start affecting you, and over time will start bringing you out of balance. We have heard it before and it's true: every person is different when it comes to dealing with stress. Remember that imbalance happens to all of us at some point in time.

It's easy to recognize imbalance when it happens suddenly. When loss of a job or a parent's death occurs, we all expect that a person will lose their balance in some way. Most of the time imbalance occurs gradually and there is no one event that can be pointed to as the cause. Slow but sure loss of balance is what most of us face on a day-to-day basis. This gradual loss is where the real danger lies. Imagine a memory issue that has been happening over the last year. Compare any two days together and it's not an issue. Compare year after year and you will find that your other fitnesses have compensated and covered for you...and covered them up.

The other major place of concern is the sheer complexity called life. If your life is simple and sane, staying in balance is child's play. It's when you have multiple fires (remember, sometimes fire is good), that it becomes dicey. Our visual image is that the balance wheel rides on a pedestal that represents the complexity of life. The lower on the pedestal the wheel sits, then the sturdier the wheel is and thus, the less complex life is at that period of time. Obviously, the higher the wheel is on the pedestal the harder it will be to keep the balance.

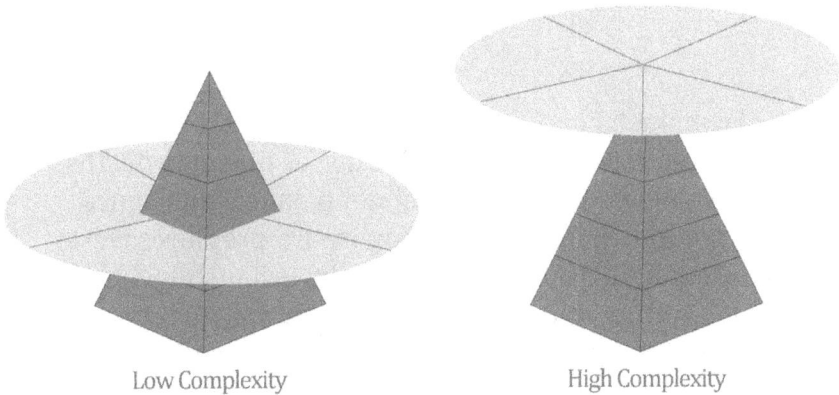

Low Complexity   High Complexity

There are three categories that can cause imbalance as it relates to complexity:

1. Internal weights. This is probably the largest area of concern because these weights are in our control and we choose not to limit or stop them. Working long hours and exhausting ourselves, practicing through our injuries and doing more harm, and not finding time to relax are some examples.

2. External pressures are items that affect our fitnesses that we have no control over. A sudden death in the family is the best example. Significant pressures on spiritual, emotional, and physical fitnesses occur instantly because the trials and tribulations of the loss of family. An exhausting level of stress results when the family attempts to understand what has happened.

3. Limitations of elasticity of the other fitnesses to cover for another fitness's weakened state. For example: If you are tired mentally, your physical fitness can only carry you so far to your destination.

If you really took control of yourself and stayed in balance, how successful would you become? What kind of mood would you be in? What could you accomplish? By the end of the day, how would you feel?

From Joel: I had gone through this roller coaster of imbalance as I went through a series of family deaths that allowed me to learn about balance/imbalance first hand. In my case, the downward pressures were emotionally, physically, and mentally exhausting. I placed a significant amount of weight on my spiritual fitness, because faith was the only thing I could rely upon during this time of my life. Looking back, I can tell that even my perceptual fitness was being stretched to cover my exhaustion. Eventually that fitness was also brought out of balance. I had lost my taste for food and listening became more of a problem. After it was all over, my wife knew that I needed to forge a personal comeback of sorts. She sent me to friends in Montana who helped me work to regain balance in my world. I slowed down to take in the environment (the sun, sky, and trees), started eating more natural foods, started to walk for exercise, began to read and write to reactivate my mind, and began to focus on the family to ensure my emotional well-being. I didn't work on any one fitness; I worked on all of the fitnesses a little at a time, and with that was able to survive and grow.

From Jeff: Experiencing an imbalance in any one area of life is challenging and daunting, but when all areas are out of balance, then you're in trouble. When my daughter was diagnosed with Type 1 Diabetes, my life was already out of balance. Things went from rough to terrible. All of my fitnesses were falling apart. I got to a point where I felt like nothing was going right. I could have focused and dwelled on the negative. I could have spent all of my time complaining, and the truth is I did plenty of it before I admitted that complaining accomplishes nothing. However, through it all, my daughter never once complained. She was her usual happy-go-lucky self. Wow! I had been spending far too much time being unhappy and unbalanced that I had been missing out on enjoying my wife and wonderful children. I decided then that I would take control of my fitnesses. I would choose to live life. I would not dwell on those things I have no control over. I admitted that complaining would get me nothing. I would no longer make excuses. The lesson my six-year-old taught me that year has shaped every day since.

The forethought of living

We think we have proven that balance should not be an afterthought. When you combine work, home, play, kids, and all of the other things, you may find that life can be complex. The issues in your world can easily drag you down the proverbial rabbit hole. If our definition of balance is true and it occurs when spiritual, perceptual, emotional, mental, and physical fitnesses are fully in support of our direction, then living in balance means that you need to set a direction for your life first.[23]

---

23 Sometimes doing your homework pays off – review your DPPV.

Do yourself a favor and make a commitment to walk the circle of balance of physical, mental, emotional, spiritual, and perceptual fitnesses. Much like a gyroscope that needs to continually spin to stay upright, we need to continually walk the circle to make sure that we stay upright. Work on every fitness a little each day, starting at the top of the circle with spiritual and then going clockwise. One more suggestion: Choose one fitness to focus on each week in order to keep you in optimum balance.

Keep in mind that as we take action on any of the fitnesses, it's not perfection that we are after, but to do and improve on a daily basis. Simple actions done now will produce results in both the immediate and long-term future. Excellent balance is required for us to walk our path and get the most from our journey!

RADICAL Persistence

There is no doubt that RADICAL Persistence is no easy task; there is a lot of soul searching, personal understanding, and improvement that is required to make sure that you have the tools in the You Toolbox and are in a position to obtain your mission. When we started this section we asked you to read and consider the following:

I CAN ATTEST THAT NO ONE WANTS THIS MORE THAN ME AND I AM RESPONSIBLE FOR MYSELF!

We hope that you now see that we didn't expect you to take this simple statement lightly. There is some significant work required to make sure that what is contained in the big granite block (BGB) will help and not hinder the life you want. The need to understand and appreciate the filters that make up absolutes, fears, perceptions, and expectations so that they put you in an advantageous position is a must. You are already one leg up on most people because of the clear understanding you now have of **R**esponsibility, **A**wareness, **D**etermination, **I**mage, **C**ontrol, **A**ffirmation, and **L**istening. RADICAL describes the power that you can have over yourself. It should be clear that balance between the spiritual, perceptual, emotional, mental, and physical areas of life is of the utmost importance.

We think it's safe to say that RADICAL Persistence is not a once-in-a-lifetime activity. You will need to care for, exercise, and enhance all of the subjects that we covered, because the better you get, the stronger you become.

Journal Entry #14: RADICAL Persistence. If you had to work on all five areas of balance at the same time, a little bit at a time, what would you do today? How would it impact your BGB? How would you use your RADICAL self to achieve it?

Fitness	What step or action can I take today that will help me stay balanced and focused?
Spiritual	
Perceptual	
Emotional	
Mental	
Physical	

I Will Eliminate All Obstacles

Excuses Removed

Some who read the following section will be angry. Good! They don't want to hear what we are about to tell them for the simple reason that it hits way too close to home. Can you imagine that? Us saying something unpopular (but true)? Like we'd ever do such a thing.

Come on. Really, could it be that bad?

Yes!

We are talking about barriers, defenses, and excuses – all which stand in our way and prevent us from taking action. We know that you are inundated with excuses day in and day out, and that it seems like appropriate behavior, and worse, even acceptable. We know that society has made it a norm, a global expectation, that you better have a reason for not doing something you promised...and it better be good. We know that even parents whom we admire and appreciate train their kids to develop excuses by asking the simple question (which they know their kids don't have a good answer for): "Why did you do that?"

We know that you may have said one of these in the past:

"The dog ate my homework."
"I didn't get enough sleep."
"I got too much sleep."
"It wasn't me."
"I didn't know."
"I didn't want to know."
"I had a headache."
"I'm sick and tired."
"I didn't want to."
"I wasn't in charge."
"It wasn't my intent."
"I was scared."
"I was bored."
"He hit me first!"
"I was doing something else."
...and our favorite, "The game was on."

Why would you ever use any of these excuses[1] to protect yourself? Why put up barriers between what you wanted to accomplish, items that you promised to get done, or commitments that you made and completing them? What is really standing in your way? It's your mission – should anything stand in your way?

These defenses are nothing more than excuses to make you not feel any guilt for whatever you promised to do. This way no one will hold your unfulfilled commitment against you. Well, that's a load isn't it? Because an excuse doesn't erase our commitment to ourselves.

Why do you need excuses anyway? Shouldn't your promise and commitment to yourself be strong enough to pull you over all of the bumps, barriers, and obstacles that can be put up along the way? Sure, it's the easy way out. But for you, it has to be different. When dealing with your own missions, you need to maintain your responsibility to keep working toward your promised land that you detailed out. You can't afford to be sidetracked or delayed; you need to keep getting through what you and life throws at you, and achieve what you want and need. Rah, rah, rah...

---

1 And just because it is not on the list doesn't mean it shouldn't be.

EXCUSES ARE MISDIRECTION, DEFLECTION, AND DECEPTION. THEY DO NOTHING FOR THE LISTENER, JUST THE SPEAKER. THEY ARE ATTEMPTS TO MAKE OURSELVES FEEL NOT GUILTY.

There is no doubt that we could have a never-ending supply of reasons why we want a good defense (whether it's real or an excuse). We get it; in our minds, excuses are nothing more than protection clauses that we invoke to keep us out of trouble or to minimize the trouble or disappointment from others. The truth is that they are words that make us feel better about ourselves but accomplish nothing. For those that have read RADICAL Persistence already (and if not, go and read it) you will see that excuses tend to be the opposite of all the ideas we discussed in the section.

We have provided the following questions to prompt some thoughts on when and how you involuntarily invoke excuses. Look at each question closely and jot down some notes on the last time they helped you use an excuse of any kind:

- ❑ Are you protecting yourself from inadequacies, vulnerabilities, or foolishness?
- ❑ Are you using excuses for self-preservation?
- ❑ Are you feeling uncomfortable or looking for a way out?
- ❑ Are you using misdirection, deflection, and deception to avoid doing something?
- ❑ Are you out of time for completing a task?
- ❑ Are you attempting to rationalize something to be true?
- ❑ Do you seek sympathy, avoid blame, or evade guilt?
- ❑ Are you perhaps avoiding the embarrassment of doing it wrong?
- ❑ Do you think you're too special (and above that kind of task) to complete the job?
- ❑ Do you lack initiative and don't want anyone to find out?
- ❑ Do you need an alibi for doing something wrong?

Interesting list, huh? Did you see things that invoked an emotional response? Are you angry at us for bringing up this sensitive topic or maybe mad that we are saying out loud what you have always known as the truth? Did you discover that you hide behind your excuses? (We did.) We hope that the list dredged up memories that you wanted to keep suppressed. The truth is that your deviations from success are preventing good things from happening for you.

But it doesn't have to be.

It's time to start identifying and removing the excuses that you use. It's time to start replying with a "yes" or "no," regardless of what society expects. It's time to live up to your expectations. Notice we said *live*. For example: "No, I didn't do it." "Yes, I watched the game instead." Tell the truth and take the punishment from which you are attempting to protect yourself. By the way, it really screws with other people's heads when you don't offer the excuse they are expecting and are conditioned to hear. This is also the defining difference between an excuse and a reason: A reason is provided and the consequence will be accepted. (It's possible that the consequence isn't fair or reasonable.) An excuse is provided to avoid the consequence.

Perhaps some founding fathers, authors, coaches, generals, and other well-spoken folks might convince you of what we're saying and why it's so important to get rid of the excuses:

> "He that is good for making excuses is seldom good for anything else." ~ *Benjamin Franklin*

> "Rationalization is a process of not perceiving reality, but of attempting to make reality fit one's emotions." ~ *Ayn Rand*

> "Never make excuses. Your friends don't need them and your foes won't believe them." ~ *John Wooden*

> "Do not make excuses, whether it's your fault or not." ~ *George Patton*

"To rush into explanations is always a sign of weakness."
~ *Agatha Christie*

"Excuses are merely nails used to build a house of failure."
~ *Habeeb Akande*

"Excuses are used to justify leaving the scene of truth without changing." ~ *Orrin Woodward*

We hope that you are convinced of the need to go deep inside both natural and manufactured defenses that mask the fears, laziness, lack of belief, procrastination, ability challenging, deflection, negativity shielding, and victim mentality issues that you hold closely.

Natural Defenses

What would this section of the book be without a little more knowledge gained about the brain? We promised in part one that we would cover this particular area in more detail and we keep our promises. A quick recap:

> The limbic or mammalian brain controls behavioral memories from positive and negative experiences, emotion, flight, fight, or freeze reflexes, and value judgments. There are three major areas of limbic brain: the hippocampus, hypothalamus, and amygdala.

Here comes the anxiously awaited material. We want a clear understanding (for those of us who aren't brainiacs) of why our natural defenses, i.e. fight, flight, or freeze, get triggered:

❑ The hippocampus (we actually have two) deals with consolidation of information from the short-term memory to long-term memory and spatial navigation. (If you ask our wives, they'll say we only have one; this part of the brain is required for asking directions.)

❑ The hypothalamus connects the nervous system to the drugstore (better known as the endocrine system) via the pituitary gland. Why is this important? Who doesn't want to know how to get to Walgreens? Actually, this is important to our conversation because of the interaction of the amygdala. The drugstore is what allows the all-powerful meds to get released into the bloodstream – endorphins, etc.

❑ When you see the bear in the woods (so to speak), the amygdala attempts to determine possible threats based on the information in short- and long-term memory. It uses everything it has at its disposal (past experience, sensory cortex) to help you make the quickest decision on whether to fight or flee. If no decision can be made, freeze is the answer. Now what we have found (which you will also find in all of the brain books – if you choose to read them) is that this flight, fight, or freeze response hijacks you from making the progress you need to make because it attempts to keep you safe and sound, even when what you want to do *is* safe and sound, really different, or really big.

❑ When flight and fight gets involved the body tenses, we become more alert, our blood pressure rises, pupils dilate, and those little bumps appear (which do not belong to a goose); it's like we pulled the trigger of a gun and our body is the bullet leaving the barrel. It's important to note that the limbic brain is not all about negative items, it's about the positive as well. Author Daniel Goldman[2] says that when a joke strikes someone as uproarious, his or her laughter is almost explosive and that, too, is a limbic response.[3]

❑ For freeze, it's a tad bit different. The mind and body have determined that there is nothing to do but stand still (think of playing possum) as the only defense. Of course, it could be that the drugstore in the mind has overdosed you with chemicals and confused the body, so it doesn't think or act. Or that standing still really is the only option.

---

2 Emotional Intelligence: Why It Can Matter More Than IQ (1996) ISBN: 978-0-553-38371-3

3 We like the idea of intense joy – Jeff, get your mind out of the gutter.

❑ When the fight, flight, or freeze response has occurred, that drugstore high has been started. It doesn't last for a minute or two; it actually lasts for eighteen minutes. During this time you basically are in *response mode*. Your job is to survive whatever you have processed as a threat. From what we have read and experienced we are no longer highly logical, emotionally strong people. We are actually not able to think clearly for these eighteen minutes. Better yet, it takes three to four hours for the hormones to totally pass through our system and until they subside, we will still be rather defensive, sensitive and prone to emotional reactions. So when you pull the trigger you create quite a long-term explosion!

The response to the response

Whew! We're glad that is out of the way. As you now know, the limbic system, especially our fight, flight, or freeze response, becomes a natural defense mechanism to keep us or get us out of perceived trouble. It makes sense that the natural design of the body takes over when nothing else wants to work. Now, for some, the pressure that it takes to pull the trigger is relatively small, while for others the pressure is relatively large; only you know which one you are.

It's probably a given that most don't actually even realize their natural defenses have taken over when after seeing a spider they run screaming down the hall waving their hands in the air like a lunatic. There are a certain number of people who don't employ good awareness mechanisms, so the start of those awesome creepy crawly moments isn't even noticed. It's nothing more than another thing that upsets them. They don't know why they left, why it happened, what occurred, and most definitely, how they can stop it (somewhat) from happening. They don't understand their triggers. Triggers are also the same items that send us down rat holes, such as getting mad, withdrawing, sudden quietness, and any other response that takes your mind away from solving the issue. It might occur when you start to go against the filters in your BGB. Remember, each of those filters keeps you safe and now you're attempting to accept new risks. Any of the triggers could get in your way because they send you down this road in an attempt to protect you from the unknown.

The question that should be on your mind is: "How can I change the sensitivity of the trigger?" Well, the answer is simple: Add more experiences (actions and decisions). Most importantly, make the additions small experiences that push you, but don't shove you. These experiences should allow you to grow your comfort zone without stretching it to the point of breaking. It should also not send you out of balance. The best anti-sensitivity trigger medication is a series of small, reasonably controlled actions which help increase the amount of pressure that it takes before the fight, flight, or freeze response occurs. It sounds so easy, doesn't it? (The truth is that if it were easy, everyone would do it.) There is no doubt that de-sensitizing the triggers that take you out of your zone requires practice.

> The good news is that the *REACH* philosophy spends a lot of time in both "A" and "C" sections to help you create, plan, and execute your missions, and avoid these triggers.

There are some definite benefits to the fight, flight, or freeze response. There are times when it's absolutely the right road to take. Let's refresh our self-awareness conversation. Those messengers of intuition that author Gavin de Becker introduced us to ("awareness buoys"), especially the nagging feelings, persistent thoughts, anxiety, curiosity, hunches, gut feelings, doubt, hesitation, suspicion, apprehension, and fear, are precursors that your subconscious has already processed. It has warned you that something isn't kosher in the environment.

The best defense is to listen carefully and act accordingly. If you choose to flee, don't think twice – get to a safe place. If you chose to fight, your odds go way up because you are aware of what is going on before it happens. And if the response is to freeze, let's hope it's the perfect circumstance and that not moving is the best answer.

The excuse

Let's be really clear: not finding and understanding what causes these natural defenses to rise in you is an excuse waiting to happen. Because if your behavior is not appropriate for the environment and you flee, that is an excuse not to do what you said you were going to do. Not listening to the symptoms of your own body (i.e. sickness) is an excuse when you miss your committed activities. And not knowing what you need to do because you are overwhelmed is also an excuse. Believe us, we have been there; something or someone caught the attention of our subconscious. We chose to ignore it, and voila, we began to make our excuses when things went wrong because we didn't want the consequences associated to our decision of not being aware.

Journal Entry #15: Your Natural Defenses.

Do you remember a time when your natural defenses of fight, flight, or freeze took over? Please describe it.

Do you remember what your mind was telling you prior to it happening? Remember the nagging feelings, persistent thoughts, anxiety, curiosity, hunches, gut feelings, doubt, hesitation, suspicion, apprehension, and fear.

What excuse (if any) did it create?

Did the excuse get you off the hook? Would you use it again?

If you had used "yes" or "no" instead of making the excuse, what would have been the outcome?

Manufactured Defenses

If natural defenses are the excuse generators of the body, manufactured defenses are the excuse generators of the mind.

Excuses are the devil's brew. It's a little dramatic but accurate. From our informal studies we learned that people will actually work harder *creating the excuse* than on *doing the work itself.* Seems ironic to us.

Why do they spend time even thinking up excuses? Answer: It makes them feel better. It's a socially acceptable and reinforced learned behavior. The simple truth is that it's a bad habit. They have gotten used to receiving sympathy and empathy from the crowd and know that if they do it again then they will get (and expect) the same results. They are deflection/sympathy junkies.[4] Why do these excuses work? Because they can both excuse their behavior and get someone to care.

What are they really protecting themselves from? They are protecting themselves from their own *failure.* If they weren't worried about failure then they sure wouldn't need to make up an excuse. Makes sense, right?

We lumped a great number of things into the word "failure" – so let's break it down a little (in no particular order):

- ❑ You're scared of your fears coming true. It could be the unknown, not knowing the next step to take, the possible truth, or operating outside of your comfort zone. Each one plays with your head to the point that it scares you and you want to escape from your challenge. Remember: Fears aren't facts; they are our projected assumptions. You are aware of the worst scenario happening (even though it hasn't) and you need to protect yourself from your future self's results because of what others might negatively say about you. Our recommendation: Get over it! There are a lot of activities out

---

4 As we talked about earlier, 26% of Americans consider themselves chronic procrastinators.

in the real world that we must get done without worry or remorse.

☐ You're lazy or a procrastinator. (Is there really a difference?) You know you made a choice, but you didn't have a plan to get it done right away and it will still be there in the morning. Quite frankly, you don't want to tell anyone that you don't have the persistence and self-discipline to do what you said. Like so many of us, you are really good at making up the necessary deflections to make sure that you aren't guilty. You would rather do something else than do what you say, so you decided that lying or trying (which is an excuse) is easier than doing – or in our vernacular, *lying and trying is dying*.

☐ You don't believe in what you're doing. You really aren't behind your own mission. You talk a good game, but you lack belief (remember our conversation in RADICIAL persistence about believe and practice). This is actually a really dangerous area because there are a lot of events out there that you sign up to do and then decide that you don't believe in yourself or them (think team, charity, partnerships, work, recreation).

☐ You are ability challenged. You have come to the conclusion (somewhat fact based) that you either have too little skill to achieve the components of the mission, or too much because you're a perfectionist. You have risen to your level of incompetence. We have met and watched both types of folks, and when the going gets tough out come their excuses on why it isn't going to happen.

☐ You are a victim. (We obviously hope you are not, but many people do fall into this category, unfortunately.) This is one area where excuses are rampant; something is always happening, and it's always against you. People, work, home, and time are always doing something *to* you. According to the victim, it's never them doing something to invoke or cause these results. It is denial at its best! You feel helpless, full of self-pity, refuse responsibility, or focus only on the problems and not the solutions.

When Joel's oldest daughter was in her teens, she loved to tell him why she didn't clean her room, do her projects, or work on her chores. She was quite the debater; she could put together a sentence from which even Houdini couldn't escape. Misdirection, deflection, and deception were everywhere. Now, it wasn't that she was lying, per se; she just didn't want to say "no." Finally, after battling, Joel finally said it: "Do those excuses work for you?" His daughter replied: "Yes, it's what happened." He retorted: "Well I'm glad it works for you, because it does nothing for me...and at the end, you still haven't done what I asked and you promised."

EXCUSES ARE LIES IN DISGUISE

Manufactured excuses are really lies in disguise; they make the speaker feel good, but do nothing for the listener. They are standing in the way of you taking full ownership of what you do. Actually, they prevent you from finding a solution and making timely progress.

We believe that excuses really only do one thing, and that is *to judge yourself not guilty*. At the end of any excuse, the undone task remains. As usual we have come up with an acronym that will help you remember those lies in disguise: **JUDGE!**

J	Justification	A reason, circumstance, or explanation to not follow through
U	Ugliness	Qualities that do not give pleasure to the senses
D	Defensiveness	To protect you from failure
G	Gratification	Not providing a source of instant satisfaction or delight
E	Entitlement	Misconceived notion of deserving certain privileges

Justification

> Justification [juhs-*tuh*-fi-**kay**-sh*uhn*][5] *n*: something such as a fact or circumstance that shows an action to be reasonable or necessary; a statement in explanation of some action or belief; the act of defending or explaining or making excuses for by reasoning.

What a fantastic introduction – thank you, free online dictionary/ thesaurus. There is no doubt that making up an excuse often takes up as much time as actually getting the job done, because we are attempting to protect ourselves from the world with the minimal amount of time we have. Some of the synonyms of "justification" really drive home the point: "vindication," "exoneration," "consideration," and "explanation." These are each pretty harsh words to protect yourself and your style of work (or lack thereof). The definition doesn't say anything about getting work accomplished, or that there is a good or bad reason why something did or didn't occur.

Obviously, there might be an excellent reason to tell someone why you have justified your behavior. It might be accurate and forthright, but even if it's true, it might not be good to do. It might be the easy way out, and/or a way to make your actions look good. Only you will know if it's appropriate for the situation.

As you can imagine, there are a significant number of excuses that one can conjure up to protect them from the outside world. Each response seems to fall into a couple of significant categories:

Time	Not enough time to do the work
Energy	At my low or max - i.e., I already give 110%
Limits	Any of these words: Can't, Won't, Didn't, Don't, Shouldn't, Couldn't, Wouldn't, Wasn't, and Haven't
Verdict	A decision was made that you or someone else deserved it

---

5 http://www.thefreedictionary.com/justification (accessed on February 15, 2013)

Time

Time is the biggest excuse we have. Can you imagine something so powerful that it will let the vision of your life take the spiral ride down the drain? It's a concept that will force you to pin up your dreams on the proverbial bulletin board called *never gonna happen*. Honestly, we believe that the time excuse is responsible for the majority of good ideas never getting done.

We claim time as the excuse for not achieving our next step (big or small), but in most cases it's not true. Why, you ask? Good question. Because we human beings are major time wasters, that's why. There is no other species that is supposedly smarter than every other animal on earth that wastes time like us. We take our time getting ready, getting breakfast, and getting out the door. We don't multi-task well, we don't optimize our day, we major in the minor stuff way too long, and when it comes to major stuff, we don't put off until tomorrow what we can do the day after. We literally waste the most precious, non-replaceable thing we have with too much TV, social media, and partying. When it comes to what we say we really want to do for the rest of our lives, we have the gall to say we don't have enough time. Ugh! Time poorly spent is the worst investment you can make!

Do you believe that you don't have enough time to actually accomplish even a small tiny little itsy bitsy minute step toward whatever you need to do? Do you think that time actually stands in your way? Hogwash! If exercise is what you want to accomplish, there's nothing that stands in your way from doing one push-up, one sit-up, or one squat. How about writing a novel? You could start by writing one line every day. Learning a new language? Learn one word a week. How about learning the harmonica, one note at a time? See, we leverage time as our justification because we think most people will understand and not question it. We are not most people! You have time. How will you spend it?

TIME IS MONEY

~ BEN FRANKLIN

We are not going to make you live through the last time you used time as your get-out-of-jail-free card (which only exists in a game). We are going to prove it by asking you to audit your current week. (If this week is not typical, pick one that is.) Make sure that you know, for your own sake, where your precious and non-renewable resource is going. For those who have never calculated it there are seven days in a week, which is 10,080 minutes. We think of it as 10,080 dollars given to you each and every week to spend as you see fit, and you are never allowed to bank it. If that dollar goes unspent, you lose it. Some people will spend it well and some not so well. What about you?

Attempt to find all 10,080 minutes in your week (be honest!). Here are some broad categories: Sleep, Food, Bathe/Dress, Relax, Improve, Work, Play, School.

We suspect that you found at least fifteen dollars...um...minutes of unused time in the last week that you could have devoted to your dreams, and you know that is an ultra conservative number! Maybe by looking at the time inventory you will see potential areas of reduction (think social media), or maybe you can outsource (really, we are serious) to someone else so you get that much needed hour to work out. We have found that most people will fill about eighty percent of their week; the rest has magically and mysteriously gotten caught up in never-never land. Which means that most people leave more than thirty hours a week on the table! They aren't quite sure where the time went, except now they know it's lost. Gone!

Obviously, when you know where your time goes, you gain control over it. You control what you spend it on and why. (We suggest spending it on your dreams coming true.) We recommend doing this exercise at least once a month to remind yourself on where your time goes. It is important that you convert this excuse from *no time* to *show time.*

Journal Entry #16: Where Did Your Time Go?

		# minutes spent	Notes
Sleep	Hitting snooze		
	Naps		
	Nighttime		
Food	Shop		
	Breakfast		prepare, eat, cleanup
	Lunch		
	Dinner		
Bathe/ Dress	Before work		showers, dressing, make-up, hair, teeth
	After work		
Relax	Family		conversations, TV
	Solo		book reading, bath
	Friends		parties, get-togethers
	Social media		emails, Facebook, Google
Improve	School		homework, class, travel
	Exercise		
Work	Meetings		
	Actual work		
	Hallway conversations		
	Phone calls		
	Transportation		
Other			
TOTAL			Total # of minutes out of 10,080

Energy

All of the energy-sapping excuses that we are about to cover might be true. It's possible that we have wasted too much energy or we don't have enough energy to get whatever we were supposed to get accomplished. Maybe we have figured out how to remove the law of physics and give more than one hundred percent to our endeavors. There are definitely times when we are tired, overworked, unbalanced, and are giving everything we've got in life to whatever cause we are choosing. And we know that when we hit these moments even thinking and planning is not in the schedule. For some, what was written is a biography of themselves and they have been at the point where they couldn't do anything more. For the rest of us, we think you have all heard the same things that we have: "I am already giving one hundred and ten percent," "I can't do anymore," "I'm at my max," "I'm too tired," or "I don't have enough brainpower left to give."

In the work environment, it's old hat and there's nothing easier than to tell your boss that you are at your max. You don't have to offer solutions (unless you're asked), you don't give facts or data, and you look pissed off or surprised that he or she could add one more straw onto the camel's back. The boss could tell by your body language alone that you were going to show what it is like to hear the camel's back break. When the boss buys it, you don't have to stay late or come in early. You leave out the fact that you have a little extra time, but you don't want to do that tedious other work.

In school, you show your parents how unreasonable the teacher is being by giving you enough homework to last a lifetime – except you must complete it in a day, and you have five teachers all doing the same thing. How can they press you like that? You conveniently leave out that you've had the syllabus for a month.

When it comes to your mission, it's easy when you get home to say that you don't have the energy to work on that project, write the next line, or review some of the homes for sale, even though these are the things that you have said will make your dreams come true.

You work harder than most at work (another excuse), you need this quality time to wind down, and it will all be there tomorrow. (Maybe it will and then again maybe it won't.) Are you prepared for the consequences?

The problem we have is that you lied to yourself. You accepted the opportunity to make excuses to make yourself feel better about your decision. Instead, you really have to exercise your capability to "just say no" (as the old anti-drug campaign recommended) and deal with the outcomes. Of course, if it's associated with your dream life, we would rather that you figure out how to do it anyway.

Limits

This little doozy of an area contains the vile and sludge by-products of the filters that you use to keep yourself safe and secure within your comfort zone. They are the world famous and mostly annoying "n'ts" (can't, won't, don't, shouldn't, etc.). They tend to fall into two specific categories of excuses: terminating and obstructing.

Terminating

A terminating excuse is a phrase that has the effect of stopping the listener (be it ourselves or another person) from asking more questions. They normally contain the words "can't," "won't," "wouldn't," and "don't." By using these words we attempt to set limits to our abilities and that nothing can get us over the hump to accomplish whatever it is we've said we'd do.

On the flip side, there are plenty of excellent arguments on when it's appropriate to use these words to support yourself and most likely support the absolutes that are inside your BGB: I *don't* do drugs, I *won't* have sex until after marriage, I *wouldn't* rob a bank, I *can't* violate my ethics so I *won't* steal.

When used as an excuse these simple words can have a disastrous effect because they make our brains stop thinking about the alternatives. Terminating excuses include:

I can't do it	Nothing more needs to be said; you have given your mind the permission to stop thinking about the issue. You've given up. Quitter!
I won't be coming in today because...	The reason is the creative part; the "won't" is the hope that they ask no more questions. The truth is there's a hidden excuse.
I wouldn't know how	This can easily be a positive if you add, "But can you help me?" If not, it becomes the stopping point; no sense in going on. Non-starter!
I don't have the skills	Definitive and very useful to others. You don't need to excuse yourself from doing or not doing anything – if you don't want to do it, then don't.

Obstructing

An obstructive excuse is a phrase that allows you to throw a wrench into the gears of progress. We tend to see these as attempts to buy some time or deflections (remember the magician's trick). Folks who use these words tend not to want to stop their progress in total; they want to set the stage because it might be really slow progress to get to their final goal. Obstructing excuses tend to include the words "shouldn't," "didn't," "haven't," "couldn't," "isn't," and "wasn't." (Granted, there are positive phrases that can be derived with these words.)

I shouldn't go out tonight	A battle with your absolutes is about to ensue. *Shouldn't* is providing, as the poker players say, an out, and you know you're not supposed to take it.
I didn't want to go to the mall, but my friends made me	Misdirection and non-responsibility. You did go to the mall, and unless there was a weapon at your head you did it of your own free will.
I didn't break the vase	In this case this is represented as a positive terminating statement. Based on tone it will probably be taken as an obstructing excuse (and most likely – if you are like the authors – you broke or helped break the vase).

I haven't decided yet	A vague attempt to use patience as your obstacle. Add facts on what you are waiting for (even if you are talking to yourself) and maybe it will work. No facts and it is a poor excuse.
I couldn't do that	The attempt to time travel and only see that it couldn't work, and the results aren't to your liking.
My family isn't supportive	Do you or do you not want this for yourself? Are you or are you not willing to meet your family responsibilities? (It better be "yes" to both.) Did they say they weren't supportive or do you feel they aren't supportive? Are they guessing at what you are doing or did you tell them?
I wasn't in charge	The person who was following orders that they knew to be wrong is still guilty.

Verdict

This is one of the hardest areas for us, because this category of excuses is used to convince yourself that whatever it was, was totally out of your control:

- ❑ Either someone played judge, jury, and executioner to you, or
- ❑ You were judge, jury, and executioner to someone else

Unless it's a court of law and the facts and data are presented in as close to a fair setting as possible, neither you nor they get to play any of the parts. This is the excuse that spousal abusers use (and bar brawlers too). No one has the right to judge the way someone looks or acts, nor does that person have the right to beat the snot out of someone else because of it. This is where politicians get to say that another country's government is wrong and then go start a war. This is where people picket each other at funerals. Well, forgive us, but that is bulls**t! We don't get to use this as an excuse to do harm, and someone else doesn't get to use it to do harm to us.

We know that this is a sensitive subject and some that are reading it will now lay their verdicts down upon us. Some folks will stop reading because we have offended their belief structure or that we are suggesting that they stop hitting their spouses – well, we are going to have to say good riddance – because "no" is an appropriate answer to anyone attempting to do physical, emotional, mental, or spiritual harm to us or you.

> **Justification Antidotes** - If you identified any excuses that you use on a regular basis, we suggest that you take a look at the following sections in the book:
>
> Time - Awareness, Determination, (R), Prioritization (A), Action (C), Habits (H); Energy - Control, Balance (R); Limits - BGB (R), Statements versus Questions (R), Natural Defenses, Phrase Erasers (E); Verdict - Control, Image, Affirmation (R)

Ugliness

A strange name for a not-so-strange set of excuses. Or a most appropriate name, since excuses are usually ugly. This category allows us to convert our five senses into excuse generators. Yes, it starts with where we look, what we hear, touch, taste, and smell, but it's not about the initial action or sensory input. It's all about how we interpret and react to them, and that is where the excuse gets created.

The problem is that when the body reacts you are leaving it up to muscle memory, filters, and natural defenses to lead the way. It makes you say the wrong things, make the wrong gestures, and scrunch up your face at an inappropriate time because you allowed your body to go into automatic mode. Worse, you might make off-the-cuff decisions without taking the appropriate time to determine if they're in your best interest. Anytime we use our senses as our defense for making us not guilty of our actions, it's an excuse. As we will keep on telling you, it doesn't mean that you or the excuse is bad. It means that it's too easy to go into automatic mode and there is nothing, we repeat nothing, that is worth going on automatic for except breathing and pumping the blood through the body. (OK, to our self-defense friends, also protecting yourself and family from an assailant.) Let's look at each of the senses.

Hearing

"I wasn't listening," "I couldn't hear you," "I thought you said..." and "I thought you heard when..." are some of the excuses that the hearing sense can generate. These are small, probably well-meaning statements, each one easily becoming deflections of why you didn't do something. Each one saps your power away from spending time on what you need to do. Another set: "He sounds funny," and "She talks too fast" could become very personal and gives your mind a toehold to create excuses.

Smell

"It didn't smell good, so it made me wave my hands and that knocked that bowl of hot soup on you. It's really the soup's fault for not smelling good." (Stop laughing.) Are you saying that never happens? It does! The world labels them as accidents and sometimes lawsuits (think *frivolous)*. Of course, kids will blurt out exactly what is on their minds; they tell us that the most common smelly excuses are "It stinks," "I don't want to go because they smell," and "I don't want to eat it because it smells" (normally while holding their nose). Why does this matter? Imagine that what you want to do might involve different types of chemicals that give off a pungent odor. Or perhaps you are attempting to create a new recipe for starving countries by using only native ingredients. Problem? Yes. Excuses waiting to happen? Yes.

Touch

You know the stuff that will set you off and create the excuse, "I'm not touching that!" Slimy, icky, and sticky all come to mind. Come on, there isn't anything even close to your fingers though you can mentally feel it; you almost don't want to touch the next page of the book (we promise it won't be sticky or icky). You are probably thinking up a good excuse not to have to touch it. Yuck to the touch of paper. What are we, savages? If it's not digital, it's gross.

The reason is that where every other sense has a limited set of receptors, touch stems from your entire body's input. The receptors' nerves are constantly helping us process pressure, temperature, and pain, and our brains attempt to process it for our benefit. Some would actually classify this as a natural defense. We believe that you have a choice on how to act or react. You know what you are doing (at least we think you do) and we believe that you have created the likes and dislikes that your brain has collected to help determine if that is a good touch or a bad touch.

For a "bad" example: It's a hot summer day, 110° in the shade and you feel the sweat under your arms. It also makes your hair stick to your head and it dribbles onto your forehead. Your toes are sticking together. (This is any day in Phoenix.) The worst part? You still have two hours before you are done working. Honestly, does that make you want to complete your goal or maybe put it off for another day because tomorrow may be cooler? We suspect that procrastination is the answer. Again, to protect us from the swath of emails and calls, the excuse might be true and valid, and you might have done the absolutely right thing by stopping, but it's still an excuse.

Taste

Sweet, salty, sour, and bitter. Sounds like an old guy attempting to impress his caregiver at the old folks home or a candy salesman – your choice. These are four of five regions on the tongue that provide you the necessary input to determine what something tastes like. So far, so good. Obviously, after tasting you give it the fairest of shakes as you determine if you like it...yeah, right. You actually use your past perceptions (those darn likes and dislikes) to help you figure out if you like it or not before you even taste it! Remember when mom told you to taste that stuff on the fork, but the stuff looked "icky"? You made a presumption that because it *looked* icky that it would *be* icky, and missed an opportunity to taste something great (or not). Oftentimes you are getting help from some of the other senses like smell, sight, touch, and distant memories ("My mom used to make me eat it as a kid!")

We have some mutual friends who don't like the texture so they won't eat the food, but when we don't tell them what we are serving, they like it. We have others that hate veggies for no other reason than they were raised to hate veggies.

Sight

This one is problematic because it allows other things to creep in, such as, loves, likes, prejudices, and hates. Just the mention of what someone else wears, the way they keep their desk, where the waistline of their pants lie, all make big excuses not to trust, converse, and/or involve another person. Need to sell your new product to a restaurant, but you don't like the outside of the building? It could have been your biggest sale. Now it's not even an attempt; it's an excuse. Too old or young is also a problem; you might turn down the best applicant, but now you have an excuse as to why you haven't found the right person. You see the grip of a concealed weapon and the person is wearing a biker's vest. "They must be a crook," you think and pull your gun before they pull theirs. Not even an excuse, and now it's a crime.

Ugliness Antidote - We suggest that if you identified any excuses that you use on a regular basis take a look at the following sections in this book:

Responsibility, Questions versus Statements, Patience, Awareness, Control (R), Habits (H).

Defensiveness

This section is about the verbal or physical exchange that sends us down the rat hole of reaction. Our category includes: Deflect, Detour, and Delay. Each has the ability to generate a whopper of an excuse all in the name of you not doing what you are supposed to do. We will not waste any time; let's get right into it.

Deflect

Your parent asks, "Did you have fun last night?"
You took it to mean, "We know what you did."
So you react and respond with, "What, are going to watch me every second of the day?!"

That, our friend, is one form of defensiveness; when what another person has said to you feels like an attack. Chances are you're feeling guilty, and your brain has given you the immediate protection of a snotty retort (which, by the way, didn't work, and now your parents know that something else went on). Or you think there is some holier-than-thou perceived expectation of you (remember our BGB conversation about expectations) and you don't know how to handle the disconnect between what you did and what they wanted. Both will result in deflective comments that are normally delivered with such emotional intent or under the poor veil of humor that it makes your comments into excuses. The reasoning: you are hoping that by putting up the excuse they will then drop the conversation and you won't be subject to any consequences.[6] We used the parent example since most can identify with it; however, we have seen the same deflective behaviors with adults at work.

These types of excuses have the greatest opportunity of preventing you from forming relationships and learning because you find it all so threatening. You find the expectations of others so daunting that you want to escape. Now, we are not experts or psychologists, but not being able to learn and pushing people away are probably not good things to do (and goes against the Living model). It could be because of doubt, trepidation, indecision, or anxiety,[7] though if not dealt with will definitely prevent you from getting where you are going. So we will give a little advice: *Listen carefully, don't take it personally, and respond thoughtfully.* Actually, this is excellent advice for all excuses not to be used. For those who have let their defensive posturing run away with their lives, get help from the professionals that can determine what is triggering this response.

Here are some great pointers about how to defuse your defensive behavior from clinical psychologist Edward Dreyfus:[8]

- ❑ Acknowledge that you are feeling defensive.
- ❑ Ask the alleged attacker whether he or she intends to be attacking or accusatory.
- ❑ Inquire as to whether the attacker is upset with you.
- ❑ Ask yourself whether this situation reminds you of other situations where you felt similarly.
- ❑ Is the question a hot button?
- ❑ Are you responding to the content of the statement/question or the tone?
- ❑ Are you feeling unfairly accused or blamed? If so, acknowledge your feelings.
- ❑ Attempt to engage the alleged attacker in a dialogue rather than a fight.

6 Guess what? They probably won't and you probably will.

7 http://www.uncommonhelp.me/articles/stop-being-so-defensive/ (accessed 11/7/2012)

8 www.docdreyfus.com/psychologically-speaking/defending-oneself-or-being-defensive/ (accessed 11/7/2012)

<u>Detour</u>

We want to cover the general words that we use on a day-in, day-out basis that act as built-in detours to achieving our goals. These general words are used to give you a way out of the commitment you made. These words aren't always used as a seed to the big smelly plant called an excuse, but in our experience it seems to start them growing. The words are "but" and "however," two nasty words that have caused their fair share of pain and suffering.

> Again, we are going to stress that excuses aren't always started because of these words; we see a high propensity of sentences that include these words.

Both words negate what a person just said; we call them *phrase erasers*. They are really dangerous when the positive goal setting statement is at the front and the negative statement is at the back, because the second statement is what is going to be remembered and treated as fact. For example:

- ❑ I want to be a guitar player. However, it will take a really long time to learn.
- ❑ I like your hair like that, but I would never have the courage to wear bangs at your age.

We want you to do a quick excuse generator exercise. As we talked about, how you structure sentences for others to hear (including yourself) actually help fester and grow that seed of an excuse into the awesome fertile soil called your mind:

Journal Entry #17: Phrase Eraser Generators

	Answer:	
I want to be:		(Dream)
But before I do anything I need to:		(Some action)
Because:		(My reason for not taking action)
...will stand in my way of making progress and being successful.		

Here are some examples:

- ☐ "I want to be a <u>writer,</u> **but** before I do anything I need to <u>return to school for writing classes</u> because <u>my lack of understanding the English language</u> will stand in my way of making progress and being successful."

- ☐ "I want to be an <u>actor,</u> **but** before I do anything I need to <u>get hair plugs</u> because <u>my looks</u> will stand in the way of making progress and being successful," said Jeff. (Just kidding! He looks really good in the dark, so he says.)

- ☐ "I want to own a <u>restaurant,</u> **but** before I do anything I need to <u>have a lot of money in the bank</u> because <u>I don't want some cheap shack and it </u>will stand in my way of making progress and being successful."

Many great dreams have been detoured by a simple word. Don't let it happen to you!

Delay

You will be happy to know that there is another set of words, ones that help us delay the activities that we are attempting to do. These are excuse landmines that people plant so that when things don't work out, they've got an excuse to fall back on. Most people, we've found, don't even see these as excuses, and in fact there are many who feel these are acceptable. These words are "try," "maybe," "I'll see," and "I know."

Let's start with *try*: *Try* doesn't imply that you will or will not do anything; it's saying that you are probably scared to admit that you can fail and so you won't give it your all. *Try* implies thought, but little or no action. Trying gives you permission to fail. In fact, by using "try" you are setting up a future excuse. "I will *try* my best," has too many outs from the success game. Try isn't enough of a commitment. Instead, eliminate *try* from your vocabulary. You can remove it as a way to acknowledge the acceptance of a task and risk. Replace it with, "I will do that to the best of my ability," and then have the courage to admit temporary defeat or failure. As Master Jedi Yoda, from *Star Wars* said: *"Do or do not. There is no try."*

Maybe and *I'll see* are cut from the same cloth. They both present the easy road; the one that carries you away from what you want to accomplish. Think of the times when you have used either of these when asked: "Can you do this for me?" You replied, "I'll see." Hmm... Is that a yes or a no? Mom asks you: "Can you take out the trash?" You respond, "Maybe." Now mom doesn't know if the trash will go out. Both of these are nothing more than delaying your real answer; we suspect you are hoping either they will forget or that you will.

We need to avoid these non-definitive answers like the plague, because by not answering appropriately you are accepting and then excusing your behavior when you don't do it (i.e. "I said maybe!"), and such behavior wastes your time and that of the person who had to listen to your excuse.

That leaves *I know*. This is a great excuse because if someone points out something that you need to improve upon or change for whatever reason, a response of "I know" puts an end to the discussion. What more can a person tell you if you already know? That's the beauty of this excuse. However, we're here to tell you that you may know, but knowing isn't doing. Sadly, the person who uses *I know* is showing that they are worse off than someone who doesn't know because if they know and still do nothing about it, then that person is showing everyone that they choose to make bad choices. Who wants to work with or be around someone who makes bad choices knowingly? So, if you *know*, then *do* something about it.

> **Defensive Antidote -** We suggest that if you identified any excuses that you use on a regular basis, take a look at the following sections in this book:
>
> Image, Listen, Control (R), Do and Improve (C).

Gratification

Hey, you like it easy, you like it now, and you want it your way! (Sounds like a burger joint commercial.) Wanting something in the shortest time is not a problem, nor is wanting it with the least amount of effort. Wanting it at a particular standard is actually pretty great! Even if you are being aggressive there is actually nothing wrong with any of them. For example:

- ❑ Fast drive-thrus for everything from food to alcohol. (Is that really a good idea?)
- ❑ Quick loading internet sites. (In 2009, shoppers would give a site between two and three seconds to display.[9])
- ❑ Aches and pains – we want a pill to cure it now.
- ❑ Instant red underlines in word documents to show misspellings. (Thank goodness for spell check!)

9 http://www.akamai.com/html/about/press/releases/2009/press_091409.html (accessed 11/17/2012)

Our question becomes: Do you change your plans or stop your actions because you *think* it will be later, slower, or just okay? Is it worth *not* stopping for food because you won't get served fast enough? What about abandoning the search for a replacement part on the web because you think the internet is too slow? You don't take an aspirin because you know the headache won't go away fast enough. You give up writing because you have to find your own errors.... Of course you won't change your plans.

Far-fetched examples? We don't think so. In our research we came across some very interesting work that drove home our point:

- Google found that slowing search results by 4/10ths of a second would reduce the number of searches by eight million a day.[1]

- Forty percent of mobile shoppers will abandon an e-commerce site that doesn't load in three seconds.

- The majority of Americans would not wait in line longer than fifteen minutes; half would not return to an establishment that kept them waiting.

1 http://www.webpronews.com/instant-gratification-in-america-infographic-2012-03

From the time of the first garden to the present, every farmer knows that you can't plant and reap at the same time. There is no place for instant gratification of their end goal; they have to wait. They have to work for it. They have to tend their gardens until they produce the food they need. You have to do the same with your mission and DPPV. You have to nurture, water, and eliminate the pests that get between you and your goal. Because whenever you *stop* what you are going to do because you *predict* that it isn't going to happen now, quickly, or perfectly, (which are all based on your perceptions and expectations and are determined, qualified, and scored by you) you have a gratification weed (excuse) growing in your garden. You have to give the mission seed a chance to grow, mature, and expand so it produces the fruit that you need not just for today, but for a lifetime.

A GRATIFICATION EXCUSE IS PREDICTING <u>NOT</u> GETTING WHAT YOU WANT AS YOUR REASON FOR NOT CONTINUING TOWARD YOUR GOAL.

There is a nasty by-product to a gratification excuse: It can make your goals go from responsibilities to chores. Goals are choices that you have picked because they will move you closer to completing your mission, which in turn helps you complete your vision and then your dreams. They are all yours, not assigned by the evil stepmother, nor a weight around your ankle preventing you from running away; they are something that you want to accomplish because you have determined that you need to.

Margaret Thatcher said it best: "I am extraordinarily patient, provided I get my own way in the end." Our advice: Don't worry about getting it right now; plan and execute so you get it at the end.

> **Gratification Antidote -** We suggest that if you identified any excuses that you use on a regular basis take a look at the following sections in this book:
>
> Patience, Control (R), Time (E), Goal Alignment (A), Doing, Attitude (C), Breaking and Forming (H).

Entitlement

Ah, we've left the best for last, and the one that will anger some of you – we guarantee it! This category deals with the excuses that are created when you believe there is some overriding privilege that you can invoke – be it age, race, creed, religion, sex, tenure, bank account, experience or education – that will exempt you from having to take action or at least equal action in order to get the same results. That's right, can you believe there are people out there who feel they deserve something for nothing? Sad but true. The only entitlement any person truly has is the right to choose. Sure, they can choose to complain about how life's not fair and how they deserve this or that because they _____ (fill in the blank).

Now, before the cheers or jeers start, we believe (and as we told you before) that if you are willing to put in the effort then the same things listed above should not hold you back. Your mission is your mission. And your effort is your effort. If you want your goal badly enough you will do what it takes – legally, ethically, morally – to get it. This category is not about society's barriers that are thrown in your way; it's about when you believe or use those same barriers to stop yourself from succeeding and/or expect others to do for you since you won't do for yourself. Given time and energy you have the ability to break down any barrier.

Because of our belief that the only difference between success and failure is the amount of time dedicated to a solution, we don't believe there are any permanent barriers. There are plenty of examples of someone who has hurdled the barriers, beaten the odds, and shown up their critics regardless of any entitlement issue they could claim. To name a few:

I'm a girl

❑ **Amelia Earhart** - The 16th woman to get issued a pilot's license.[10] Earhart's name became a household word in 1932 when she became the first woman, and second person, to fly solo across the Atlantic. She did it on the fifth anniversary of Charles Lindbergh's feat, flying a Lockheed Vega from Harbor Grace, Newfoundland to Londonderry, Ireland. That year, she received the Distinguished Flying Cross from Congress, the Cross of Knight of the Legion of Honor from the French Government, and the Gold Medal of the National Geographic Society from President Hoover. In January 1935 Earhart became the first person to fly solo across the Pacific Ocean from Honolulu to Oakland, California. And then she soloed from Los Angeles to Mexico City and back to Newark, N.J.[11]

---

10 Long, Elgen M. and Marie K. Amelia Earhart: The Mystery Solved. New York: Simon & Schuster, 1999. ISBN 0-684-86005-8

11 http://www.history.navy.mil/faqs/faq3-1.htm (accessed on march 4, 2013)

- **Col. Jeannie Flynn Leavitt** - Not only is she a decorated fighter pilot, she has broken through gender barriers few thought possible. She was recently named the Air Force's first female wing commander, commanding 5,000 airmen at Seymour Johnson Air Force Base in North Carolina. Twenty years ago, when she had completed part of her training, she was told that if she wanted to be fighter pilot she would be the first to do so and would draw attention. "I said, 'Well, I don't want the attention, but I want to fly fighters more than anything,'" she responded.[12]

I'm not Caucasian

- **George Washington Carver** - Born into slavery in Diamond, Missouri, around 1864. The exact year and date of his birth are unknown. Carver went on to become one of the most prominent scientists and inventors of his time, as well as a teacher at the Tuskegee Institute. Carver devised over a hundred products using the peanut—including dyes, plastics and gasoline.[13]

- **Jackie Robinson** - born in Cairo, Georgia in 1919 to a family of sharecroppers. His mother, Mallie Robinson, single-handedly raised Jackie and her four other children. They were the only black family on their block, and the prejudice they encountered only strengthened their bond. From this humble beginning would grow the first baseball player to break Major League Baseball's color barrier that segregated the sport for more than fifty years. In 1947, Brooklyn Dodgers president Branch Rickey approached Jackie about joining the Brooklyn Dodgers. The major leagues had not had an African-American player since 1889, when baseball became segregated. When Jackie first donned a Brooklyn Dodger uniform, he pioneered the integration of professional athletics in America. By breaking the color barrier in baseball, the nation's preeminent sport, he courageously challenged the deeply rooted custom of racial segregation in both the North and the South.[14]

12 http://abcnews.go.com/blogs/headlines/2012/10/female-fighter-pilot-breaks-gender-barriers/ (accessed on February 10, 2013)

13 http://www.biography.com/people/george-washington-carver-9240299 (accessed on February 10, 2013)

14 http://www.jackierobinson.com/about/bio.html (accessed on February 10, 2013)

Too old

☐ **Fauja Singh** - Started running marathons at age eighty-nine, and is still running today (he's currently 101).

☐ **Col. Harland Sanders** - According to his 1974 autobiography, before Harland Sanders became world famous, he was a sixth-grade dropout, a farmhand, an army mule-tender, a locomotive fireman, a railroad worker, an aspiring lawyer, an insurance salesman, a ferryboat entrepreneur, a tire salesman, an amateur obstetrician, an (unsuccessful) political candidate, a gas station operator, a motel operator and finally, a restaurateur. At the age of sixty-five a new interstate highway snatched the traffic away from his Corbin, KY restaurant, and Sanders was left with nothing but a Social Security check and a secret recipe for fried chicken.[15]

Too young

☐ **Greg Grossman** - Not your typical teenager. He's a culinary prodigy with a career that some seasoned professional chefs might envy. At the age of fifteen, he has already headed up a catering company in the Hamptons, launched a culinary research group, and recently returned from Spain where he attended Madrid Fusion with Gerry Dawes... Oh, and he's still in high school.[16]

☐ **Jack Andraka** - In December 2012, fifteen-year-old Andraka won Intel's prestigious Gordon E. Moore Award along with other top honors at the corporation's annual Science and Engineering Fair, the world's largest high school research and science competition. He created a simple dipstick sensor to test for levels of mesothelin, which is a biomarker for early-stage pancreatic cancer that's found in blood and urine. Andraka's prize-winning invention means patients could be armed with a simple method to detect the disease in its earliest incarnations, before it becomes invasive and when it still has a chance to respond to medical care.[17]

---

15 http://colonelsanders.com/bio.asp (accessed on February 10, 2013)

16 http://www.restaurantgirl.com/qa_with_15yearold_chef_greg_gr.html (accessed on February 10, 2013)

17 http://www.takepart.com/article/2013/01/27/jack-andraka?cmpid=tp-ad-outbrain-general (acc. 2/10/13)

The question becomes, can *you* remove whatever social, cultural, or economic barriers reside in your own mind to make progress? Yes, we know, we aren't being realistic. Those guys and gals above were flukes, and times were different. Nope. Nada.

We don't agree. First and foremost, remember that your dreams don't have to be realistic. They were designed to have no boundaries for a reason – to stretch you way past your comfort zone. Flukes or not, the people above succeeded because of their drive, wants, hopes, and desires. They wanted something and they went out and got it. They didn't use excuses; instead they went out in the world, suffered the bumps, bruises and scars of their endeavors, and made progress. They were living. Nothing, we repeat *nothing*, happened overnight for any of them. It took time, focus, and dedication. For some of them it took many temporary defeats before they found success. And by the way, times aren't different now (actually they might even be better); the amount of help available today is mind-boggling! The web with all of its flaws and misinformation doesn't discriminate who it helps. You can find a lead on almost every topic given you want to put in the effort. There is someone, some organization, or some place to go to get help, but only if you are willing to type on the keyboard and press enter. So there is nothing that any of us are actually entitled to outside of our given rights by the land we live in.

Here are the most popular excuses that come from entitlement:

- ❑ **"I deserve it" or other arrogant behaviors**. No one deserves anything from someone else. (Harsh, isn't it?) You only deserve to have the opportunity, the same as everyone else. There is no need to exaggerate your own importance or abilities.

- ❑ **"I have already put in my time" (age, work, experience).** Your age and previous experiences got you to where you are today, so congrats, but that doesn't mean that it will take you to where you are going. You have the responsibility to make the necessary adjustments to what you have done, or maybe start from the beginning (bottom rung on the ladder) to get what you want.

❑ **"They have deprived me; it's only fair."** "They" are exactly whom? And "fair" is exactly what? And what is your definition of "deprived"? There is nothing fair about this world and no matter how much is attempted it will never match up to what everyone wants. Personally, we believe that no one should expect or consider that others will have the same definition or expectation of fair.

❑ **"I don't want to work for it" or non-effort behaviors.** If this is your excuse, then this is not the book for you because nothing happens when nothing happens. If you are relying on luck to be your ticket home without actually doing anything then you will be disappointed.

❑ **"Me first," self-importance, lack of gratitude or other selfish behaviors.** If your belief is that you come before all others no matter what – including your own responsibilities and obligations – then it's probably going to be a big problem for you as you progress. There are too many people, events, and commitments that will be required for you to achieve your dream.

> **Entitlement Antidote** - We suggest that if you identified any excuses that you use on a regular basis take a look at the following sections in this book: Responsibility, Determination, Image, Control (R), Mission (A), Doing, (C), Breaking and Forming (H)

Excuses Simplified

Well, you've heard them and you are probably tired of them, but all of these excuses stand in your way of success: Time, energy, limits, verdict, senses, detract, detour, delay, pain, pleasure, arrogance, age, work, experience, fair, non-effort, gratitude, or selfish excuses. The good news is we can simplify and narrow this down to three easy words. We discovered that all of the categories that we wrote about seem to be able to be described in one statement:

COMPARSION, COMPLAINT, AND COMPLACENCY ARE THE PRIMARY EXCUSE ENGINES OF LIFE.

Seeing how you match up to another (fictitious or real) will take you down paths that are impossible to win, because as we all know, no two people are exactly alike. Whining and complaining to others or to yourself wastes energy and time, and prevents you from taking the necessary steps toward your goals and dreams. Not doing what should be done when you need to do it is to lose those moments forever.

How do you avoid comparison, complaint, and complacency? Review each of the Antidotes sections; study them, use them, and improve upon them. Break out of the status quo and start being aware of what you say and how you say it. Catch yourself making an excuse and replace it with a simple "yes" or "no" answer and accept the consequences for your actions. Remember, talk isn't cheap – it's free! You can blame anyone you like (person, thing, society, circumstance, history), but at the end it's really *your* fault if you didn't do what *you* said you'd do. It might get others mad because you have broken the social convention of not giving the rest of the story, but it will be worth it because you will start figuring out pretty quickly that when you remove the excuse, you increase the productivity. Actions speak volumes, words say nothing, and excuses are empty words.

Removing excuses is all about conditioning the mind, body, and spirit to accomplish what you want. It's making sure that any perceptions and expectations that are set are the ones you set for yourself. You need not give up any responsibilities to motivate yourself because it all falls on your shoulders. A lack of motivation means one thing: you have chosen to be lazy. (Remember, you make the choice!) Being lazy will not make your dreams come true. Period.

Journal Entry #18: During the last week what excuses have you used?

At home (family, chores, grocery shopping. etc.):

At work (coworkers, assignments, leaders, etc.):

At play (teammates, exercising, hobbies, etc.):

It Is All About The Choices I Make

Accurate Missions

Most people are experts when it comes to talking about the things they're going to do to achieve their goals, dreams, etc. If talking were an Olympic sport, it would be the most popular by far. People will go into great detail about the life they would like to be living. Why is that? We like to say most talkers suffer from a case of verbal diarrhea. However, the real reasons are that talking requires:

- ❑ No commitment
- ❑ No action
- ❑ No planning
- ❑ No starting point
- ❑ No finishing point
- ❑ No reflection
- ❑ No achievement
- ❑ No potential failure
- ❑ No chance of success
- ❑ No pain
- ❑ No getting off the sofa

Imagine if the talkers spent as much time pursuing their goals as they did talking about them. Where would they be and what would they accomplish? Too many people mistake talking for accomplishment, and it isn't the same. Don't get us wrong; talking with a friend about your goals, missions, visions, or dreams is perfectly natural. It's even a good idea. Sharing your ideas with others is a great way to get feedback and input. Even if the feedback isn't what you want to hear, you can still use constructive criticism to help make sure you're on the correct path. Sharing can even be fun when it's used as a motivator.

Then why do some get stuck here at the talking stage? You know the answer. Getting started isn't easy.

Accomplishment requires dedication and sacrifice. That sacrifice can and should include the removal of things that will *not* help make your dream come true. Stop and think about this: who gains from sitting on the sofa not doing or thinking? It's not you. You gain nothing and lose far too much. You can't lose weight or make more money. You can't go here or there by sitting on your butt and you can never get back lost time. People who park their caboose on the sofa after work are the epitome of the dying model.

Dedicate yourself to living the life you want by doing what needs to be done, even if it means that there will not be a lot of time to relax. How about this for a thought: if you are making your goals a reality, would that not fill you with a sense of well-being better than the sofa ever would, and wouldn't that well-being make you relaxed?

First Plan

Think of any World War II movie: the mission was assigned, the details were described, the team picked, and a plan created with the expectation of success (think Plan A). All necessary tools were obtained and then the team did their ultimate best to execute the plan. They even planned for contingencies. Never was it a plan for making them all heroes.

PLANNED OUT, THEN EXECUTED.

They didn't get caught up in not having all of the data (though they always had just enough). They made sure that everyone had the skills and understood the risks. They invoked the military's 6 Ps: *Proper Planning Prevents Piss Poor Performance*. None of the members ever forgot what the real mission was about or how important it was to complete it successfully.

Well, that is our plan for you, but without all of the literal battlefields and life or death situations. The battlefields will be the figurative kind where it's you against your status quo.

For the rest of this section we are going to concentrate specifically on missions and what they should consist of, and how to make sure that they get done. It's about the specifics of the expected results, the people involved, the training necessary, the tools needed, and contingencies required as they relate to living the life you want.

Before anyone gets any ideas that it's too hard to plan their lives because they have tried before and it never worked out – Hogwash! You can. To be a part of the Living model *you will need to live in the now and also plan your future*. You can have all of the fun you like, just make sure that the fun doesn't stand in the way of what you really want out of life. You get to have a balanced life; however, you can't make excuses if you make choices that throw your life out of balance. You know exactly what you have to bring to this party in order to get what you want, and we're going to provide you with the map to get you there.

> When we introduced missions we gave a simplified definition that it was the combination of Goals, Actions, and Results. If you're interested, the dictionary[1] agrees with us (and we're darned excited about it) in two of four of their definitions: *1) an important assignment carried out; 2) an important goal or purpose that is accompanied by strong conviction; calling or vocation.* Actually, the last definition is the best; it has this entire book wrapped up in one little statement – you have purpose, goals, conviction, and calling.
>
> ---
> 1 http://dictionary.reference.com/browse/mission (accessed Jan 5th, 2013)

Definition Replay - We suspect that some of you are starting to have definitions and words bounce around in your minds, especially dreams, vision, missions and goals. So, we are going to attempt to show the differences between each:	
Dreams	Wants, needs, and desires that break the realistic, normal, and stereotypical bounds. They let you think big and without limits. They are represented in your mental and emotional fitnesses. They aren't even specific except to help answer: "What do I want to do when I grow up?" They don't do anything except to allow you to open the door to a new world and ignite your passion and purpose.
Vision	Long-term future of yourself in four distinct areas: Home and Family, Education and Career, Community and Service, and Hobbies and Recreation. This is the opportunity to mentally time travel into your future, determine what you want this end result to look like, and return to the present to plan the next major destination on your journey. Visions aren't always 100% realistic, but they are 100% optimistic. You will have found a comfortable window of execution (i.e. ten, fifteen, twenty years).
Missions	A collection of goals, actions, and results that will keep moving you toward your vision. There will probably be many missions required to accomplish your next vision. Each one, which is three to eighteen months long, is a step along your path and one you must accomplish before you can make it to the next. Missions require your absolute attention, determination and resolve to get accomplished, each one providing the results that you require.
Goals	Short-term expectations of yourself that will have an observable and measurable achievement within a fixed timeframe. This is more than a moment in time; it will be in the near future and will probably be more realistic and pressure oriented than all of the other areas. It should be; any goal you make should be achievable.
The differences between the four stages are: boundaries (realistic, normal, and stereotypical), risk, time, effort, and expected results.	

Missions Are Hard Work

If missions were easy, everyone would achieve their dreams and we would live in a place called Utopia. No one would wait, complain, or become distracted from their destiny. Of course, you are realistic enough to know it won't happen, not because it can't, but because it's hard work. Some folks will use all of their well-manufactured excuses to help protect the outcomes that they didn't work for. For others, their natural defenses will kick in and they will run as fast as they can away from what they wanted. If you can believe it, at the end some folks will actually be surprised that they didn't make it happen. Others will take a big step forward only to fall two steps back, mostly from making the same mistakes over and over again, all the while claiming that they are new and original ones. To us, this is sad, really sad, because it doesn't have to be this way.

You know that if you play in the mud of mission accomplishment, you're going to get dirty – and you want to get dirty! Actually, if you are attempting to stay (figuratively) clean while you are executing your mission, trying to keep your dress prim and proper – you are probably over-planning and not taking enough action (more in the "C" section). You are probably wasting time, energy, brainpower, and all available resources on the wrong things. Stick your hands in the mud, get dirty, and start working on what you want.

It doesn't matter how high, how long, or how much work it will take. You know that you can put forth the effort required and move up the success mountain. If you really, really want it, you can and will make it happen. Of course, to every "up" the mountain there is a potential "down." Don't fall into the trap of paralysis by analysis. This is where you think and plan and talk, but never take action.

Let's take a small journey:

> We are putting you at a base camp in the middle of a climb up a mountain. We'll call it Camp Decide. You have worked hard to get to this camp; not everyone

in your party has done it. Some never left the parking lot after looking at the tall mountain in front of them. All they saw were the supplies that they would have to carry, the distance they would have to hike, the fact that they don't like the cold and they have no intention of getting dirty. They have already given up and nothing will change their minds. They are perfectly fine with staying in the parking lot, even though they know they will be there for a really long time.

Some of the members of your group gave up after a short while. They took the hike to the first camp, but when their summit appeared too far away, the trek too long, and the trail too muddy, they made the easy choice and quit. What is interesting about them is that they chose not to go back to the parking lot; they wanted to stay at Camp Survive for as long as they could get away with it. The Camp has food, drink, warmth, but little success. However, to those in the parking lot, these people at Camp Survive sure look successful. Every so often the inhabitants of this camp will get a flash of energy and head out on the trail only to be turned away by the elements, a lack of supplies, or, more importantly, a lack of planning. They didn't plan for the next phase of their trip and so go back to the warmth of Camp Survive where they can live safely. They can tell their friends that they started their climb up the mountain and follow it with a plethora of excuses, and not take one ounce of responsibility for their situation. They will shrug their shoulders and say, "I tried."

As for you, you were much more than an occupant. You looked at the mountain and saw the challenge, planned the next part of your trip well, and forged your path to this spot, to Camp Decide. You know that you cannot stay here forever; you will either have to move forward or go back. The good news is that for a limited period of time you have the choice to be patient and determine what you want or should do next. You took the time to relax as you planned the rest of your journey. The bad news is that you don't have all day; the path to the next camp is clear for now, but there are storms-a-brewing and not much time to make the trek. Camp Decide has limited food, water, and shelter. What are you going to do? You can either go back to Camp Survive where you can join your friends in a feast of misery, or worse, go to the parking lot where you can look up at your dream of climbing this mountain from the safety of your car and always regret your inaction, but use excuses to justify your failure. If you retreat you wasted the most valuable resource that once used can never be reclaimed, time. Or, you can forge ahead. It's your choice.

You choose to climb. Leaning into the wind, as the elements take their toll, you hunker down and move forward despite the numerous challenges that await you. The wind is harsh and biting (much like the comments from acquaintances who don't appreciate your mission), you are cold, your eyes are burning, your stomach growls with hunger, your throat is parched, and you are so very tired, yet you keep placing one foot in front of the other, in the direction of your choosing, which happens to be the summit. You are on the unmarked, never before hiked Strive Trail! You are learning every step of the way, you are taking action, making no excuses as you figure out how to get over the hurdles of your journey to the top, and you have made a promise to yourself to never, ever give up. You take a moment to catch your breath and realize that you are truly living life and it feels amazing.

One morning, after what feels like and might have been days, weeks, months, or years on this mountain, you see the summit. You look back to where you started and cannot see a thing. You know it's down there, somewhere behind you. Looking forward again, you take the last couple of steps. You are ready to plant your flag at the summit of what once seemed like an impossibility. What began as a crowd of excited, anxious people has turned into a crowd of one.

You have reached the top of this mountain, but instead of going back down to Camp Survive, you see the next mountain in the distance and at that moment decide to climb it as well. Why not? You now know you are capable of anything to which you set your mind. Your friends and family might think it's altitude sickness when you tell them, but you know that if you can reach the summit of Mount Thrive, you can get to the next one with little trouble because now you know how to achieve, succeed, and reap the rewards of each journey! You are living and it feels great!

This Die to Thrive continuum is the path that we are all on. As Curly said in the movie *City Slickers*, "The secret to life is one thing." He was right. Looking back and then forward, you will know that one thing. That one thing is different for each of us. We all have to get out of the parking lot and get to our summit, and then the next and the next and so on.

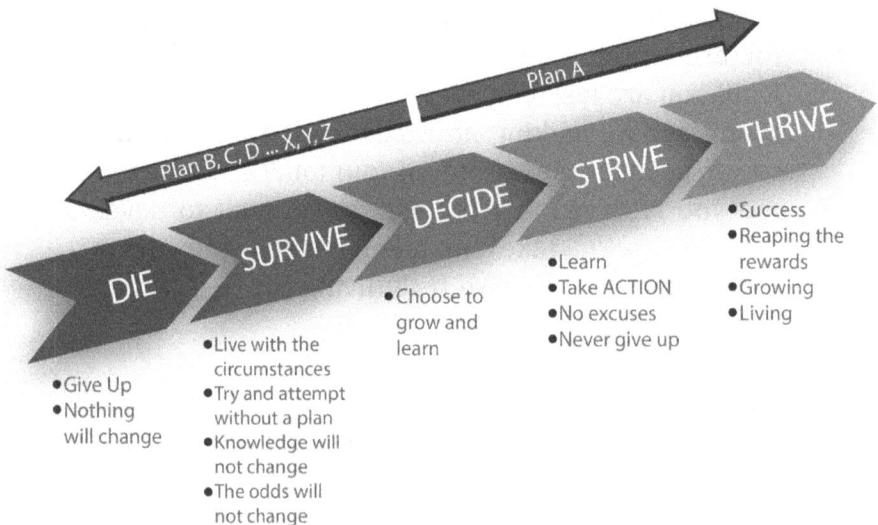

Plan B, C, D ... X, Y, Z

Plan A

DIE

SURVIVE

DECIDE

STRIVE

THRIVE

- Give Up
- Nothing will change

- Live with the circumstances
- Try and attempt without a plan
- Knowledge will not change
- The odds will not change

- Choose to grow and learn

- Learn
- Take ACTION
- No excuses
- Never give up

- Success
- Reaping the rewards
- Growing
- Living

The steps are easy:

- ❑ **Die:** This is the parking lot, and as we discussed at the beginning of the book, dying takes place when you are not growing or learning. You have given up on what you wanted. You have correctly come to the conclusion that nothing will change.[1] Dying is a fact. People are proving it to be true every day.

- ❑ **Survive:** You are prepared to live with the circumstances. You might try and attempt to make a change, but you have no real plan. You're hoping luck will take the place of planning and action. Many people like to say those at the top got lucky because it makes them feel there's hope for them to live that life without investing all of the time and effort required to change dreams and goals into reality. You're not looking to gain in knowledge, and you have done nothing to change the odds that you are faced with, yet you haven't totally given yourself over to the dying model. If you stay at this point for too long you will slip into Die without even knowing it. It's so easy that you won't even be aware that it's happening and you may never know.

- ❑ **Decide:** This is the critical junction point of putting your words into measurable actions. It's hard work (which is why so few choose this path) to go to the next level and real easy to go back down (which is why so many choose it). It's up to you to choose where you want to be. That's one of the great beauties of life...you have a choice. Some might argue that the choice we speak of is the ultimate freedom that people have, and they'd be correct. We hope you are figuring out that "discourage or encourage" leads to effective application if you practice either one. You get the results you accept. It's your choice, always has been, and always will be. What will you decide?

---

1 We said correctly, because if you don't make the change then it won't happen, and thus you have proven the statement true.

❑ **Strive:** This is about understanding where you are going, planning your journey, learning the skills needed, and growing as a person. There is nothing static about your world and in your mind there is no going back. Forward is the only direction you now accept. You do not feel entitled. You earn the life you deserve. Life is now about living...finally! You do not waste time or energy in making up excuses to protect your image or lack of actions. You're a person who makes decisions, lives with the consequences, and strives to live each and every day.

❑ **Thrive:** You have achieved success, you are reaping the rewards, and you are always moving on to your next challenge. You have realized that it's still easy to become complacent and that the slide down to Die (the parking lot) is always available, but it is not an option for you. You have chosen never to take it! Failure is no longer an option and never will be again. Excuses are for cowards who are not willing to accept responsibility for their own lives. Living is for those, like yourself, who have found that obtaining the life you want is the greatest of all freedoms and is truly a gift to be enjoyed.

Climb the Mountain

Folks, this is not some mystical, magical ride that you are going to take. There is no gondola, sky tram, train, or donkey (okay, there might be an ass or two on the trail) that is going to hoist you up without you working for it. The hike up the mountain is going to take planning and action. What will you need to get to the top of a mountain so high that few will take the trip? What needs to be different about you than all of those guys and gals watching from the parking lot? The answer: you will need to have will, skill, and ways.

- **Will**. This includes the right attitude, confidence, determination, and guts all rolled up in one package. It is the focus of intent, desire, and hope aimed toward your mission. Viktor Frankl, in his book *Man's Search for Meaning*,[2] recognized that "[a] man who let himself decline because he could not see any future goal found himself occupied with retrospective thoughts." In the case of the concentration camps of World War II, retrospective thoughts meant that without *will*, the man would soon die. It didn't matter if he or she was in good health or not, without the *will* they found no reason to find the *way*.

- **Skill**. This is the easiest to describe and we will let the dictionary do the talking for us: it is *the ability to use one's knowledge effectively and readily in execution or performance.*[3] The only test is if you can or you can't do something. Do you have the abilities that you need to make the mission come to an appropriate, successful conclusion? If not, what *skill* do you need to find your *way?* Now the question about *skill* is how truthful can you be about yourself, and how hard do you want to work to get the *skill* you need to make this mission successful?

- **Ways**. To make sure that your mission is successful, you need as many paths as possible. This contains your original plan (you know, the one that is perfectly timed and perfectly mentally executed). It also includes knowing that there will be numerous obstacles that can (and will) stand in your way, and regardless of what you are up against you know that you will get through them. *Ways* is about the planning process. Remember what author Shane Lopez talked about: "Anticipate obstacles and create multiple pathways..." (We think Mr. Lopez gives great advice.)

The good news: *will*, *skill*, and *ways* aren't just about the external activities of the mission; they affect our internal activities as

2 Man's Search for Meaning, Viktor Frankl. Beacon Press, 2006, ISBN 978-0-8070-1426-4

3 http://www.merriam-webster.com/dictionary/skill (accessed March 5, 2013)

well. They can provide much needed clarity by helping you filter your filters. Yes, more help in figuring out which absolutes, fears, perceptions and expectation filters you should take along for the ride. Your BGB (that well-protected comfort zone) can use the power of *will*, *skill*, and *ways* to help you break through which thoughts, conversations, plans and actions you need to take. *Will* gives you the courage to make the change, *skill* provides the knowledge to choose what changes to make, and *ways* gets your mind to think of the much needed alternatives so the changes will hold.

Are you ready for that hike to the next level?

> If your comfort zone is getting in your way, closely review your BGB. Compare it to the four destinations. Ask yourself which of these filters will stand in your way of getting what you want and which ones will keep you firmly on your path. Ask what is giving you the *will;* what is providing the *skill*; and in what *ways* do they help. Remember, you're taking a trip for the rest of your life; it's important that you pack light, stay flexible, and travel efficiently.

Unfortunately, we know there are some of you that are currently reading these words and saying to yourselves: "It's too far," "it's too long," "It's too high," or "I don't have what I need." (Of course, we don't think it's you.) So we want to provide a little mentorship if you are still struggling on that massive one-inch step forward toward your future. Here it goes:

YOU ARE IN CONTROL OF YOU.

You are in control of the wiggle room you give yourself. You are in control of the dream, vision, mission, goal, and stretch that you accept. You're in control of the time and breaks you take. When you hike and how high you hike is all up to you. Perhaps the answer is to not stretch as much, to add some boundaries, or not put yourself out on a limb (especially if you don't like heights). Do what you know you can do.

The goal

As we already talked about, within each mission there are interrelated goals. These goals are imperative to your success. They need to provide a clear understanding of the outcomes that you expect, need, and desire. As described, goals are short-term expectations of you that will have observable and measurable achievement within a fixed timeframe. Each goal will be in the near future (think one day to four weeks) and will probably be more realistic, optimistic, and pressure oriented than all of the other areas. Having a clear understanding of the goals in your mission and asking all of the appropriate questions will give you a great start toward accomplishing your vision and ultimately your dream.

Just to complete the picture: Every goal can have one or more actions, which can have one or more results, and definitely have contingencies being planned for. With that out of the way, let's get planning.

GOAL	An observable and measurable result achieved within a fixed timeframe.
ACTION	Something accomplished or performed.
RESULT	The outcome of your endeavor(s).
CONTINGENCY	An alternative plan of action that will allow your results to match your goal.

The biggest question most have, especially if they're not familiar with goal setting is where to start. Our answer is pretty simple: Anywhere. Remember that you're planning, not doing. At this time it's about putting thoughts on paper. You have the opportunity to change, alter, remove or refine anything that you have written. No real risks are being taken.

You might ask, what goals should be included? Any and all is probably the best answer for now. We recommend that a goal be big enough to be able to think about and choices can be made on how to achieve it. It should also be small enough to achieve without triggering any of your natural defenses. You want goals that have meaning, and clear objectives that are obvious as to what they will achieve for your life. Though we recommend a period no greater than four weeks, we will not tell you that all goals will need to be accomplished in one day, one week, or one month. That will be up to you. Only you know what you can achieve, but remember to be honest with yourself when setting goals. Think of each goal as a climber's anchor that is placed in the mountain. Its job is to help you hold your position as you go upward, so be sure to place that anchor correctly because all of your weight will be hanging from that little point.

We have said it before, yet feel it's important to remind you, that you need to stay focused and put ideas onto paper. Goals are no different. Don't let your goals wander aimlessly around your head. This is your plan to complete your mission and you have the right (and we really recommend this step) to make sure that you can see your plan on a daily basis. You don't want to leave it up to memory as to what was or was not included, because memories can be tricky.

Start breaking down your first mission into easy-to-understand goals, statements and ideas. Don't worry about the order or the details. If you find yourself stuck, get together with some friends, mentors, or family and talk it out. They can be a terrific sounding board, even if they don't agree with or like your goals. You need to then ask the following questions to probe your psyche for the detail. It's important to have the right specifics behind each and every goal. Start with your first goal of this mission:

❑ **What is the goal?** Your goal should be concise, condensed and very specific. It should be something that is tangible when completed.

❑ **Why this goal?** Understanding the reason behind the goal will allow you to muster the attitude, energy, time, and resources to accomplish it. It's important to remember that this goal should be attainable and reasonable. It should be big enough to stretch you, but small enough not to invoke your defenses.

❑ **When does the goal need to be done?** Specifically - date and time. This will help keep you on track and focused.

❑ **What is the priority of this goal?** The priority is only about which one you start first and which one gets the resources when resources become a problem (i.e. time, money, energy). Beware of attempting to skirt the rules by making a #1a, #1b, #1c. In the immortal words of Duncan MacCloud from the TV show *Highlander*: "There can be only one..." then a #2, #3.

❑ **How do you know when it's completed?** If you can't or don't know where it starts and how it ends, then you will have a problem completing it. Being specific with the metrics of completion will also allow you to understand if the progress you are making is appropriate.

❑ **What resources does this goal need in order to be completed?** Time, money, energy, technology, process, and people should all be considered and reviewed to determine what resources will be required for this goal to be accomplished. Most are in your control. Needing other people's help normally requires you asking them. We recommend being forthright about the risks, rewards, and resources you require from them.

❑ **How does the goal interact with other goals?** Very few goals stand alone. They normally require something from a previous goal and will be a part of a future goal.

❑ **Is this goal congruent with where my future is going?** It's important that for every goal you make, for every step you take, that you will be watching to make sure that they all line up with your vision of life. Compare each goal to your future self: Home and Family, Education and Career, Community and Service, and Hobbies and Recreation.

We suggest that you now go through the process of doing this for each and every goal. As each goal passes the test, write it on a white index card. These are now your Goal cards.

In alignment or outliers

If done correctly, there should be a stack of white index Goal cards sitting in front of you. Place this stack off to the side. Next, take all of the activities you do in a month and write them on a different colored set of index cards on the same table. (We're using the example of a red set.) We will refer to this set of cards as our activity cards.

Now place your white goal cards on the table and match the red activity cards to each of your goals. It will be safe to say that all of the red activity cards that you laid down are in alignment with your goals – they support and/or accomplish what you want out of each respective goal, because as we all know, actions speak louder than words.

If, when you're done, you're still holding red cards in your hand, then these activities are not supporting any of your goals and are considered *outliers* (we could probably spell them *outliars!*) These activities are wasting your time, don't support your mission or goals, and are costing you in terms of time, money, or energy (usually all three areas at once). If you're holding a red activity card that you really, really like, there's a good chance that you're attempting to justify its existence by placing it on a goal so you don't feel guilty about holding it (this is the out*liar* part). Don't do it!

Next, take a closer look at each activity card you're still holding in your hand and determine if you should still be doing that activity. If not, get rid of it. It's possible, for whatever reason, that some outliers are a choice that you have made and are not willing to change. Sleeping in on Saturdays might not accomplish anything toward your goals or missions, but you have decided to do it anyway. Freedom of choice is a beautiful thing.

String theory (at least our version of it)

It's very important to understand which goals come first, second, and all the way to last to accomplish your mission. Take a moment and take those pesky white goal cards and determine which one you can start with now, which ones have to wait until another one is done, which ones have a timing issue (can't start school for a month), and which one will be the last activity that completes the mission. If you were to take the white goal cards and lay them out on the floor with your mission result at the top, your first goal would be at the bottom. You literally could take a string and connect each goal to the next one up until you reached the final mission at the top. If goals #1 and #2 had to be completed before #5 got started, you would attach a string from #1 and #2 to #5. There are always timing issues as they relate to goals, so do your best to stagger your starts and your ends, so you're not attempting to get everything accomplished on the same day. Also, do your best to structure your goal setting so that you don't waste time going backward; up and forward is best and most efficient.

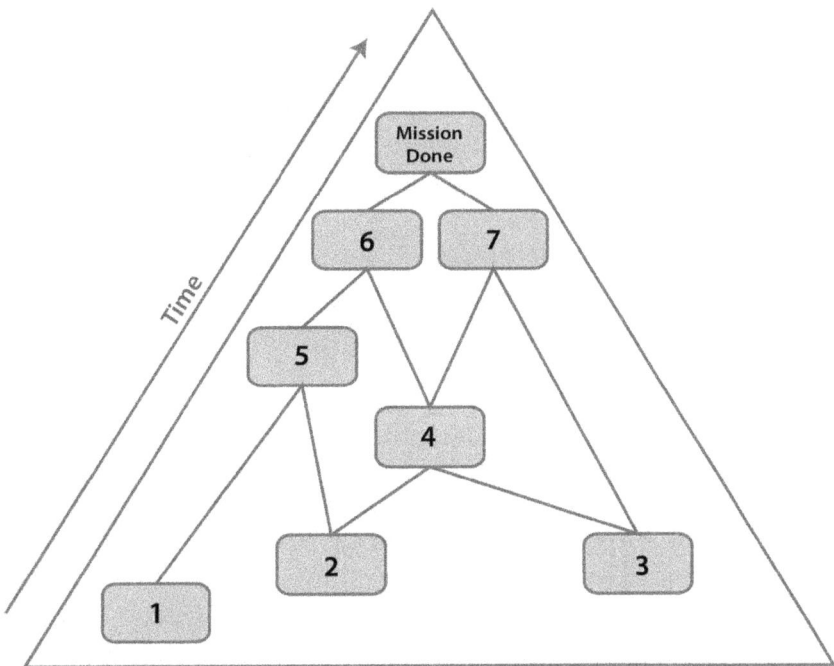

Hopefully when you have completed this task you will have something that is shaped like a mountain – to stay with our theme. Of course, as you can imagine, if you lay all of the missions out, you should see the interconnectivity between each of them as well.

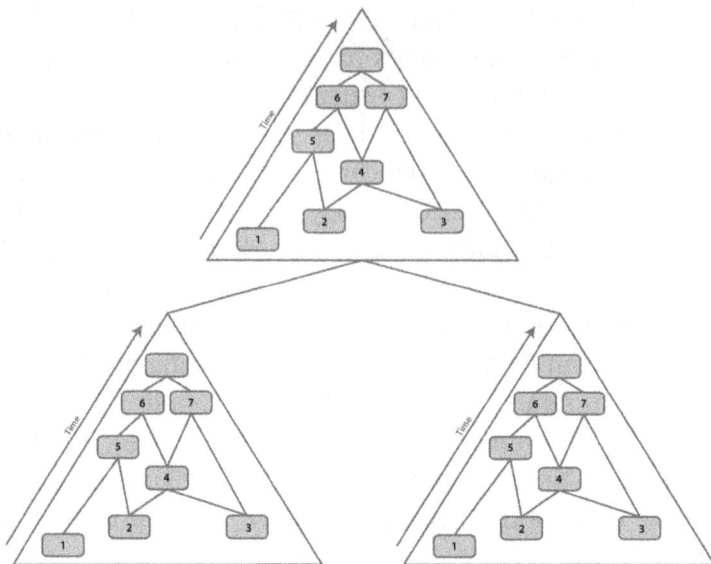

If you have a goal that you want to get done, but you can't seem to connect it to the other goals in your mission or to any other missions, then you have discovered the goal version of outliers. A choice needs to be made: Do you waste the time to accomplish something that isn't going to help you?

Now that you have laid it all out, it's time to determine if you have everything you need to support your mission and get your result. Ask yourself the following questions:

- ❑ **Do you have repetitive goals (multiple goals attempting the same result)?** If yes, you know what to do – whittle it down to one.

- ❑ **Do you have missing goals?** If yes, go back through the process. Define the goal and connect it up with the other goals. Now, we don't recommend adding every bathroom break, snack, or workout. Just the big items that get you to take the next step.

- ❑ **Are there some goals that are too big, thus invoking your natural defenses?** If yes, break them down until they are understandable, manageable, and don't tug on your limbic system's trip wire.

❑ **Do your goals or missions contradict one another?** If yes, make the tough decisions and decide in which direction you want your life to go.

❑ **Are your goals stated in a negative tone?** If yes, remember, words are powerful. You will either be motivated or suppressed by what you write. We recommend changing the words into a powerful and positive phrase or statement.

Before you go on: If you have added, changed or removed any of your goals, go back through both processes (in alignment or outlier, and string theory) and determine that you have the appropriate interconnectivity of your everyday actions with your future results. We'll wait for you.

Doing requires planning

When it comes to doing what you said you'd do, it helps to have a plan. In fact, it's a must. Did you know that planning is actually a form of doing? As we said, attempting to get where you want to be without a plan is worse than sitting around just talking about it. Here's why: all too often those who go and do without a plan get frustrated, angry, and end up quitting. They then say things such as, "I tried," "I'm never going to be anything or do anything," or the worst: "I knew it wouldn't work!"[4]

Of course, we know you're not an excuse maker. You aren't going to fail before you even begin. You will not create a self-fulfilling prophecy other than your dream of success. The others didn't have a plan to follow, but you will! You won't have to say a word, because your plans and execution will speak for themselves.

There is a story from one of Joel's mentors and friends, Neil Jarvis, who had the goal to "Come to America." He was told to write fifteen steps to achieve his goal. The first fourteen were about planning,

---

4 We love that excuse because if you knew it wouldn't work and yet you wasted your time and resources doing it, what does that really say about you?

and the fifteenth was about taking real action: "Pick up the phone and call someone in America."

Your turn: Take every white goal card and flip it over. Think about and then write the fifteen things that you need to do to accomplish each goal.

In a timely fashion

Time isn't going to stand still for you.

Picture this: You stand at the bottom of a down escalator. This escalator represents the finite amount of time you have to accomplish the mission at the top. The amount of time in which you *must* obtain your expected results from this mission is at the top step far above you; when it gets down to the bottom you're out of time. Remember the lesson on patience: you need the right amount of time to make the right decision. Take too little time and you might get the wrong result; take too much and you might miss the opportunity. This is exactly what is happening in your mission or goal. Don't get to the point where you have run out of time, but are still short of your mission.

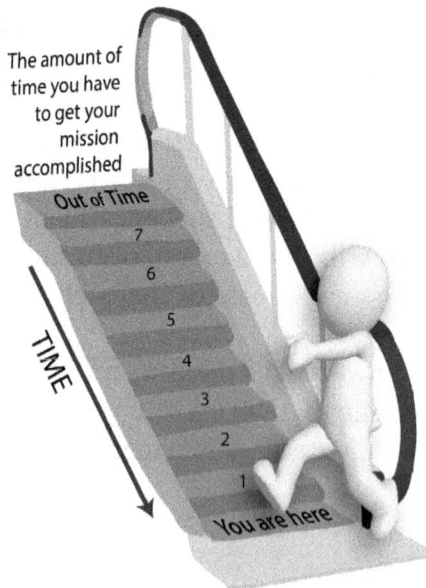

The amount of time you have to get your mission accomplished

Out of Time

7
6
5
4
3
2
1

TIME

You are here

For example, let's say you have seven goals that need to get accomplished in seven months.[5] At the start, you can easily spread out the goals across the time escalator and can reach each step before running out of time. You have spaced each goal accordingly and when you complete your last goal your out-of-time marker will be at the bottom with you. Mission accomplished.

However, a common scenario may go something like this: goals 1 and 2 went well and were completed on schedule. Then you decided to take a small break as a reward for your hard work. The bad news is that time didn't stop moving, so when you returned to working on your goals you felt a new pressure to get them done because your timeline hadn't changed, but your amount of available time had. Now you have to re-space the remaining goals over a shorter period of time. Here's where the rushing around to finish your goals begins, and it's often the start of lame excuses that no one wants to hear. You need to be sure that you get all of the bunched up goals out of the way and still get the others completed before the dreaded out-of-time step arrives.

Of course, you know that there is only so much you can really do with the amount of time available and at some point that buzzer is going to sound. Don't you want to win the prize when it does? (It's kind of like winning or losing on the game show *Minute to Win It*.)

Let's keep moving forward (pun intended). You get goal #3 out of the way, but #4 takes a greater amount of time than expected, and as a result the rest of the goals begin bunching up. It really doesn't matter as long as you remember that time doesn't stop moving. Never, ever! Time is coming at you at the exact same pace as before, but you haven't managed it correctly.

You got so caught up in goal #4 that goals #5, #6, and #7 back up to the point that there is no way you will get them done in the time remaining. You have a problem (maybe more than one). Give yourself another couple of moments and "out of time" becomes a reality. What will you do?

---

5 For simplicity, each goal is going to take one month and progress will be in a linear fashion.

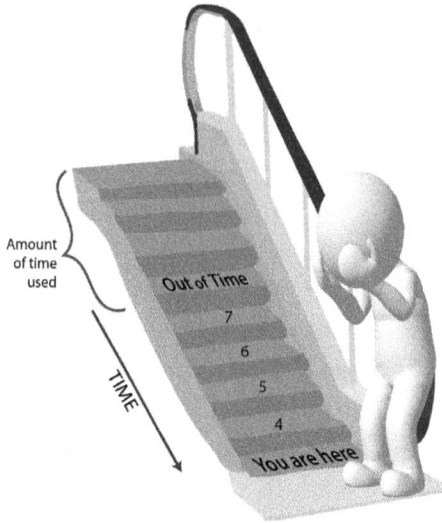

In the grand scheme of life we can always come up with reasons to not do something that we should do or promised to do. We can excuse our behaviors, our poor time management skills, or whatever else we can think of in order to feel better.

These can't be your reasons for not completing your mission. The best advice is to know and recognize an excuse when you see, hear, or use one. We really want you to plan your way to what you want, so when you do it, it's done!

So the question becomes: If you find yourself behind in your goals, and out-of-time is approaching fast, what can you do?

You probably said:

- ❑ *Stopping or removing a goal.* This is going to take too much time so strike it off the list. The problem is, why did you have it on your plan to begin with if it wasn't important? You went through a lot of trouble to set the goal because it supported the mission you were on. You have chosen this mission, the goals that have gone in, and the results that you expected. You were doing it for reasons that only you know, and now because you didn't use your time wisely this part of the mission is no longer important to you.

This isn't meant to be depressing or accusatory, just a wake up call. We don't want anyone to waste valuable time or, even worse, not achieve what he or she wants. To waste time is wrong because you can't get any of it back. Keep that in mind the next time you're bored. Now, if you have found that your goal was really superfluous to your plan and that you lied to yourself that you needed to accomplish it for your mission, then by all means learn your lesson and get rid of it.

❑ *Skipping a goal.* If you're saying to yourself that all you need to do is skip one of your goals, that's fine. Of course, we will ask: Why are they in your mission in the first place, in this particular order? There is a reason why this goal was placed in this mission in this order, so don't lose the information. Maybe you're thinking that you'll give yourself more time? If that was an option why didn't you do that in the first place? This can be harsh, but we don't want you to put anything in your mission that doesn't belong. You must be honest about the goals you set and the purpose of those goals.

❑ *Replanning a mission.* Out of all of the fix-it solutions this is probably the hardest to argue. You know you're out of time; you know that something has to be done because you believe in your mission. You can enter replanning mode and reset your time escalator to the beginning (who is going to know except you?), but that's the easy way out. What we recommend is taking a look at why it happened (learn those lessons) and then replan and rededicate yourself to your mission.

If you have a good plan and are able to work efficiently and plan for contingencies, the time escalator is not all bad news. Your efficient planning has allowed you to be ahead of schedule. When an unforeseen circumstance arises, you now have some leeway to deal with the circumstance and still remain on track to accomplish your goal in the time you've allotted.

We could caution you against giving yourself too much time or breaking your goals into units that are too simple, which may mean you aren't working at maximum efficiency, though it really doesn't matter if your end result is what you want. We would rather you take a lot of small steps to obtain your dreams then take a few giant steps and give up. The mission is to always make progress, never scare yourself away from what you want, and stay balanced in your life.

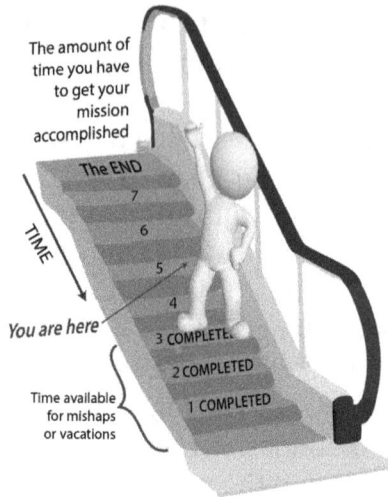

For any mission to work you must have a clear and understandable timetable. Open-ended timeframes give you too many outs for not achieving them, and will lead to excuses and drag out the amount of time you need to obtain results. You need to require of yourself that any mission or goal have a specific target end date. We actually shy away from statements like *two weeks* or *next month*. Once you have the specific end date and time, you can know how to place your goals on your time escalator, and this will allow you to stay focused and on target.

Get some help

An area in which you may find support and encouragement is with a mentor. Some may think this is an antiquated approach, and those people would be dead wrong. Having the luxury of going to a mentor, someone who's been there and done that, is invaluable. They may not have taken the same route you're taking to the summit, but they know what it takes to be one of the few to reach it, and that is where their experience and knowledge will become a great asset to you.

Choose your mentor wisely. A mentor can be anyone you respect or admire. Usually, you want to choose a person who has achieved some of the goals that you're working toward, but that's not required. We suggest that you choose a person who has taken control of their life, is following the living model, and is a person of action. Beware of the talkers who talk the talk, but never walk the walk.

We have found that most people who have conquered their summits are more than willing to share their knowledge and experience with someone who is serious about accomplishing their own goals and dreams. Keep in mind that your mentor will want to see you succeed. However, they will not want to have their time wasted by someone who is not a doer. In order to get the most out of your engagements, you absolutely must be prepared when you and your mentor meet. You should always have your journal or notebook handy in order to review your plan and progress. You should have a list of questions and a place in your notebook to jot down your mentor's answers and suggestions. Your mentor will not always agree with your plan or goals, but that's okay because it will cause you to prove why what you're doing is going to work, and in the process you may find that there is a better way to get to where you want to go. A great mentor will think of you holistically and care about all of your activities because they want to make sure that you're headed in the right direction.

> **Journal Entry #19: Who is your mentor going to be?**

Obstacles along the path

We would like you to now take just a moment and quiz yourself on each of your goals and think about the obstacles that you might face. Take each white goal card and think out the possible problems and obstacles and what you can do about them:

❑ **Biggest problem area.** (1) Break up the goal into smaller pieces to make it more manageable; (2) Ask yourself (or your support team) the best way to minimize the problem; (3) Determine if there is a way to remove the goal from your plan and still get your mission accomplished.

❑ **Scares you or stretches you way outside of your comfort zone.** (1) Split up or shorten the goal. Your natural defenses are working overtime and you're about to pull the trigger. Don't! (2) Might need to work on your BGB to release yourself from some of your own fears, perceptions, and expectations.

❑ **You need help with _____.** (1) Might be missing some goals that help reduce your need for help; (2) Reach out to your support team. Go to the individuals who can help you the most. (Please don't use guilt, threats or promises to get their help. Ask for the help you need.) (3) Split up the goals into more manageable segments.

❑ **You can already see failure and frustration.** (1) Go back and make sure that your DPPV is in alignment; (2) Work extremely hard on removing the appropriate filters and excuses from your existence.

We Love It When a Plan Comes Together

We think you have all heard the expression, "I love it when a plan comes together." Well, that's exactly how you should feel right now. You should enjoy seeing the mission (mountain, hill, whatever peak-like structure that tickles your fancy) that you have made come to life. You should feel great about breaking down your vision into missions that stretch you enough outside your comfort zone so that you can make progress in the direction of your goals.

Of course, you should feel good about separating the mission down into manageable goals. You can see how all of the goals interact with one another, and especially how they support one another. You have, at a minimum, figured out your first step toward Plan A (for those that don't remember, Plan A = Your Future Results in the four destinations). You should have a well-thought-out and executable first mission if you follow the steps that we are sharing with you. Whether or not it works will be strictly up to you and your ability to avoid excuses and stay focused.

Give yourself a pat on the back. You have accomplished more in understanding your path than most people do in understanding their home budget (which this process can be used for too!) You, our friends, have started to run up your mountain. You have started a journey that is going to take you to your future.

We do have one test that will validate if what you have written will get you where you want to be. As we talked about way back at the beginning, when you're creating your vision you will need to mentally time travel to your future in the four destinations (Home and Family, Education and Career, Community and Service, Hobbies and Recreation) then come back to the present to plan your journey. Using the power of mental time-traveling, can you see the end of your first mission? Don't be cursory; be specific. Actually go to your future and see the impact of your decisions and results. See how this mission effects your:

- ❏ Home and Family
- ❏ Education and Career
- ❏ Community and Service
- ❏ Hobbies and Recreation

We're hoping that you see your immediate future and like it. You like what life will become when you *Live The Risk*.

Extra credit climbing

Now if you're an overachiever, there's nothing stopping you from applying the same mission planning techniques that we just did for the next three missions that you had in JE #9B. You will probably need some white index Goal cards, tape, string, and a pen.

Allow a mission to be at least three to eighteen months, which will allow you to break down the broad steps that you need to take to get your vision of life. When a mission is seen in total, the comfort zone stretching will be felt. Also, it's expected that as you get three to five years out, the details associated with each mission might become a little fuzzy, which is perfectly okay. Looking at only a maximum of the top four missions is therefore appropriate.

Break down each mission into its appropriate goals, and then ask the following questions:

- ❑ What is the goal?
- ❑ Why are you doing this goal?
- ❑ When does the goal need to get done?
- ❑ What is the priority of this goal?
- ❑ How do you know when it's completed?
- ❑ What resources does this goal need?
- ❑ How does the goal interact with other goals?
- ❑ Is this goal congruent with my future?
- ❑ What are the biggest obstacles I need to plan for?

Small Stones Build Big Pyramids

Chip Away

We believe that *"only action is action"*[1] and everything else is talk. You can't achieve what you want by *talking* about what you're going to do. You need *action* to make progress. At the end only doing is living.

If you want to be a participant in the Living model, keep taking action until your last breath. Keep putting one foot in front of the other in a direction of your choosing. The only way you get what you want is by...you've got it...*doing*!

Doing is Living >>> **Living is Action**

Now, we know this is not a new concept. Mahatma Gandhi said, *"The future depends on what you do today."* He didn't say, "Your future depends on what you might do tomorrow, a week from Thursday, or next month." *Do* is a two-letter word that holds a lot of power.

---

1 Attributed to Skip Hancock.

Our definition is:

> ## To *do* means taking action now without the worry of success, failure, remorse, or excuse

It's not about random movements and claiming them as "action." What you want are specific movements that have the greatest opportunity to move you toward your mission, visions, and dreams. This is really, really important. Waving your arms in the air is doing something, but if you want to fly, it will be nothing more than wasted time and energy.

All actions need to happen at the right time and for the right reasons. Yes, it's true that when push comes to shove doing something is better than doing nothing at all. But doing the wrong things when you know that there are right things to do is not a good use of your time, money, or energy.

There is a quote from martial arts grand master Edmund K. Parker that says, *"To hear is to doubt, to see is to be deceived, to feel is to believe."* It's normally spoken when someone doesn't believe that a particular self-defense technique will work. The instructor then says the quote, demonstrates it on the questioner, and viola, the questioner believes because he or she felt the impact personally. And that is the moral of this story; you need to feel your actions personally.

You can't afford to hear your own words and expect belief. We suspect that you have seen this behavior day in and day out in many areas (think government and corporate America). Politicians, industry leaders, and advertisers have made a science out of telling us what we want to hear through their speeches and commercials only to find out weeks later that it was not like that at all.

You can't afford to "see" something and immediately decide what it means (probably leveraging your BGB filters). Think about how two eyewitnesses have completely different versions of a crime. They have both witnessed the exact same situation, but because they have filtered the information it takes on a different slant for each one.

Your key to success is to bypass your external applications (hearing and seeing) and internalize instead. Yep, let it get inside of you. The experience stays with you much longer and its effect is much more intense. "Feel to believe" is the cornerstone of taking control and leading yourself.

Doing is....	Doing may....	Doing may not...	Doing is not...
Taking action and control	Require change	Provide instant results	For the fainthearted
Developing patience	Involve risk	Always be fun and games	For quitters
The only way to get from here to there	Lead to temporary defeats	Be popular with your peers	For making excuses
Applied effort	Cause a rash	Provide equal time to relax	Waiting for others to take action
Rewarding	Be painful	Look flashy or cool	About the future

A.C.T.I.O.N.

Remember the beginning of the definition: "To *do* means taking action..." Well, this is a hidden gem because "action" is actually a great acronym that stands for **A**bsolute **C**ommitment **T**o **I**mproving **O**urselves **N**ow.[2] What excites us about these six words is the amount of energy compacted within its little frame. It encompasses the attitude, knowledge and skill that is being invoked to accomplish your current task. It's all about doing in the current moment and it has one result in mind: improvement. It's to make sure that you're improving yourself each and every moment, no matter how much time it takes.

> ## "YOU CAN'T BUILD A REPUTATION ON WHAT YOU ARE GOING TO DO."
> ### ~ HENRY FORD

A very personal story from Joel: Isn't it interesting what people think about when they compare themselves to someone of more skill? They decide that they're not good enough, that they shouldn't even attempt it, or that they shouldn't even participate in the event, activity, or sport. Think about the amount of time that is spent thinking about how "not good" they are!

I noticed this when colleagues and I were meeting to organize thoughts for a new book. A wonderful friend, personal mentor, fellow author and excellent writer, John, said something to the effect of (and I'll paraphrase): "I will be glad to be the editor. I am known for my extreme grammar editing skills." Now, this is important; it's true, John writes and speaks very well! His blog is filled with entries of well-written material. I am honored to know and work with him. With all of that praise, my mind released a fear so powerful that it became my only thought and it was mentally paralyzing!

---

2 ACTION™ is an acronym created by Lawrence Robinson II at his Attitude First Training Center in Phoenix Arizona. Used with permission.

Here is what my mind was saying:

- John will read my stuff and find out that I can't spell.
- He will announce to the world that I can't construct a sentence.
- All of the jokes that my family told when I was young about my spelling and grammar will be true and now he will start telling them as well!
- He will tell my friends that I can't write.

To be honest, all I could think about was that I would never have skills like John. Actually, I would never even come close. My mind kept planting seeds of doubt that made me question if I should even attempt this project or any other writing activity. Ugh! This fear was so mind-numbing that I even stopped listening to the other folks who were in the room. Fortunately for me the meeting ended, but I could tell that I was still wondering if this fear was true.

I know, I know, sanity should have prevailed – I can't be that bad...or can I? I have written more than two dozen articles, self-published one book, and am working on several others. I really needed to make this fear go away or it would end my future as a writer. So I began to look at the facts:

I was born in the Bronx, New York, and grew up in Queens, New York, and Los Angeles. We only spoke English at home. I have never taken a foreign language in school. My mom, aunt, grandparents and sister loved to write. You would think that the odds for literacy would be in my favor, but nope. All those who have read my working drafts will know one thing to be true: I struggle with language. I even joke that English is my second language and I only wish I knew what my first one was.

I remember as a child that I would become very frustrated with English teachers who only marked the words that I got wrong: a grade of "F" for the ten words I misspelled! My thought was: what happened to the ten words that I got right?

I barely passed an English class in high school. In college my soon-to-be wife would edit my papers so at least I got a "C." The articles I write today go through several editing cycles

– and still there are grammatical errors, wrong tenses (darn those tenses!), and misspellings. MS Word's spell check tool is my best friend; the squiggly lines are a joy to have around. The red one for misspelled words and the green one for grammatical mistakes – love them! I am waiting patiently for a blue line to underline the sentences and paragraphs with mixed up tenses. I am comforted knowing that there are a lot of people from history who have had the same problem: John F. Kennedy, Albert Einstein, George Washington, Winston Churchill, and even the bestselling author Agatha Christie, but they were famous; the world seems to have looked past their issues with spelling and grammar. The facts were supporting the fear and not me. What was I supposed to do?

Fast forward a couple of weeks to when my wife and I were driving from Phoenix to San Diego. With thirteen hours of thinking time on this round trip adventure, I was replaying this fear of writing in my mind. I suspect we have all had the same type of conversations about someone or something: I wish I had John's skill. Why can't I have John's writing skill? Darn John's skill. What I could do with John's skill. Can I, would I, should I...etc.

Nine hours into the trip and it hit me. No, not another car. It was a thought that changed my perspective. I decided what a waste of time it was to be afraid, envious, or jealous of John. He has done all of the right things to sharpen his skills. I should be...no, I am proud of him; ecstatic that he listened to those teachers in school, internalized the lessons, and is able to use his skill to get his message across. He has been blessed by a higher power with his natural talent. I need to employ my latest learning of self-awareness, turn this fear into personal strength, and realize it has nothing to do with John or his skill. It has nothing to do with my comparison to him. It has everything to do with me!

So what that it takes me two or three times longer to create an article? Does it matter that it requires me to hire an editor to correct the books that I write? Should I be ashamed that I have asked my wife to read my material so at least there aren't blatant mistakes within the paragraphs? The answer to all of these questions is: "It doesn't matter."

The only thing that matters is that I do the action. I need to keep getting my thoughts out of my head; I need to keep applying my pen to the parchment, and I need to keep learning the rules of this language. Yes, I have a weakness, but I will not let it stop me! I will not look for perfection in my writing; I will continue to do and improve.

I need to reach out to colleagues who have the skill, and hope they will share their knowledge with me. I need to learn from my mistakes, I need to improve my vocabulary, I need to actively learn the appropriate syntax, and most importantly, I need to keep doing what I enjoy! When I hear the jokes (remember I make them about myself as well), I need to know that they are just that: jokes, nothing more and nothing less. They only bother me if I am bothered by them.

So, if you're like me, and are one of the millions with thoughts of not being good enough, especially when you're comparing yourself to others...if you're mentally beaten down by jokes... if you're thinking that your skill set in the martial arts, writing, running, real estate, investing, any sport, or other talent should stop because there are others who do it better...if you don't think you have the proficiency you need to be successful...I hope that you will stop doing yourself a disservice.

Take it from me; you're already ahead of the game. Most people who have the skill tend not to use it to propel themselves forward. You're living your dream by taking action and learning to become better! You're getting past your own internal mental, emotional, physical, and spiritual barriers and doing it! Give yourself a pat on the back when you succeed. Congratulate yourself when you learn and apply a new lesson. Pick yourself up off the ground when you fall. Most importantly, continue to learn with every success and failure. It doesn't matter what anyone else says or does; you're doing it to the best of your ability!

Personally, I don't know if I'll become famous for what I write or if my works will be just for me. I do know that I am honored by those who read my message and humbled by their feedback![3]

---

3 Article posted on Joel's Facebook notes on June 30, 2010. Edited, of course, for grammar and punctuation.

If Joel wants writing to be a significant part of his dream he can't let comparisons, complacency or complaints stand in his way. He needs, no matter what, to keep taking daily action toward his Plan A. If he stopped right where he was when someone told him that he didn't write well or if Jeff believed that he couldn't be successful as an entrepreneur, then both of them should have stopped and given up. But we followed the Five Rules of Doing, which catapulted us to success.

These Five Rules of Doing include:

1. Allow yourself permission.
2. Understand the pitfalls.
3. Stay very aware of your situation.
4. Learn from everything.
5. Choose to do.

Rule #1: Allow Yourself Permission

One of the biggest hurdles that you place in your own path is that you have not given yourself permission to take the action and experience the success that you deserve. You stand in your own way most of the time. Sure, you talk a good game when you need to do something, but you often wait around until someone else – be it a spouse, boss, the government, police – tells you that you can start. If you're waiting for permission for something that you know you need to do...then give permission to yourself and do it! We know it sounds kind of hokey. The truth is, if you don't, who will?

Time to be honest

Much of the time you have decided on taking actions that you have neither the will nor skill to accomplish. The good news is that it hasn't stopped you, yet. Let's get this out in the open: if you haven't come to grips with what you can and can't do, then there is a good chance of setting yourself up for failure. And we don't want you to fail![4] We want you to give yourself permission to be honest and identify every place where you have a deficiency and figure out a way to plug it, minimize it, or remove it. What are the things you need? Be specific about the skill and where you can get it.

Honesty is also about understanding and accepting the current truth and then putting forth the effort to change the future truth. It's true that the best of plans might need to change and often do. You probably know someone who keeps working toward a goal the same way as they have done before, except they have never been successful (not even once). Why do they keep at it?

If you're honest with yourself, you will be conscious and proactive as to why and when your mission or goal is not working and make the necessary changes. Keep in mind, we are not saying give up or abandon what you want. We're saying to dig deep, check your ego, and make a change to be more successful.

Listen to the anxiety

There is no doubt that you are going to have some significant anxiety-filled moments as you take action. When you do, we don't want you to give up. Sure, there are going to be times when it is nothing but "nose to the grindstone" activities because some unexpected thing has happened and it's up to you to find a solution. Anxiety helps inform you that:

❑ You could be out of balance (i.e. RADICAL Persistence).

❑ You're not using your resources (time, money, energy, people) properly.

❑ You might not have the right plan.

❑ You might not have the will, skill, or ways (thus, you are missing goals).

---

4 People who fail don't write great book reviews or give recommendations. People that succeed do.

It's really important that you do not ignore this helpful anxiety. When it occurs take a moment and rebalance yourself, readjust your resources so they work for you and not against you, and get the right skills by adding them into your plans (and yes, that might change your timing). Each might alter your plans, but not your overall mission.

We ask you not to sweat the small stuff; just keep plugging away. Because something is stressful or anxiety-laden in your life doesn't mean that it equals failure. You could view these moments as taking a different path toward the same mountain peak. Oftentimes, while on a different path you may experience, learn, and acquire new skills that you wouldn't have gotten on the original path. Take every opportunity to learn and grow.

Known versus unknown

Lastly, giving yourself permission means giving yourself the ability to question and to ask yourself more detailed questions than anyone on the outside would ever ask, such as, "What if?" "Why?" and "Why not?" The ability to question gives you the opportunity to focus on the unknowns in your actions and to make them known. It also gives you the chance to practice changing the perception of your situation.

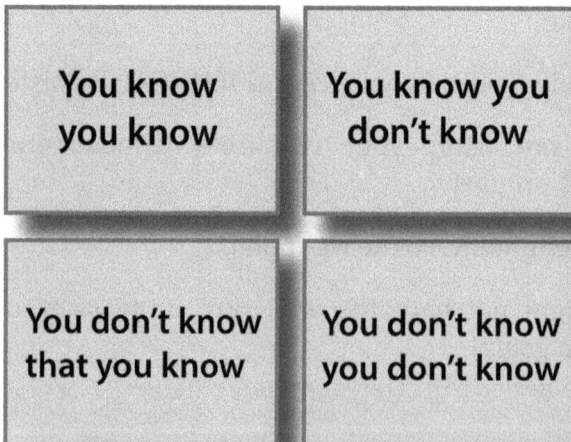

You know you know	You know you don't know
You don't know that you know	You don't know you don't know

Look at the picture on the previous page; it represents the four broad categories of knowledge. The upper left represents what and how you know to do the things you do. Easy to fall back on what you know, because...you know it. Beware, this is where the trap is: When we keep repeating what we know without thought (think automatic pilot), we will keep getting the same results each and every time. Good news: if we're getting good results, then keep it up and look for better ways to get more results.

For example: Let's take Henry Ford. In the years before 1908 he built many cars, and he built them well, but none met his dream of building a "motor car for the great multitude."[5] On October 1, 1908 the first Model T rolled off the assembly line. The car revolutionized American transportation. If Ford had stayed put with how he was building cars he would have been living what Albert Einstein called the definition of insanity: "Doing the same thing over and over again and expecting different results." Henry Ford wanted different results. He wanted to get out of his known knowledge box to determine if he was doing the right things, and he wasn't worried about making mistakes (remember, he started in 1903 with the first Model A), which, of course, would lead him to one of the other three boxes in our graphic. Plus, we're sure Mr. Ford didn't want to be insane.[6]

To avoid insanity, you would travel over to the top right box. To anyone that makes the trip, it's a solid admission that you know you don't know something and thus you're up to finding other resources to help fill in the blanks. You will ask what will hopefully be some amazing questions. At some point in time you will accept what someone else says as fact and move on.

Be careful; you can listen to everyone and gather their opinions, but if you want an answer to your question, do independent research. When *you* come to the conclusion that *you're* right, then move forward. It removes the excuses and the blame. Back to Ford: He was smart enough to know that he didn't have all the right information to improve his own design, so he actually hired the right people,

---

5 http://media.ford.com/article_display.cfm?article_id=81 (accessed March 1, 2013)

6 Nor do we. Although, do the insane know they are insane?

such as motion-study expert Frederick Taylor, to make the jobs on the line more efficient.

It sounds like utopia, doesn't it? Well, it's not. Staying on the top right of the model can also waste a lot of time. It can leave you in *analysis paralysis* (AP), the no man's land of data gathering that prevents you from making a decision. For those that have never been to the AP, we applaud you. For those folks who have visited and knew they are staying too long, good for you. For those that have set up shop in the AP, we want to kick you in the rear end because you haven't figured out that you have wasted time and accomplished nothing.

The bigger problems are on the bottom of the model. Starting on the bottom left, "You don't know what you know" is learning the lesson and forgetting it. It's when you start wasting time and energy in accomplishing the same thing again and again (see Original Mistakes in Rule #2). You're reinventing the wheel over and over, not asking the questions from the top of the model, and not making decisions. We think this is the worst of the four categories because of all of the waste that can occur. Do you think Ford could have produced ten million cars unless he challenged his own thinking? He actually asked those "what if" questions and filled his knowledge with enough information that by 1913 he created the first moving assembly line. He never relaxed thinking he knew how to solve the problem; he kept playing between the two top boxes which made a significant impact in his life, and as a result all of our lives.

As for the bottom right, it represents the dead zone of "You don't know that you don't know." There is no opinion that you're seeking, because you don't know to seek it. It would be a shame to be lost in the dead zone because you'd be no better than a zombie walking aimlessly. Ignorance may be bliss, but it's also nothing more than the dying model perfected. The only way out is to purposely build a ladder and climb out.

We wish we could tell you some great story of how you can tell you're stuck in this box; quite frankly sometimes it requires a poke in the eye, over and over again, for you to realize it. Here are some moments that will normally say you're in this box:

- ❑ When you ask the question, "Why is this happening?"
- ❑ When you use the statement, "I didn't know."
- ❑ When you feel mentally lost.
- ❑ When your anxiety or fear states are raising their ugly heads.

Journal Entry #20: What Do You Know? We will assume that you know the things you know. Let's start looking for opportunities within the other areas. (Be honest.) Write down details of your current problems/situations and let's determine what to do:

❑ **You know you don't know.** Determine what or to whom you can talk to give you some ideas that will provide some clarity. Now go talk to them.

❑ **You don't know that you know.** Look past your own ego and what you think are the answers and make sure that you're not reinventing the wheel.

❑ **You don't know that you don't know.** Look at the list and determine the items to which you can say, "I don't know" and get some help.

Rule #2: Understand the Pitfalls

Folks, it comes down to this equation: Goals + Actions = Results. Doing what you need to do, and when you need to do it, will provide you with the greatest opportunity for success. It really is about the mindset. The problem occurs when within every good mindset there seems to be some...how do we say it...bumps, gorges, and cliffs. So this rule is all about the pitfalls that we may face and how to avoid them:

- ❑ Pitfall 1: Complexity
- ❑ Pitfall 2: Heroic behaviors
- ❑ Pitfall 3: Original mistakes

Complexity

Some of us get lost in the complexities that we think are around every corner; they appear to be waiting for us to be unsuspecting and unaware. Complex situations are nothing more than intertwining simplistic ideas or actions that when combined create an illusion of complexity, but really require *sophisticated* answers. The only reason why it's complex is because we have made it complex. We have allowed it to be more than what it really is! Complexity is an energy-waster. We need to break our conditioning that a hard job requires hard work and that a complex problem requires a complex solution.

Each task should be as sophisticated and simple as the last time you went to a bookstore. Did you think long and hard if a book you wanted would be money well spent? Did you ask your friends and family? Did you rethink your own opinion because of a review that you read? Or, did you jump in with both feet, pull a book off the shelf and buy it? Did you even think about the costs spent on looking for a book and wondering if it was worth the time? The bookstore is easy and simple for most: see the pretty cover on the bookshelf, check out the words on the back, ask the lady at the desk, make a decision and go to the cash register. You aren't going to worry about a $25 book – it might not be good after reading it, in which case you get rid of it quickly, or it could change your life and you buy copies for friends and family. The only decision you have to make is, are you going to buy it or not? Simple. You're not going to put a committee together and agonize over this little decision. Darn simple. Every one of our actions needs to be this way. We need to break down our decision into small, simplistic steps.

Think of the next complex task you will do. Now, apply the "15 Things" process to it that we discussed in Accurate Missions. Keep writing, breaking it down, and simplifying. When you're done, take action on the simplest item on the list. Then do the same for the next item and then the next. Keep taking action until all the steps are completed. Next time, when required to do a complex task keep breaking down the angst and trepidation into simple activities so you can get them done and stay in control. As you continue to develop, you will give yourself the opportunity to turn simple actions into more sophisticated results.

Heroic behaviors

In the process of doing there are times when we do too much. You probably have experienced putting all of your waking hours into an action; you give up family, friends, sleep, and food to get something done. The problem is it lasted too long.

Heroic behavior has its place; it's meant for really short bursts of time (and we mean *short*!) If you think about it, you attempt to apply it way too long to mask the problems from incomplete planning, poor use of time, lack of resources, and bad decisions. Working harder doesn't equal success.

Our reasoning: You're expecting yourself to hold your energy at 100% for too long of a time, and thus become fatigued. At some point in the near future you will not even be close to running at optimal speed. If you've ever crammed for an exam the night before, you know what we're talking about. At some point your body will become tired and your energy will decline as you continue to push beyond your limits. At worse, illness will creep in and force you to take time off, and it will be more than you want, but at this point you have no choice because your body is now out of balance.

The human body can't take heroics as a state of being. The moment that the adrenalin wears off, you're going to deplete every source of energy you have: physical, mental, emotional, and at some point, spiritual. The human body is not made to keep going and going and going with no rest or relaxation. We believe that the optimum amount of energy one should give is about 75% overall, not 100% (except for the rare occasion). And we can prove it.

Grab a really big, heavy book. Hold it straight out so your arm is parallel with the floor. This represents one hundred percent. Don't sway or lean on anything. That book is attached to your hand and floating in air. Continue holding it. It's getting harder and harder to do so, isn't it?

Now bend at the elbow to about forty-five degrees with your elbow close to your body and hold the book. Again, don't sway or lean on anything. Easier? This is seventy-five percent. You could probably stay here for a really long time (try it if you want, but we don't require it). Attempt to hold this pose for ten minutes, except every so often hold the book out again at 100% for thirty seconds. Can you do it?

Welcome to the appropriate use of heroic behavior. You can burst to 100% anytime you like, as long as you are not expected to stay there for a really long period of time. The good news is that the more you experience 100% for short periods of time, the better you will be at dealing with it. Let heroic behavior be a technique that is used on rare occasions, not the tool that you use on all occasions.

Original mistakes

We can hear you: You don't want to make a mistake. We feel for you; we don't want you to make one either, except where growth and learning reside. We think we have driven home the point that we would rather you do something than sit around thinking and worrying about it. Because all the time you waste worrying about making a mistake is a mistake in itself. The time wasted will add up to an incredible amount and you will have nothing to show for your efforts except delay.

Return to our *"do"* definition: "...without worry" was added for the reason that if you're doing your best at the moment and you believe what you're doing is morally and ethically sound, can you really be wrong? Unless a court of law is judging you or you care about what your peers think, we're going to believe that every action you take has the capability of being the best action at that time. There is a little right in everything we do, and at most times there is a lot of right.

You will discover that some mistakes will enhance your understanding of what you're doing. We are not talking about the ordinary, run-of-the-mill type of mistakes. This is about making the original mistakes that you have never heard or seen anyone else (or you) make before.

Can you imagine the excitement of trying new things, taking chances, doing what some think is impossible when you aren't worried about making new mistakes? Remember, we are not talking about taking unnecessary risks and repeating mistakes that others have made. But if, at the time of making a decision, you could make it without the fear of overreacting to an imperfect decision, can you imagine what you could accomplish? The possibilities are endless.

To risk something is Living; To risk nothing is Dying.

Some of the greatest accomplishments of the current era held some risk or another, and some were great original mistakes, including Post-It Notes, penicillin, Velcro, potato chips, ice cream cones, chocolate chip cookies, microwave ovens, corn flakes, the Frisbee, and Silly Putty.

How you can implement original mistakes in your own life:

- ❑ Forgive yourself and others when you or they have stepped out and taken a logical chance in an effort to achieve their goals.

- ❑ See the triggers of negative self-talk and self-bashing that you do when something goes originally wrong. Stay positive.

- ❑ Recognize where your comfort zone starts and ends and make the adjustments in order to allow for original mistakes to occur. Stretch yourself into the unknown without triggering your natural defenses.

- ❑ Keep the communication paths open to all those involved. This helps others realize that this is no longer an original mistake.

- ❑ Recognize that this mistake is a temporary defeat; it's not failure. Brush yourself off and get back to doing. Refine your actions. You're less likely to do things that might cause you temporary defeat in the future.

When was your last original mistake? Did it follow the original mistake rules? How did you deal with correcting it?

We are not naive enough to believe that original mistakes can't affect other people. If they do, help them understand through your actions. First, be honest. Don't hide, don't shun, don't excuse, and definitely don't lie. Prepare your logic and attempt to learn. You need to be a strong-willed individual, because those you disappoint or hurt through your mistakes might not be pleased and you will risk your relationship with them. We make no promises as to what will occur, except those who take the high road vs. the low road tend to always come out ahead. Original Mistakes is an excellent tool to keep you doing, taking ACTION, and not fearing failure.

Rule #3: Stay Very Aware of the Situation

Here is the issue that we see when folks get down and dirty with doing. They become myopic. They seem to get so into their tasks (which is a good thing) that they forget to look around and take in the scenery (which is a bad thing). We are not talking about wandering around not paying attention; we are talking about paying attention to one thing so deeply that you miss other opportunities around you. In the art of doing you need to be aware of what is happening so you can take advantage of it when and if needed.

There are four distinct areas for staying aware: 1. Understand the snare of the obvious, 2. Be focused and flexible, 3. Prepare thoughtful contingencies (sounds nice, doesn't it?) and finally, 4. Relax as you panic (sounds weird, but we'll explain).

The snare of the obvious

Imagine for a moment that a speaker standing on the stage of a large darkened auditorium begins to give her speech. Because of the bright lights she can't see past the edge of the stage. She begins with the same hopes and dreams that this speech will be accepted like the last time she gave it. Five minutes into the talk, the joke she just told gets a groan from the audience. She still expects that all will be okay – just as it was the last time. This is a large audience (same size as always); she is comfortable on stage (like always). She can see her slides on the projector (they look good and bright, as always). Oh no, another statement, another groan. The entire thirty-minute presentation goes the same way. She is glad to get through all of the actions that she promised. Finally, like she always does, she asks for the house lights to be brought up and finally sees what she had missed. Her audience were all in their twenties and her material was geared toward senior citizens. They didn't understand her because she expected a different audience. She assumed the obvious and was very wrong.

We would like to tell you that this never happens, but it happens all the time. You walk into a situation, problem, or opportunity thinking you know everything you need to, only to find out that some of the obvious things you assumed are wrong. Be it external or internal, communication starts with the assumption that you communicate well! In reality, you tend to give parts of stories and half-pictures when you talk to others (and even yourself). Actions are filled from top to bottom with communication. If you're building a shelf, you're telling yourself about the type of wood, brackets, and nails to use, and if you're going to build it well, you better be giving yourself the right information. If your action requires others, you better make sure that you tell them what they need, what to expect, and what you have assumed.

How many of you have been in a classroom or a meeting where you did not understand what the speaker was saying? What could have been the outcome if someone would have raised his or her hand and asked a question without embarrassment or ridicule? You never want to be the speaker of whom no one asks any questions, only to find out later that no one absorbed any of the information, and they missed out on the value that you thought you were providing.

"Never assume the obvious" (our form of NATO) is a simple, powerful four-word phrase to help you remember that assuming the obvious is a productivity killer. NATO reminds you to not work under the pretense that either you or those with whom you work know all of the facts and details.

The obvious assumption	You	Others
What is said or done is clearly understood	Never assume that you understand what others are saying without paraphrasing it back to them. If their actions are unclear then double-check – remember, the achievement of your dream could count on them.	Never assume that others understand what you're saying or doing. If your actions require others to understand then you best be sure that they do.
Questions will be asked	Ask the questions that need to be asked of yourself and others (especially if you make the comment, "I can count on that to be true"). Check your facts.	Never assume that others will ask the questions if they don't understand or need more information to do their work on your behalf. Double-check their knowledge.
The situation is known	Don't assume that you understand another's situation.	Never assume that others understand the situation like you do. Explain it and have them repeat it.
Wants the same outcome	Make sure that you understand why you're doing the things that you're doing. If you don't get it, why would anyone else understand?	Never assume that others want the same outcome as you do. Others might not place the same level of importance on the items that you are.

The focused and the flexible

Let's say you're a real estate mogul, like Jeff hopes to be when he grows up. You're working on getting your property ready for rental. You know that time equals money and if you delay bringing the property to market it will cost you. Out of the blue, someone you know asks if you would give him advice on buying his first rental. It's not in your mission to help others, actually far from it; your intent is to grow your net worth by growing the number of properties you own. If you stop now and delay your mission, you might miss the window of opportunity to rent it during those critical summer months where most of the rental moves take place. What do you do? This is the question that Jeff faced during his goal to acquire rental properties.

His whole plan was predicated on obtaining a certain number of properties in a given time period. By keeping his nose to the grindstone and getting work done at the newly acquired property, it would have rented for the maximum amount and he'd be right on target. The good news is that *isn't* what he did. Even though he was focused, Jeff was smart enough to be flexible. He understood that there might be an opportunity within his friend's question. He knew that he might be able to put his real estate license to work by helping folks find their first property, which in turn would provide much needed capital to achieve more of his goals. He might be able to take on the management of properties for others, which would also give him more of an income, again supporting his bigger dream (Jeff is the king of small chips, and he's not even insulted by such comments).

Can you imagine what could have occurred if he had missed the opportunity? He would have worked at the rental until it was on the market. He would have rented it and collected the rent every month. He would then have started working on acquiring his next property. It would have been slow going for him to get out of his then current profession of teaching.

Instead, Jeff took advantage (in a good way) and created even more chips so he could get to his dream. He had no issue in changing his mission for the better. Now Jeff has his own properties, many others under management, an active real estate career, and he offers mentoring to others on their quest to buy their first rental property.[7]

You can't always control external events, even when you're committed to your goal. The path may change. Some new challenge may pop up that takes you in an entirely new direction. By being flexible you can adjust your actions to take advantage of the new opportunity, yet still remain true to your goal. Flexibility is not just the art of making lemonade from lemons, but making lemon pie and lemon margaritas too! It ensures that you're always reviewing what is working and what isn't so that you can change your approach when necessary. No one can anticipate the exact outcome of any venture; flexibility allows you to make the most of whatever does happen and make it work for you.

Just like patience, flexibility is something that you should bring to the party. It's yours to use; it's not something that others can give you. Flexibility is one of the tools in your You Toolbox that helps you take advantage of a situation; it continues to help you stay in an action mode. The key to flexibility is that it allows you to bend and weather the events that arise and make the most of them. Those who are not flexible will break; they will lose focus. They will give up and quit.

We are making focus sound bad and flexibility sound great. That is not always the case. There are times when a laser-like focus is exactly what you want to have, and where flexibility gets in your way or allows your mind to wander way too much. It's important that you take those little mini-breaths to look around and make sure that you're choosing what you want to do in any given moment. Remember, you're not assuming that there is only one way to accomplish your action and you don't regret what you have chosen to do. Regrets anchor you in the past and keep you from spending time on your future.

---

7 This is exactly how Joel bought his first rental property.

Prepare thoughtful contingencies

No one wants to talk about it, and fewer want to plan for it, but we all need a back-up plan. You don't want to be surprised if your Plan A gets blocked and you have to take another route. Before anyone gets the idea that this is the same as a Plan B, C, or D - it's not. You have the same dreams, visions, and goals...just a different set of actions to get you to your end result. It's still Plan A, but you were smart enough to embed a contingency clause.

After all of that planning we did in Accurate Missions, could we be telling you that you really haven't figured it *all* out? That is exactly what we are telling you, especially if you're living even a little outside of your comfort zone (BGB). You have taken on risk, and that means that there is a chance something might not work exactly as planned. For example: you're planning on obtaining a loan from the FHA to buy your next house and it doesn't get approved, yet you're planning to buy the house anyway (it's all part of Plan A). Having a secondary option (or third or fourth) to achieve this goal is a good idea. Think of it as a different path to get up the same mountain. The peak is still the same, just the route has been changed.

We are sure that you're tired of hearing it, but remember you're living *your* mission. Let's make sure that you have planned for some of the big contingencies so you don't get lost and you don't lose hope. The question that we often get is, "Should every move I make require a back-up plan?" If you did that would be cool, though our practical answer is no, of course not, especially if you have some experience in what you're doing and have actions planned in small enough increments. Experience will give you the knowledge and will tell you how to get over the proverbial hump because you have done it before. Having small actions planned gives you the opportunity to make small detours.

Journal Entry #21: No Regrets

Go back into the regrets you have in life. Recognize the mistake and learn from it. Did you see any interesting and connected opportunities that crossed your path that you ignored because you were so involved in what you were doing? How can you make sure it doesn't happen again?

Using any unsuccessful goal, what could you have done differently to change the outcome for the better?

Relax as you panic

A bad situation has lit the proverbial match. You can smell the sulfur as the fire starts burning. You're speaking to yourself and others as frustration at the situation sets in.

This negative situation has entered your psyche and begins to play havoc with your mind and emotions. Frustration begins to alter your attitude and brings you down physically, mentally, and emotionally. It slowly weakens your control over yourself. It starts to magnify the issues. Frustration starts to sensitize the triggers to your natural defenses, putting them on notice that something is not pleasing you in the situation.

How do you blow out the match before it lights the fuse? By welcoming the frustration and seeing the value of the situation and what it can teach you. By doing this you will be able to make the frustration a jumping board for positive events. Frustration has the capability to help you identify a problem, giving you ample time to figure it out.

Some might ask, why would you want to welcome the one item you don't want? Because by feeding the frustration you're going to make the flame on that match bigger and bigger. You're going to get angry, you're going to forget your values, and you're going to play dangerously close to the edge. That match is going to light that fast-burning fuse toward panic.

Of course, some folks don't listen. That match was dropped and the fuse was lit. You can see the burn mark on the ground as it quickly makes it way to the mounds of TNT at the end. It burns and winds its way toward the finale. Frustration has unleashed the power of negativity. You have started to become afraid of your creation.

> Some folks use the word "worry" or "fear" vs. "afraid." To us, it's same thing. It's born out of our psyche and manifests as possible negative facts in our thoughts and actions. In RADICAL persistence we spent a lot of time on fears (which can include worries and being afraid); it was one of the four major categories inside of the Big Granite Box (BGB). When the feeling occurs, whatever actions you are doing or about to do are plucking on those strings and the noise results in causing you concerns.

How do you handle being afraid? The only way is to recognize and conquer it. We suggest that it's time to find those mentors and friends who will give you much needed facts to calm you down and alter your path. Start listening closely. Start taking action in small steps. Ask yourself what you're really afraid of. See if you can figure out why you lit the fuse and how to put it out.

Sometimes you may get so caught up in watching the fuse burn that you don't ever put it out. You will probably find yourself far from a relaxed state of mind. The result is a big bang!

The bang you hear and feel is the feeling of panic as it relates to the situation. Panic occurs because we no longer think we have command over our environment, our activities, or the timing of our actions. It's not necessarily that someone else has control; it's that *we* do not have control! Panic is not having another driver cut you off while driving home from work. Panic occurs when that happens and there is a wall on your right and a semi speeding up behind you! At work, panic can occur when multiple things go wrong in quick succession or when items that should have already been accomplished start to pile up and your manager is asking for all of them *now*! Panic is when you think you're running out of time!

Panic can occur when every action you attempt fails – or at least you think it does. Panic sets in when your attitude is not at the level that you need it to be so you can achieve your task. Panic can be instilled by the brilliance of others or by the comparison of their attitude shining brighter than yours.

Panic is the feeling of failure before it happens, the loss of confidence, lack of a plan or strategy, lack of internal balance, or loss of accuracy. To panic is to put your mind and body severely out of balance. Panic sets our senses to a heightened awareness, which allows us to survive. Its flaw is that it does not give us a chance to act and sends us, instead, into a very unproductive and dangerous tailspin.

Frustration, worry, fear, and panic are natural reactions to abnormal events, to activities not yet experienced, or to being overpowered by fright or anger. To regain balance you must be able to relax and stop the burn and be patient for the right solution. Panic and patience are the invaluable ingredients of any offensive and defensive action against what you have perceived as a bad situation. Panic will notify your brain of the issues, and being relaxed will allow you to hear and act upon them.

Relaxation is an internal experience to calm the nerves. It lets you take a break from the situation that you're in and gives you an opportunity to think about it in a calm setting. It allows you to have the opportunity to see all of the issues and the possible solutions. Relaxation gives you the opportunity to regain your internal balance and accuracy.

The renowned Mayo Clinic says that practicing relaxation

techniques can reduce stress symptoms by slowing your heart rate, lowering blood pressure, slowing your breathing rate, increasing blood flow to major muscles, reducing muscle tension and chronic pain, improving concentration, reducing anger and frustration, and boosting confidence to handle problems[8].

> Don't sell relaxation short. It doesn't have to be meditation, medication, visualization, or progressive muscle release; it can be taking a small hiatus, such as a nap or a good night's sleep. It just needs to be a break from the action.

Rule #4: Learn From Everything

There is definitely a great by-product of taking action and it's the opportunity to enhance your own skills by learning from what you did and improving on them for the next time. Learning while doing is the hidden gem. You have the opportunity to alter your current course, change your productivity, and affect your future paths. Give yourself the opportunity to learn by welcoming wrong moves, doing and improving, and refining and reviewing.

Welcome the wrong moves

We wish we could tell you that you aren't going to make wrong moves, and that the chips will always land exactly where you expect them to each time you set out to accomplish one of your goals. We can't; there might come a time when something you're driving toward doesn't work out. Maybe it's a wrong goal, the possibility of a bad mission, or that the actions you took didn't work. It happens. The world is filled with missteps. What can't happen is that you become discouraged or disengaged by your temporary defeat.

---

8 http://www.mayoclinic.com/health/relaxation-technique/SR00007 (accessed March 1, 2013)

Sometimes when things don't work out it can seem like the end of the world, but it hasn't occurred yet. We promise that the sun will come up the next day, and guess what, you get another opportunity to accomplish your dream and to create the next chip. So brush yourself off, look at your mission, and determine another way to climb the next step. Go back to, and maybe simplify, your audacious goals, or make the steps smaller (too much stretch outside of your comfort zone is not always a good thing). Maybe you haven't allowed for enough time. Step back, refine, change, or remove as you see fit and as needed.

Even in the worst of circumstances we should never sit on our rear ends, cry, wish it to be different, and take no actions to make it so. Treat this fall as nothing more than an opportunity to see what the ground is like; get back up, brush yourself off, take a breath, and keep moving forward.

Take a moment to honor your past: Take a look at your past experiences, determine which ones were wrong moves, and figure out what you should have done. What do you think the outcome would have been if you had made the changes? Now that you know, what will you do about it?

> You can never guarantee that you will avoid every fall. You *can* guarantee that you will always get up. Staying down and giving up is the Dying model.

Refinement and review

Can you imagine how boring life would be if we only took our first action and stopped there? No refinement required, no worry, no wonder, no happy accidents, no nothing – just do it and be done. There'd be nothing left to achieve, no new situations to keep you on your toes. We guess we would all be standing around never expecting anyone to make the next move.

Humans must be constantly challenged to feel a passion for living. Avoid complacency like the plague it is. Complacency is the beginning of the end because once we've settled on it, then the living model is no longer being followed and we're on the downhill slide to death. To ensure we avoid complacency, we should never stop reviewing what we know and what we do. Let's not catch ourselves saying, "I am too old to change," or "You can't teach an old dog new tricks." We should treat these words as nothing more than an excuse to stay in a rut and not take responsibility for creating the life we desire. Those of us wanting to take control and create energy will cherish the opportunity to further refine ourselves!

We need to want to challenge ourselves, continue to learn, welcome change, and grow.

Complacency's enemy is action. Take a moment and let's improve one thing in each area of your current four areas of life: Home and Family, Education and Career, Community and Service, and Hobbies and Recreation.

And don't forget that you're never alone! If you want to refine and review your actions, it's best that you review them with others that have done something similar to whatever you're attempting to accomplish. It's time to bring in your friends, family, and even some strangers if you think they will give you the appropriate, honest, fact-based reviews that you need.

Do and improve

Think back to when you were growing up and going to school. From a child's perspective it seemed all about rushing you through and memorizing "stuff" in order to pass the next test. Were you there to learn and experience or just get through? What would school be like if you got to experience the material each and every day with the objective to do and improve? A place where you would be compared to your own standard of where you were yesterday, so that today could be better. What if school were not a place for perfection, but for practice (at least in your mind)? What if you were expected to push past your comfort zone and given methods and techniques by which to practice, and then, only be tested on doing and improving consistently? Would you want to go to school?

How would this "do and improve" philosophy affect your business life? If it became less important for you to get promoted and more important for you to do and improve, could you see any changes that might occur? Imagine the new discoveries that might present themselves. Imagine the challenges you might be faced with; how excited would you be? How about your personal missions? Could you take away any of the pressure by not expecting to be 100% perfect today at what you do, but doing better than what you did yesterday?

Let's get real; perfection is a nirvana that no human being will achieve. For at the moment that you achieve it, where do you go? Nowhere. Instead you should take every action as a way to do and improve as it relates to the last time you did that action. Raise the bar on yourself and keep improving.

The opportunity to apply this way of thinking to your own actions is right now. You don't have to wait for permission. All you have to do is remember three items:

- ❑ You need to do whatever you're taking action on to the best of your ability.
- ❑ Stand up for what, why and how you did it.
- ❑ Learn from it.

Ask yourself: in what areas of your life are you striving for perfection? Are they holding you up before you move onto the next goal or mission? If yes, why? In each of the areas, what actions can you take right now that will help cement the behavior of *do and improve*?

Rule #5: Choose to Do

You need to see every choice you make as a do/take action moment. There are no ifs, ands, or buts – just a decision to move in the direction of your choosing. There are no judges, juries, peers, bosses, significant others, or family. No one but you. Your only purpose is to take one more step. That's it. At the moment of doing you don't even care about good or bad (because that would be planning); all you want is to take action. There will be plenty of time to wallow in the outcomes or pat yourself on the back. Your job right now is to take the next action and repeat.

You know that if you can keep applying yourself and doing, you will achieve what you want. Hopefully, you want more than just to apply yourself; we want you to dedicate yourself to the new version of your life.

Those who are dedicated are never held back by circumstances. Barriers or defeats will not deter them. They give their all, and they believe that their actions will help them achieve their goals. Doubt is not an option to those who believe.

If you're not choosing, you're letting things happen around you. You're reacting, and you probably turned over control to someone else. No choice (which is really a choice in itself) will allow a vacuum to form within your mind and as we have discovered in nature, vacuums are not tolerated. That empty space will be filled with overreacting, unhappiness, fear of failure and excuses. You will say things such as, "I can never catch a break," "It seems everything is going against me," and "Isn't anyone on my side?" Or, perhaps you'll say, "Why do bad things only happen to me?" "This isn't fair," and "I don't know why I even try." Here are two more for good measure (we're on a roll): "I guess this is how it's supposed to be," or "The only luck I have is bad luck."

We would be remiss if we didn't talk about those folks who lose interest in their own actions. These are folks who are doing and then get bored. They wander to the next project or idea because their own dreams, vision, and missions are not strong enough to keep them on their paths. Their actions are so big or complex that they lose patience with themselves. They continuously move out of the world of doing and only see that the finish line is too far away. They complain that there are too many tasks between here and where they need to be. They see too many decisions between where they are now and where they are going.

We hope that you're not one of them.

You know, even before you take action there is only one of two roads to decide upon (and we're not talking about the high road or the low road). It's either going to be the road that is well marked or the road that is unmarked. One makes you feel comfortable and the other a little lost. Both roads are going to require you to do the same thing: make the decision to take it and then move forward.

To end, Ben Franklin asked himself two questions each and every day: "What good shall I do this day?" and each evening: "What good have I done today?" Mr. Franklin, we couldn't have said it better ourselves. The bookends of "Do" and "Done" need to sit on everyone's desk. They need to remind us that we have a responsibility to tolerate only the behaviors in which what we said we would do, we have done.

Journal Entry #22: Do and Done

What will be between your bookends of Do/Done today? What actions must you take today to stay on track to your goals and mission?

Do you hold yourself accountable for your actions? What will occur if you don't get them done?

What obstacles can you foresee getting in your way? How will you remove them?

Continually *REACH* In Order To Live!

Habit Forming

We would hate for you to get all the way to the H in *REACH* and think that you could put it down and go on to the next book. We obviously want you to retain, use, and repeat what you have learned from all of the actions that came before this in each of the other sections: Living Model, DPPV, RADICAL Persistence, Excuses Removed, Accurate Missions, and Chip Away. Of course, if you have the ability to internalize what you read, implement 100% of it into your life and have infused it into your DNA (kind of like Marvel Comics' Wolverine), congrats; you are better than we are.

For every other non-mutant individual who has read the sections, congrats on having made some progress toward altering how and what you do so you can bring to life your own Living model. This section is for you![1]

Habit Forming is about internalizing and repeating what you want to retain and use for life. It's about taking the best of what you have learned and keeping it at the top of your mind so that it's a part of your brain and muscle memory (like breathing). We can hear those inner voices saying, "Yeah, I'll remember what I need to do." Wrong.

---

[1] Not to mention that it makes you our kind of people even though we really would like to be Wolverine.

Without everyday practice, what you have learned will not stay on as a permanent part of you. You need to learn to take the information and internalize it. Let's get dramatic: You need to burn it onto your soul so you don't ever, ever forget it because it's that important to your future successes and happiness.

Now, let's flip the coin over. You want to get rid of a bad habit like smoking. According to the 2012 Surgeon General's Report, very few people start smoking after age twenty-five. Nearly nine out of ten adult smokers started by age eighteen, and 99% started by age twenty-six.[2] You know it's bad for your health. You understand the long-term repercussions that you will face by smoking. You have calculated the price you're paying. Yet, you keep on smoking. Your common sense will agree with the possible benefits that you will get from stopping: The toxins will leave your body after ten days. If you quit before the age of thirty you reduce your risk of dying from smoking by 90%, and if by the age of fifty it's fifty percent. Your breath and clothes won't stink, and you'll have more disposable income. These should be great arguments, but some folks still won't stop. The following are the statistics that will tell you about how hard it is to break a bad habit:[3]

- ❑ 70% of smokers want to quit altogether.
- ❑ 40% of those want to quit this year.
- ❑ 7% will succeed at quitting smoking on their first attempt.
- ❑ 3.5% who quit smoking, go cold turkey.
- ❑ 50% that quit will relapse while intoxicated with alcohol (not surprising; it suppresses the mind's control over itself).

Besides the drug-induced cravings and all of the negative effects, smoking points out that repetition and routine are the keys to the establishment of any habit. Ben Franklin – much more intelligent than us and one of our favorite persons of action – once said, "Early to bed, early to rise makes a man healthy, wealthy and wise."

---

2 http://www.cancer.org/cancer/cancercauses/tobaccocancer/questionsaboutsmokingtobaccoandhealth/

   questions-about-smoking-tobacco-and-health-why-do-people-start

3 http://www.statisticbrain.com/quitting-smoking-statistics/ (accessed on 5/27/2013)

Establishing a routine is the beginning of a habit. Once formed, those good habits (sleep, study, work, family, prayer) become the groundwork that allows you to find success.

The Pros and Cons of Habits

We cannot stress enough that you're responsible for the habits you have. And by no means are these habits like little people with big hairy feet (hobbits), but rather the things we do as part of our daily lives. You accepted every habit you have as the way you'll do business for yourself. A habit is a subconscious response, much like when you:

- ❑ Drive home from work and you don't remember the trip (it's a habit).
- ❑ Cut your food into pieces before eating, all of the time (a habit).
- ❑ Wash your hands after using the potty (a habit - and a good one).
- ❑ Drinking when depressed (a habit - and a bad one).

We all acquired habits in the same way. Someone or something laid down the first track and pounded in the first stake – you, parents, teachers, friends, or family who wanted you to behave a particular way – or maybe you did it because you liked the response. The rest was up to you; you continued to build on it, by repeating the behavior, until the track was laid and the caboose just rode it without thinking.

Think about the habits you have. Write down as many of the habits you have (write in code for the ones you don't want anyone to know you have). Here is an incomplete list of topics: grooming, dressing, eating, drinking, communication, sex, drugs, family, exercise, work, sports, friends, relationships, driving, sleeping, acting, writing, talking, spiritual habits. Review your list and ask these questions:

- ☐ Are you being honest with yourself about your habits?
- ☐ Are you worried what others might say?
- ☐ Are you worried about how others might react?
- ☐ Why do you do the things you do?
- ☐ Do you remember the first time you did this thing or acted a certain way back before it was a habit?
- ☐ Do you still see the value and reason or are you a creature of it?
- ☐ Have you let your habits become an excuse?
- ☐ How many do you wish you had?
- ☐ How many do you want to get rid of?

The biggest questions to ask are: What is the value of these repeated items? Do they help you succeed?

Here is a summary of when the brain is on habits. The basal ganglia, especially the striatum, is where the mind lays down the tracks upon which habits ride. These tracks are composed of the synaptic paths that hold your previous thoughts, decisions, and actions together. The good news is that as we ride the rails, the tracks become more and more embedded into the gray matter. Thus, when we fall into the appropriate situation for the habit, we will use them without question; we follow the same tracks that we have always used, with no real thinking (ah, the automated response[4]). Every time you pass over those tracks, they sink a little farther into your fertile mind as if they were ruts. If you've ever driven on a dirt road, getting out of a rut is hard to do. We had better make sure these ruts are the ones we want and need. If not, it's time to build some new tracks (new synaptic pathways) so when the habit gets used it goes in a direction of your choosing.

Check out appendix B if you want to know what occurs inside of the brain when it deals with habits.

---

4 In case you wondered, the sciences suggest that there really aren't any 100% automatic "no thought required" habits since the brain still controls the activities we do.

If you always write with your left hand, attempt to write with your right (vice versa if you write with your right hand). Do this for one minute. Write the alphabet, numbers one through ten, and then write your name. Feels wrong, doesn't it? Nothing works like it did with the other hand. It felt almost like a stranger was writing it. If you practiced you would probably improve. So, if we asked you (which we aren't going to) to learn to write with your non-dominant hand, what are the odds that you will get better? Good. Well, if you did it long enough and didn't have the other hand available to you, what are the odds that you could make writing with your opposite hand the new habit? Also pretty good.

Next time you brush your teeth or shave, attempt to do it differently. Start from the opposite side. Attempt to do it for a full week.

"Rafael Nadal is a Spanish professional tennis player. He has been ranked #2 on the ATP Tour for a record 158 weeks and became #1 on 18 August 2008. Nadal is only left-handed when he plays tennis - everything else he does with his right hand! As this video released by Nike shows, he would not manage very well in a left-handed world. Rafael began playing tennis at age four, guided by another uncle, Toni Nadal, who remained his coach on the professional tour. In his early years, Nadal (who wrote with his right hand) played left-handed tennis with both a two-handed forehand and backhand. When he was twelve, however, his uncle encouraged him to adopt a more conventional left-handed style. Nadal stuck with his two-handed backhand, but switched to what became his signature one-handed forehand, the stroke that was credited with lifting him into the sport's upper echelons."[1]

1 http://www.anythinglefthanded.co.uk/famous/rafael-nadal.html

Not All Habits Are Good

There are times when we have internalized things we probably shouldn't have. In the framework of *REACH*, it might be that you make excuses and don't chip away at your goals. If that is the case, we need to figure out how to jettison those from your mind so that they don't put you on the wrong path.

By now, someone out there in the land of self-help books is quoting some author who talks about doing this or that for X number of days[5] and by doing so will change the habit. For those who have proven that a certain number of days does indeed work, fantastic! Keep going. For those who haven't, stay tuned; we aren't giving up on you, and you shouldn't either. Personally, we were unable to find any clinical proof that backs up a specific number of days. Even practicing all of the time doesn't guarantee that the new habit stays and the old habit goes away. There are folks who have been sober for years only to go back to drinking because something triggered that old response, such as a significant emotional event. There are some folks who give up a lifelong obsession in a moment (see next box). And there are folks who no matter how many times or how long they diet (be it under or over X amount of days), they still have a problem and need to diet again.

> Joel's grandfather-in-law smoked unfiltered cigarettes for more than fifty years. Now, he wasn't a light-up-once-a-day guy; he was light-the-next-one-before-the-first-one-was-out type guy. He smoked from the time he was thirteen. He was the type of person that every brand wanted as their loyal customer. He would smoke when he was ill or well; it didn't matter. Each puff of smoke clouded the windows of his house (his wife didn't smoke). Then one day, after being threatened with another proctology exam with a long wand by his doctor, he gave up the habit in a moment. Literally! For more than ten years until the time he passed away, he didn't have another cigarette.

---

5 We have seen 8, 14, 21, and 30 as the most popular answers.

The saying "I'm gonna drop you like a bad habit"[6] is a lot easier said than done.[7] Science proves that those good/bad habit tracks will always be there, and unfortunately they are easy to find if you ever go looking. The research tells us that we need to actually make new tracks (those synaptic pathways), and make them a much more inviting journey to take. We need to bypass the old ruts altogether. In keeping with the train theme, we want to create the switch box so our dream liner doesn't take the old track.

How to Create a New Habit

How can some folks kick a habit or create a new habit in a matter of moments while others can't? Well, outside of the theory that some are predisposed by genes, mental wiring, and the psychophysical world, none of us quite understand. For others, there does appear to be several qualities that keep showing up that allow habits to be formed.

The qualities we found for building new habits are:

- ❑ Visualize your success
- ❑ Take the path of least resistance
- ❑ Understand risk and reward
- ❑ Learn, repeat, and verify
- ❑ Know your triggers
- ❑ Keep it simple and small

"WE ARE WHAT WE REPEATEDLY DO. EXCELLENCE THEN, IS NOT AN ACT, BUT A HABIT."
~ WILL DURANT

---

6 It appears to be a line from the movie *Rocky*.

7 We only wish it was easy to drop a bad habit because there'd be no such thing as addictions.

Visualize your success

To see the future, return to the present and plan your journey. This is the definition of *hopefulness* that we gave way back at the beginning of this book. Well, the same process works right here. You need to ensure that you have a clear understanding of what and why you want to do something, especially if you're going to continuously do it. You need to understand why you want this new habit, make sure that it provides you with a strong sense of direction, and know that you can clearly understand the results it will provide. Remember, this is not a one-time event; a habit is here to stay, so make sure it's the right one.

At this point you're pondering, *What do I want to achieve as a result of this new habit?*

Consider it the surveyor's map to where your tracks are going to be laid. We suggest that your answer have deep intellectual, emotional, and spiritual meaning for you. No wishy-washy mumbo-jumbo, but a powerful end in mind to allow you to have a new beginning. Now, we will caution you, do not cheat the system. Do not take any old borrowed answer (i.e. exercise fifteen minutes a day) and think you have done it. Make sure that you have a clear and deep understanding of the habit you want to create. We suggest you see it from the points of view of both yourself and others:

- ❑ Time
- ❑ Health and/or energy
- ❑ Financial
- ❑ The five fitnesses (spiritual, perceptual, emotional, mental, and physical)

It's important to understand what the success of your new habit will be when you lay the new track down and allow your train to ride its rails. When you visualize your future with this habit, don't think it's about the first time (though that is important); also think about your success the tenth and hundredth time. Keep it front and center, all of the time. Take a sticky note and write your soon-to-be new habit on it. Place it upon the surface that you will see the most as the habit gets executed. If it's changing the way you brush your teeth, then put it on the bathroom mirror. If it's to not snack at home, put it on the pantry and fridge. If it's kissing your spouse every day before you leave for work, put it on your spouse. (Kidding! Actually, the front door would be appropriate.) If this habit is accessed in multiple places, make multiple notes. Don't assume that you will remember. Don't take it on chance – make it a new habit.

Take the Path of Least Resistance

Be it water or wind, nature has repeatedly shown that it will take the path of least resistance when attempting to go from here to there. Well, the same is true for the habits that we take or do not take. The rails that we ride semi-automatically are the paths that have shown us to be of least resistance in our lives. We need to go out of our way to make what we want the easiest and simplest way possible in order to help us stay on those new tracks. How, you may ask? Well, it comes down to three things:

1. Understand that we move away from pain or we go toward pleasure.
2. Establish both barriers and passageways.
3. Make it comfortable and enjoyable.

Pain and pleasure

The path of least resistance is governed first by the pains and pleasures in our life. This is not a new concept, and some of the greatest self-help gurus in the world, such as Anthony Robbins, talk long and hard about this topic. For the folks who have not heard about it, we will give you the lowdown. And for those who have heard about it, this will be a brief review.

Pain and pleasure are the emotional, physical, mental, and/or spiritual associations that you make in regard to what you want to do. They are your true motivation for wanting to change or keep something in place. For some, the pain associated with an event will repel them from ever participating in the event, even if it's considered pleasurable. ("I love ice cream, but I'm lactose intolerant so I will never have it!") For others, the pleasure they will receive from the event will outweigh any pain that they might endure. ("I love the way I look in this bathing suit so working out – which I hate to do - is so worth it!")

Beware, it's not as easy as saying that pain is bad and pleasure is good. We have found there are scales for both. One side is attractive and the other side is repulsive. Repulsive is a big "NO, I AM NOT DOING THIS!" Whereas attractive is a big "I CAN'T WAIT TO DO THIS AGAIN!"

Now comes the hard part. Are you more repulsed by the pain and more attracted to the pleasure? Think about the habits you want and ask yourself if the process to obtain them repulses or attracts you. That can give you some valuable insight into why you have or haven't pursued them.

To help you navigate the path of least resistance we want you to make a clear and concise association between what your new habit will be and what it will help to solve. The deeper the feeling of repelling or attracting, dissolving or creating, the better the opportunity you will have of keeping the habit around for good. We will caution you that if the associations are weak and feeble, your train will lose traction and jump the track back to whatever it did before. Those old tracks are always lurking and waiting to be rediscovered. Be careful!

For example, you want to create a new habit that involves not drinking alcohol. Think of the troubles, tribulations, and negative issues that alcohol causes for you or those around you. Create assumptions about what the negative effects will have on your job, family, friends, health, sanity and bank account. Associate the negative issues that have or will occur. Remember, make it clear, powerful and believable – feel the effects in your gut!

Another example: You want the habit of exercise and physical fitness. Think of the satisfaction that you will get from how you will look and feel, not to mention seeing the benefits from the medical side (lower blood pressure, less body fat, longer life), what you can now eat (higher calories because you will burn more, quicker), and how your spouse will see you (you'll be too sexy for your shirt!). You might even find that compliments from your friends are a pleasurable reward.

When forming a new habit, determine the motivation. Are you going away from pain or going toward pleasure? Your motivation needs to be strong, specific, direct, and forthright. Remember, you want this habit more than anything else, because this habit will help you fulfill your dreams, goals, and vision.

Establish both barriers and passageways

"The water will flow where there are openings," said the elder to the young child. "If you put a rock where you don't want the water to go, the water will then go someplace else."

This is exactly what you need to do when dealing with soon-to-be new habits that need to take precedence over old habits. The fact is that you have tracks of past habits littering your mind. You have to be very deliberate and methodical when you strategically place rocks in your way, so the path of least resistance is your direction. The need to remove the opportunity of using old pathways has got to be a part of your decision-making process. You also need to make sure that the paths you want to take are open, willing, and accepting.

The simplest of barriers or passageways can be as small as cues and reminders, like a sticky note from the previous section, a string around your finger, or a coin in your pocket. It can be the reciting of a poem or pledge each and every morning so you can keep your direction front and center. Or, it can be avoiding the people, the process, and/or the technology that draw you back into your old habits.[8]

---

8 For those who are thinking big - we must caution you that everything you pick will either support or hinder you.

People

- **Passageways to help you obtain the path you want**: You want to surround yourself with folks who encourage, support, and help you follow-up on your habit. There is an excellent possibility that they already display the skills and abilities that you seek. These are folks that you want to associate with because they will help you install the tracks and the switches needed to make this habit permanent.

  Folks for supporting your habits are picked after you have your direction clearly in mind. This will prevent you from following another person's vision of your life.

  The people that surround you should be mentors that will model and mirror the behaviors you want.

  If you want to stop smoking, then hang out with friends who don't smoke. Go to places that are smoke-free. Encourage people to remind you (kindly) of the benefits (preachy gets annoying).

- **Barriers prevent you from taking the wrong path:** These are folks who display, request, encourage, or demand a behavior from you that would take you off your path. They probably symbolize the qualities that you are attempting to block and/or replace. The hard part is that a relationship that has this much power can't remain partially there, at least not until your new habit is ingrained within you.

  So, let's go to the extreme. Take any brainwashing or mind-control story that you have heard. Each starts the same way: take the individual away from their friends, family, and routine and place them among others who think, act, and obey a certain way. (Scary if you're doing it to others or others are doing it to you.)

  For example: If you don't really want to stop smoking, continue to hang with the friends who smoke, go to bars that let you smoke (especially if you understand your triggers), shop by yourself at the convenience store where you always buy your cigarettes.

Process

- [ ] **Passageways to help you obtain the path you want**: The order in which you do things is a powerful method to cement or block a habit. Make sure that you're using a process that encourages you to stay on the straight and narrow. Design want you want, the steps that you will use, and execute flawlessly until you get your results. We caution you not to change your process everyday because it will keep your mind guessing as to what path it should take. Give yourself time and energy to cement your will upon your mind. Build those right ruts.

- [ ] **Barriers prevent you from taking the wrong path:** You're probably going to follow the same process time and time again. So it makes great sense to alter the process to alter your behaviors. If you want to drive a different way to work, then attempt to get up at a different time, add some regular activities before you leave, exit your street from a different direction, and park in a different space. We know it sounds silly, but remember, you're attempting to get yourself out of a groove that is deep and entrenched; you have to do things differently if you want to jump the track.

Technology

- [ ] **Passageways to help you obtain the path you want**: Determine what technologies you can surround yourself with that will help support your new habit, be it TV, radio, computing, paper, pencil, manuals, etc.

  For example: a writer wants to stop writing by hand and for the first time ever use a PC. The best way is to remove the technology of paper and pencils (including pens, markers, etc.), and put the PC front and center in their workspace. Get the writer training so the PC is not so foreign; give tasks that allow them to get used to the environment.

- [ ] **Barriers prevent you from taking the wrong path:** We are surrounding ourselves with more technology than we know what to do with. We can watch a show on our TV, and transfer the show to our phone and then to our tablet. A person can get hooked on the accessibility of information and forget the reason why they were looking it up. What you listen to, watch, read, and type on all have the capability to lead you on a different path than what you have intended. If you're breaking a "gaming" habit, you probably want to remove games from your phone and computer. Not looking at the sports page in the newspaper or online will help. Not listening to all-sports all-the-time radio is probably appropriate.

Regardless if it's a passageway or barrier, whatever you place in your way to help your new habits or prevent your old habits from happening needs to be a deliberate placement in your river of life. You can't use a pebble if you're attempting to stop a gusher; it needs to a boulder (or several boulders). You need to work diligently and honestly in figuring out which people, processes, and technologies are appropriate to change what you want to change. This process and step is not by any means a "one and done and move on" type of change. Most people, us included, will find that this process takes time, and for some it could be a lot of time. If that is the case, be sure to keep chipping away in order to continue moving toward your goals and dreams while you're working on the new habit or habits.

Comfortable and enjoyable

This subject seems like a no-brainer. If you want to take the path of least resistance, then make it the most comfortable and enjoyable path to take. Seems like quality advice – because it is! No one in their right mind would want to take a path that is rocky and alligator-ridden if there is an easier choice. No one wants to climb unnecessary stairs and leap tall buildings to get to the next building when there is an elevator and a sidewalk nearby. Absolutely no one wants to change their habits when they like and enjoy their old ones and have already made up their minds not to change.

To make something more comfortable and enjoyable we have found three simple measures to employ:

❑ First, find higher value in the new habit than the habit you're currently committed to using. Make sure that your reasoning is clear and concise and that it's 100% believable by you (it doesn't matter if others believe your reason). Make sure your reason (the value) for your new habit is created by you. Even though you can model your value after someone else, we actually suggest that you don't take their words and actions verbatim; there are too many excuses that can brew today and screw you tomorrow.

❑ Second, establish your new habit with great enthusiasm. If you aren't excited about what you're doing, then who will be? Don't expect others to jump up and down because you're making changes. It's up to you. You need to be positive, passionate, proud, and grateful for what you're about to accomplish because you will do it as long as you're focused on the outcome whether anyone else is happy for you or not. Do it for you!

❑ Lastly, you need to have the right attitude to accept, honor, and stick with your change.

Understand risk and reward

Every habit that we attempt to change holds a certain amount of risk that might trigger our natural or manufactured defenses. We have a responsibility to ourselves to hold off what could be a paralyzing and debilitating response by being honest and open about the risks that we might face. You need to make sure that you have already planned the appropriate contingencies in case the risks and pitfalls occur. The good news is that if you accomplished the *visualize your success* portion of Habits, you have already come to grips with what you might face. Think of the obstacles, setbacks, issues, and risks, and plan how you're going to overcome the snowball in your path before it becomes an avalanche.

A word of caution: Since you have identified and planned for the risks that might occur on the way to laying down your path, you cannot get sidetracked with thinking that every pothole will lead to a detour, which is also an excuse. Sometimes you need to build a bridge over the pothole. In other words, if you want this habit bad enough, sometimes you plow through your obstacles, setbacks, issues, and risks when they occur instead of spending a lot of time looking for another way around. Remember, this habit has been created by you for your own reasons, so please keep that thought front and center.

It would be detrimental to only talk about the bad and not the good. If you want new behaviors, then it's appropriate that you give yourself some rewards when you achieve them regularly. We're not suggesting that every time you do the right thing you give yourself a cookie, which is just another form of mind control. We're suggesting that at certain intervals you reward yourself for achieving what you set out to do. The secret of success is making sure the reward:

- ❑ Has a clear time frame. (After twenty-five workouts, buy yourself something special.)

- ❑ Appropriate for what you're attempting to accomplish. (Spending the day at the lake after completing the big assignment.)

- ❑ Supports your habit. (So no cookies if you're attempting to eat right.)

- ❑ Continues to encourage your accomplishments. (Perhaps an "Atta boy!" is enough.)

The goal of all rewards is to give yourself a pat on the back for doing a good job and to encourage you to keep doing what you're doing. Pick things that help you continue to achieve your new habit. Remember, there is no room for partial commitment when it comes to achieving what you want. You need to want, to crave, and to stay fully committed to your own new habits. You need to keep driving over those rails so they become a quality and worthwhile path.

Learn, verify, and repeat

To develop a good habit is a beautiful thing; it helps you mentally categorize the actions, problems, decisions, and results that you received. It also allows you to build up and predict outcomes because you have seen and hopefully remember the results from previous endeavors. As discussed, it's a mechanism that helps you simplify and it provides for a little automation within your lives.

When we learn improperly and practice incorrectly, new problems will occur. This is because we will rely on and semi-automate the wrong steps or cues. (You've carefully built the new track – great! It goes right through that alligator swamp, and in the wrong direction – not great!) The only train that will travel on those tracks will be a crazy train. Can you imagine after working to embed a new habit in the neural fibers of the brain how difficult it will be to change after finding it lacking or going in the wrong direction? Tired from the activity of putting it there, fresh from the training sessions that you painstakingly provided your mind, you're now going to attempt to wipe the slate clean – like shaking an Etch-a-Sketch? It ain't gonna happen. We want to avoid mistakes before they happen or at least recognize and correct them as soon as they do.

"I AM SLOW TO LEARN AND SLOW TO FORGET THAT WHICH I HAVE LEARNED. MY MIND IS LIKE A PIECE OF STEEL, VERY HARD TO SCRATCH ANYTHING ON IT AND ALMOST IMPOSSIBLE AFTER YOU GET IT THERE TO RUB IT OUT."
~ ABE LINCOLN

Mr. Lincoln said it best, and this is exactly what we want from you for your new habits. Because this habit is staying on your permanent record, we want you to be:

- ❑ Deliberately slow in your learning.
- ❑ Sure that you have learned it the right way.
- ❑ Be repetitive in your practice of it.

We want you to make sure that what you are committing to your neural network is exactly what you want and need it to be. In truth the old adage of "practice makes perfect" should read "plodding practice makes it perfectly permanent." A mouthful to say, but still true. Slow down and take your time with each of your scratches. (This sounds so wrong! Honest, it's just a rash.) Don't rush through your activities just to say "done is done" and only record the beginning and the end. Give yourself a chance to mentally record the journey.

A word of caution: Don't get stuck in the wrong routine and do nothing about it. Remember to validate your work; don't etch too many marks on your steel plate only to realize that the scratches don't align. Be honest with yourself and remember to visualize success. You're bound to have missteps, take unplanned detours, and on occasion forget what track you're supposed to be on, so as frequently as feasible, ask yourself these questions:

- ❑ How do I know what actions are correct for this habit?
- ❑ How can I prove that I am taking the right actions to ensure that my new habit sticks?
- ❑ Have I applied my new habit today?
- ❑ Am I keeping track of what I do, when I do it, and why I do it?

Check your train wheel alignment regularly so that you'll always know how your train is going to ride on the tracks.

Keep reminding yourself that you must ride that rail continuously, daily and regularly, especially if it's a replacement for another line of track (another habit). Once and done does not a habit make.[9] The more regular and consistent you are in your practice, the deeper the scratch and the greater importance the new pathways will take on in your mindset. We suggest that you attempt the habit at the same time each day (or multiple times each day), and find a routine so that your actions are implanted into muscle and brain memory.

---

9 We are sure that Shakespeare said it or wished he had.

Know your triggers

You think you are in total control of yourself, habits, and actions. You think that you are your own puppet master, pulling your own strings so you can get your expected and desired responses. At some point in the day (this is a hypothetical scenario because you never lose control, right?) you suddenly lose control and find yourself going down a path that you weren't expecting. How does this happen?

- ❑ A guy stops short in front of you and you swerve into the next lane.
- ❑ Looking at the time on the clock you suddenly become hungry (up until you saw the clock you weren't hungry at all).
- ❑ A person said something in a certain way (or the way you interpreted it) and you become defensive and maybe even offended.
- ❑ You smell the morning coffee and suddenly you're grabbing your first smoke of the day.
- ❑ The setting sun makes you reach for your first beer.

It appears that we are in control unless someone or something else figures out the trigger to our automated response...and then they are in control.

Remember Pavlov's dogs? Russian Physiologist Ivan Pavlov discovered that a particular signal could produce a conditioned response. In his experiment, it was the sound of a bell that made his dog salivate. Interesting, because that is what triggers habits.

You have, during your lifetime, associated a certain signal or trigger with a habit. It's actually quite ingenious to take what could be a multi-step process and mentally file it under a simple word, sound, action, or event. Why waste your time in filing away all of the steps when one thing will do? Of course, if you want to break a habit or at least the association with the habit, you really have to start figuring out your triggers and signals. We suggest that you review many of the things you learned in RADICAL Persistence (especially the A, D and C sections), as well as in Excuses Removed for appropriate triggers:

RADICAL Self Category	How it applies to triggers
Awareness	Self-awareness gives you the opportunity to unravel the mystery around you. If you want to figure out a habit, attempt to catch yourself doing it and then write down everything you're doing before the actions took place. Was it a person that entered the room, a statement made, a telephone call, the sun in the morning, the moon at night, making a cup of coffee, or the alarm clock going off (to name a few)?
Determination	Determine for yourself if the signal and response works for you. It could be the perfect thing or it could be the worst thing.
Control	It's important to remember that you're in control of yourself. No one is entitled or required to pull your strings and trigger your habits except you and then only in the way that you want.

Excuses Removed Category	How it applies to triggers
Natural Defenses	The fight, flight, or freeze responses are all governed by triggers that respond to your comfort zone. The more perceived risk, the higher the chance that a habit will be invoked to save you.
Manufactured Defenses	Every excuse listed in the section has a trigger that helps protect your ego from harm. Remember, we are attempting to judge ourselves not guilty.

Of course, it works the exact same way if you want to create a habit. Determine the most likely thing or event that will help you remember to establish your new pathway. Remember, you're filing a process away in that gray matter and it's important that it's well associated with your DPPV, mission and goals. It's a case of the ends justifying the means. Do what you must in order to get the life you desire.

> If you can identify the trigger or the habit, you have a great opportunity to make a choice whether you want to keep it or not. We are not judging anyone for the habits they have and we aren't pretending that no habits or only good habits are possible.

Discovering triggers for an old habit

❑ What tends to be the trigger that sets the habit into motion each time? List all triggers no matter how insignificant.

❑ What is the best way to de-emphasize this trigger? Can you put up any barriers? Can you remove the trigger or at least reduce its frequency?

❑ How would you feel if this habit and trigger were to go away?

❑ How do you start implementing your trigger reduction?

Developing triggers for new habits

❑ What is the most likely trigger or signal that you can use to enable you to remember the habit you want to create?

❑ What steps can you take to make sure your trigger elicits the correct response?

❑ How will you feel when this habit is cemented in your psyche?

❑ How can you use the path of least resistance to help develop this new habit?

Keep it simple and small

Have you ever had one of those really bouncy balls that always took off in a different direction than you expected? It was bad enough when you were attempting to bounce one of the balls, but when you were attempting to get two or more going, *fuggedaboutit*! Those stupid balls went wherever they wanted and not where you wanted. That is exactly what happens when folks attempt to create or alter too many habits at once. Everything is in motion and nothing is really getting done. Much like in Chip Away, the art of dealing with habits is to make sure you're keeping it very simple, which in this world means focusing on one and only one, and keeping it small and manageable.

Here is an old question you may have heard: How you do eat an elephant? One bite at a time. Well, this is very true for habits. The need to concentrate on one habit at a time along with the need to make it mentally, physically, emotionally, and spiritually small enough to handle is the key to successfully building that new habit. You have a responsibility to yourself to control your natural and manufactured defenses from getting in the way as you reroute and lay new tracks upon which to ride. Give yourself the space and time so you can design and implement the habits you choose. You're attempting to rewire your brain; you're laying down new tracks and attempting to close off old ones, and you want to make sure that you have a great plan and carry through on the appropriate actions to make this work, and work correctly. You don't want to be wandering from one area to another; you want to deal with one. Got it?

The reason to keep the changes concise is the realization that everything is fine and dandy when it all goes your way. At the moment it doesn't, your reaction will be to return to the most comfortable (regardless if they are correct) things that you do. In a fight, you might be trained as a martial artist, but if someone catches you off guard and forces you to react, you might suddenly be that kid who wildly starts swinging his hands to keep his attacker away, or worse, stand there taking a beating from the bully. Reaction can be reduced to not having a plan and not having awareness of your surroundings. People who do nothing but react are excuse experts.

Simple and small also provides the opportunity as we alter, add, emphasize, or de-emphasize our habits. It gives us the chance to change what is inside our BGB because a lot of our absolutes, fears, perceptions, and expectations are based on habits that we have obtained at an early age. Thus, if we can figure out what we don't want (or at least how to make it the last track we would ever take) we can actually make room for new habits, ideas, attitudes and beliefs.

The Benefits of Habits

At the end, you get the behaviors that you tolerate and you get the behaviors you track and reward. This is true with how others respond, and this is definitely true for how you will respond to yourself. There is no doubt in our minds that what you tolerate of yourself is what you're going to do. Unless you *want* to make the change, alter the habit, or block behavior from happening, then it's not going to happen. Period!

There is no one strong enough (outside of the heavens) to force you to do something that you don't want to do. If someone wants you to diet, but you don't want to...guess what, it isn't going to happen. If you don't want to stop drinking, no matter how much guilt is applied, it isn't going to happen. A smoker is never going to quit until he or she actually wants to, so why waste time and energy asking them, or trying to guilt them into doing something they don't want to do? History keeps proving over and over again that if people don't want to do something, they will not do it.

The good news is that when people put their minds to a problem and want to solve it for themselves, then anything is possible. When you want to change something in yourself and you have the correct controls and tools in place, you will be able to do anything!

You have the secrets to:

- ❏ Visualize your success
- ❏ Make it the path of least resistance
- ❏ Understand the risks and rewards
- ❏ Learn, repeat, and verify that all of those scratches on the steel (your brain) are exactly what you want
- ❏ Know your triggers so you can prevent or accept when to invoke your habit
- ❏ Understand that by keeping your challenges simple and small you have a greater chance of success

You also have the tools for putting up barriers across the tracks so the habits that you choose to remove are not easily accessible.

There is no doubt that by ensuring that the correct habits are formed, you have raised the bar for achieving bigger and better things, even if it's one small step at a time. You need to keep raising the bar until there are no more bars to be raised, which should coincide with your last breath.

Journal Entry #23: Quality Control. Pick a new habit that you have been working on and ask the following questions:

Can I visualize my success when this habit is fully in place?

What actions have I taken to prevent old habits from interfering with this new habit? Do I understand the obstacles, risks, and limits to establishing my new habit and following through with it? (Take the path of least resistance.)

How can I prove that I am taking the right actions to ensure that my new habit sticks? (Understanding Risk and Reward.)

Am I keeping track of what I do, when I do it, and why I do it? (Learn, repeat and verify.)

Do I understand what sets me down the path of using this habit? (Know my triggers.)

Can I simplify and minimize the complexity of my new habit? (Keep it simple and small.)

Welcome to Your Beginning

Something happened to the status quo in our lives on those hikes and runs three years ago. Were we lost or had we found ourselves in a place we didn't expect?

To tell you the truth, we weren't lost at all and neither are you. We didn't believe in ourselves. The idea that we could still take control of our lives or that we could go after our Plan A was so outside of our comfort zone that we were surprised it was even an option. To think we still had choices was surprising. We suspect that you have found the same.

You have choices available to you and all you need is to decide to make them.

All the steps we took you on in this book were the same steps that we took on our personal journeys. Sure, our words became more concise. We dropped the things that didn't work. We researched the items that we couldn't explain. Once we had the answers, then we knew we had a book worth sharing.

Let's recap the seven steps to *Live The Risk* called life:

1	I want to grow	There is a clear difference between living and dying. To live requires constant growing and learning.
2	I believe, I can, I am, I will	If dreams, passion, purpose and vision are aligned they are your Plan A.
3	No one wants this more than me	The need to determine what keeps you safe, RADICAL, and balanced is a must.
4	I will eliminate all obstacles	You have no use for natural and manufactured excuses that are protecting you from consequences.
5	It is all about the choices I make	You have a plan to achieve your missions.
6	Small stones build big pyramids	There is no replacement for doing what is required.
7	Continually *REACH* in order to live	The need to have the right habits is imperative to your growing and learning.

We will leave you with one last request: Do for others what we hope we have done for you. Have the courage, compassion and willingness to contribute in order to help make this world a better place. Share your knowledge and be an inspiration and example to your friends, family, and future generations.

Most importantly, remember to embrace life and encourage others to start living. There is no doubt in our minds that it's a lot better than the alternative.

So, we're going to say it just once more for old times' sake:

IF YOU'RE NOT LIVING...
YOU'RE _____!

We have come to the end of our journey. You have turned your drop in the proverbial bucket into a tidal wave of personal action, challenges, and energy. You now have the methodology, tools, and questions to tap your courage and travel this new course. You have redesigned yourself not in our image, but in what you want for yourself. There is no doubt in our minds that when you decide to *Live The Risk* called Life, you will find what you've always wanted.

Think big, start small, and enjoy it all!

Jeff and Joel

Drop us a line at:
Website: www.LiveTheRisk.com
Twitter: @Live_The_Risk
Facebook: LiveTheRisk

P.S. There can only be so much that we can write in a book and still expect folks to read it. So what we didn't include in the book, we put in our workshops. If you find that you need a more comprehensive journey or want to continue learning about the steps we have outlined in this book, check out our website for workshop dates and offers.

> To obtain updates, workshop
> information, and other exclusive
> materials delivered directly to your e-mail,
> please register at:
>
> **www.LiveTheRisk.com/Advantage**

IT IS NOT THE CRITIC WHO COUNTS;
NOT THE MAN WHO POINTS OUT HOW THE
STRONG MAN STUMBLES,
OR WHERE THE DOER OF DEEDS COULD HAVE
DONE THEM BETTER.

THE CREDIT BELONGS TO THE MAN WHO IS
ACTUALLY IN THE ARENA,
WHOSE FACE IS MARRED BY DUST AND SWEAT
AND BLOOD;

WHO STRIVES VALIANTLY;
WHO ERRS,
WHO COMES SHORT AGAIN AND AGAIN,
BECAUSE THERE IS NO EFFORT WITHOUT ERROR
OR SHORTCOMING;

BUT WHO DOES
ACTUALLY STRIVE TO DO THE DEEDS;
WHO KNOWS GREAT ENTHUSIASMS,
THE GREAT DEVOTIONS;
WHO SPENDS HIMSELF IN A WORTHY CAUSE;

WHO AT THE BEST
KNOWS IN THE END THE TRIUMPH OF
HIGH ACHIEVEMENT,
AND WHO AT THE WORST IF HE FAILS,
AT LEAST FAILS WHILE DARING GREATLY
SO THAT HIS PLACE SHALL NEVER BE WITH THOSE
COLD AND TIMID SOULS WHO NEITHER KNOW
VICTORY NOR DEFEAT.

~ THEODORE ROOSEVELT

Appendix A: The Passion Questions

If you can answer "yes" to all of the following questions, then congrats! You have passed one of the tests that have stumped most people. You can maintain control, keep moving forward, and handle the successes that you will have. You don't see failure, because problems are nothing more than annoying hurdles that need to be cleared. You can see and obtain your future by constantly making choices. Most importantly, you accept responsibility for what you want to be and where you are going. Congrats, you are able to take the next step along your journey.

If you can't answer "yes" to all of them (and we mean *all*), then we would tell you that your passion isn't going to support where you want to go. Sure, you will make some progress, but at some point in your future the batteries will run low and you won't have the energy to keep moving forward. Go back and really think about your dream or vision, strengthen it, and make sure it's yours. If your starting place was passion, we suggest that you refine what you think until you can answer "yes" to all nine questions.

	The Passion Questions © 2005 – 2013 L.E. Robinson II & JS Levinson	
	Answer "yes" or "no" to all of the following questions:	
	Section I – Energy Giver	Description
1	Does my passion fill me with energy?	Thinking about your dream / passion / goal / vision gives you a boost (motivation).
	Section II – Raising the Bar	
2	Am I a student of my passion?	Commitment, constant learning, and seeking out new thoughts / answers.
3	Am I becoming an expert in my passion?	Am I seen by the community as adding to the intellectual property of my dreams / passion (i.e. thought or action)?
4	Does my passion force me to raise the bar on myself?	Am I willing to use new approaches to do what hasn't been done and to risk failure?
	Section III – Who Am I?	
5	Are my 'values' and 'culture' in support of my passion?	If your passion goes against either, it will be very hard to pursue. Values and culture are the two hardest areas to change.
6	Do my friends identify my passion in me and see the positive results that it brings?	Friends don't have to agree. Or do I need new friends because these are holding me back?
	Section IV – Success and Failure	
7	Am I willing to fail at my passion and then keep on attempting?	You view failure as nothing more than a temporary defeat and an opportunity to go in a different direction to achieve what you want.
8	Does my passion apply to both work and home life?	Your passion has become a part of you. Every moment is an opportunity.
9	Am I willing to give up material things to obtain my passion?	Am I willing to give up being at home each night with my significant other, friends, and family, and replace it with being on the road accomplishing my dream? Am I willing to move and leave everything else behind? Am I willing to take a risk?

Appendix B: The Brain Side of Habits

The basal ganglia (or basal nuclei) are a group of nuclei of varied origin in the brains of vertebrates that act as a cohesive functional unit. They are situated at the base of the forebrain and are strongly connected with the cerebral cortex, thalamus and other brain areas. The basal ganglia are associated with a variety of functions, including voluntary motor control, procedural learning relating to routine behaviors or "habits" such as bruxism, eye movements, and cognitive, emotional functions. Currently popular theories implicate the basal ganglia primarily in action selection. That is, the decision of which of several possible behaviors to execute at a given time. Experimental studies show that the basal ganglia exert an inhibitory influence on a number of motor systems, and that a release of this inhibition permits a motor system to become active. The "behavior switching" that takes place within the basal ganglia is influenced by signals from many parts of the brain, including the prefrontal cortex, which plays a key role in executive functions.

The main components of the basal ganglia are the striatum (caudate nucleus and putamen), the globus pallidus, the substantia nigra, the nucleus accumbens, and the subthalamic nucleus. The largest component, the striatum, receives input from many brain areas, but sends output only to other components of the basal ganglia. The pallidum receives input from the striatum, and sends inhibitory output to a number of motor-related areas. The substantia nigra is the source of the striatal input of the neurotransmitter dopamine, which plays an important role in basal ganglia function. The subthalamic nucleus receives input mainly from the striatum and cerebral cortex, and projects to the globus pallidus. Each of these areas has a complex internal anatomical and neurochemical organization."[1]

You didn't think that we would miss the chance to give another brain lesson, did you? We don't know about you, but when we first read the research (it happens that Wikipedia had the best write-up) we found ourselves in a bit over our heads. (Surprised? Not so much.) In a nutshell, according to MIT professor Ann M. Graybiel, the striatum (the portion of the basal ganglia) is part of the learning and memory machinery of the brain. She continues to say that the striatum is involved in the type of procedural or implicit learning resulting in automated responses and that if lesions are made in this region after the period of learning, the animals tested have difficulty remembering how to do the task.

Excerpt from *MIT News* - October 29th, 2012:[2]

> MIT team experimentally simulated with rats trained to run a T-shaped maze. As the rats approached the decision point, they heard a tone indicating whether they should turn left or right. When they chose correctly, they received a reward — chocolate milk (for turning left) or sugar water (for turning right).
>
> To show that the behavior was habitual, the researchers eventually stopped giving the trained rats any rewards, and found that they continued running the maze correctly. The researchers then went a step further, offering the rats chocolate milk in their cages but mixing it with

1 Http://en.wikipedia.org/Basal_ganglia (Accessed March 19, 2013)

2 http://web.mit.edu/newsoffice/2012/understanding-how-brains-control-our-habits-1029.html

lithium chloride, which causes light nausea. The rats still continued to run left when cued to do so, although they stopped drinking the chocolate milk.

Using optogenetics, a technique that allows researchers to inhibit specific cells with light, the researchers turned off IL cortex activity for several seconds as the rats approached the point in the maze where they had to decide which way to turn. Almost instantly, the rats dropped the habit of running to the left (the side with the now-distasteful reward).

Disclaimer: So before anyone gets their shorts in a bind, we are not suggesting that you perform optogenetics on yourself to get rid of any habits. We don't encourage any personal testing on animals (or humans!) to prove our points.

Notes